The publisher and the University of California Press
Foundation gratefully acknowledge the generous support of
the Anne G. Lipow Endowment Fund in Social Justice and
Human Rights.

D0901837

Journeys

GENDER AND JUSTICE

Edited by Claire M. Renzetti

This University of California Press series explores how the experiences of offending, victimization, and justice are profoundly influenced by the intersections of gender with other markers of social location. Cross-cultural and comparative, series volumes publish the best new scholarship that seeks to challenge assumptions, highlight inequalities, and transform practice and policy.

Journeys

*Resilience and Growth for Survivors of
Intimate Partner Abuse*

SUSAN L. MILLER

University of California Press

University of California Press, one of the most distinguished university presses in the United States, enriches lives around the world by advancing scholarship in the humanities, social sciences, and natural sciences. Its activities are supported by the UC Press Foundation and by philanthropic contributions from individuals and institutions. For more information, visit www.ucpress.edu.

University of California Press
Oakland, California

Library of Congress Cataloging-in-Publication Data

Names: Miller, Susan L., author.
Title: Journeys : resilience and growth for survivors of intimate partner abuse / Susan L. Miller.
Description: Oakland, California : University of California Press, [2018] | Series: Gender and justice ; 5 | Includes bibliographical references and index. |
Identifiers: LCCN 2017054876 (print) | LCCN 2017059022 (ebook) | ISBN 9780520961463 (Epub) | ISBN 9780520286085 (cloth : alk. paper) | ISBN 9780520286108 (pbk : alk. paper)
Subjects: LCSH: Intimate partner violence—United States—Case studies. | Resilience (Personality trait) | Posttraumatic growth—United States—Case studies. | Abused women—United States—Case studies.
Classification: LCC HV6626.2 (ebook) | LCC HV6626.2 .M555 2018 (print) | DDC 362.82/924—dc23
LC record available at https://lccn.loc.gov/2017054876

27   26   25   24   23   22   21   20   19   18
10   9   8   7   6   5   4   3   2   1

In loving memory of my wonderful parents,
Marilyn and Kenneth Miller.
You are so missed.

And, of course, to my amazing son, Connor.

Pain nourishes courage. You can't be brave if you've only had wonderful things happen to you.

—MARY TYLER MOORE, 1986

Contents

Acknowledgments

No book is ever written in isolation. I am surrounded by many people who enrich my life, support my goals and dreams, and offer comfort, adventure, insight, and tenderness at just the right times. I first would like to acknowledge the women who participated in this project—their grace and strength and selflessness are laudable and very much appreciated. My chosen field of study keeps me in contact with people whose lives I find inspiring. The women behind the stories in this project are humble, determined, vulnerable, and courageous. They falter at times but persevere despite the volatility of their lives. They are astute problem solvers, a trait that applies to all survivors, not just the ones portrayed here who left their abusive relationships. I am impressed by their unshaken integrity, their commitment to their children and others they cherish, and their determination to keep moving forward. They have not stayed stuck ruminating but instead have used their experiences to help themselves and others. I thank you all for your time, your graciousness, and your openness and willingness to share your personal stories. I hope my work amplifies your voices and demonstrates how people can grow, rebound, resist, and hope in the face of trauma, fear, and abuse. These women are inspiring, but so are other survivors of abuse who may still be trying to start their journey to live violence-free. I applaud all of you.

This book also owes much to my own sources of support: family, friends, and colleagues. I am deeply nourished by their care. My beloved parents—my first storytellers and exemplars of social justice activists—passed away during the writing of this book, and my friends and family provided much support when my own resilience faltered. A big shout-out especially to my twin sister Lisa, my son Connor, and my cousins Kathy Miller Gillmore and David Miller for all of their love and restorative laughter.

I owe a big debt to LeeAnn Iovanni for her incisive comments on earlier drafts of this manuscript and for fun times in Denmark and on the Delaware beaches. Here's to many more years of true friendship! I am so fortunate to have many wonderful friends and colleagues to thank as well for conversations and distractions: the Joseph DeRosa Sr. family, the Becker family, Lisa Bartran and Janna Lambine, Michelle and Morgan Meloy, Georgia and Arthur Scott, Nancy Getchell, Lisa Larance, Kim and Ray Book, Blanche and Stephanie Creech, Frank and Ellen Scarpitti, Lisa Hull, Joan Klint, Leslie Sherman and David Wakeley, Lisa Laffend, Toni Essner, Mareta Gallagher and my fun-loving book group, Melanie Stone, Angela Gover, Rosemary Barberet, Sue Osthoff, Kristen Hefner, Emily Bonistall Postel, Ronet Bachman, Margaret Stetz, Jennifer Naccarelli, Cynthia Burack, Gerry Lewis Loper, Ruth Fleury-Steiner, Alesha Durfee, and the awesome birthday women—Carol Post, Jessica Schiffman, Debbie Hegadus, and Judy Schneider. Thank you to my graduate school professors at the University of Maryland who honed my thinking and research skills, and inspired me in ways I still feel today: Ray Paternoster (Emperor of Wyoming, whose memory lives on), Sally Simpson, and Vernetta Young. I appreciate the expert transcribing help from Carolyn Peck and Stephanie Creech, and office support from Deanna Nardi-Gurcz; a big shout-out also to so many of our wonderful graduate students at my university with whom I have collaborated on research projects or had the pleasure to teach. Finally, I must acknowledge the many welcome interruptions from the newest member of our family, Max the wonder dog, in addition to "the girls" who camp out in my office, cats Sophie, Molly, and Pippi.

Perhaps it has become obligatory to thank one's editors, but here I cannot be effusive enough. The team of Maura Rossner and Claire Renzetti is one that all authors wish for. Their support, insight, and caring, not to mention their supersmart input, were invaluable. I thank them with much enthusiasm. The insight from editorial assistant Sabrina Robleh and the reviewers, the production expertise of Emilia Thiuri, and the superb copy editing by Elisabeth Magnus are also reflected in the book, and I thank all of them with much gratitude for their careful reading.

Preface

More than one in three women in the United States have experienced rape, physical violence, and/or stalking by an intimate partner in their lifetime (Black et al. 2011).[1] In this book I refer to these actions as intimate partner violence and abuse (IPV/A). I made a deliberate choice to use *IPV/A* rather than *IPV* or *IPA* or *domestic violence* (*DV*), since *IPV/A* is a broader term that encompasses a wide range of victimizing acts committed by a previous or current dating partner, lover, or spouse. Most intimate partner abuse does not consist of the stereotypical physical violence but rather is best characterized by coercive control (Stark 2007) and other behaviors such as financial abuse (Adams et al. 2008), stalking, pet abuse (Hardesty et al. 2013), cyberstalking (Southworth et al. 2007), spiritual abuse (Dehan and Levi 2009), proxy abuse (Melton 2004, 2007), and paper abuse (S. Miller and Smolter 2011; overall, see also Belknap 2015, 392–93). I also recognize that nonphysical abuse can be more frightening (Crossman, Hardesty, and Raffaelli 2016) and can cause greater long-term trauma and emotional scars for some victims/survivors than physical violence (Fleury-Steiner, Fleury-Steiner, and Miller 2011). My acronym *IPV/A* is more inclusive: it can extend to some women in my study who did not "count" themselves as "domestic violence victims" because their abuser was not physically violent, but whose horrendous emotional abuse was nonetheless profoundly controlling and traumatizing. This term varies across disciplines—and thus practitioners and scholars—with some relying on the term *domestic violence* while others use *abuse and maltreatment*. I believe that *domestic violence* is a weak euphemism that does not fully convey the panoply of tactics and the gendered power aspects of this violence. Some of the women I interviewed, however, did use this term, and in being true to their voices I use their word choices when I quote from their narratives.

Heterosexual IPV/A is deeply gendered; these relationships of power and control between women and their male abusers are inherently asymmetrical.[2] Gender also reinforces the social reproduction of domination as practiced by key criminal justice and legal institutions, which often eclipse women's agency and resistance. While victims of ongoing IPV/A need immediate protection and assistance, knowledge from the scores of women who have experienced IPV/A in the past and who are now living violence-free can potentially aid victims/survivors at all points in the process. Some of these women stay closely connected to the movement against violence against women, even becoming activists, while other women no longer self-identify as victims or publicly disclose their past experiences. Many women remain haunted by victimization, yet still describe themselves as living vibrant lives in which they are not only surviving but thriving. Moving from such adversity toward creating lives that repudiate violence and victimization entails a host of changes and challenges. While abused women exhibit enormous courage and resistance even when enmeshed in violent relationships, their escape and subsequent journey reveal even greater resilience and resourcefulness as they handle the dangers and myriad obstacles while moving forward.

This book explores the resilience, challenges, and journeys of thirty-one survivors of IPV/A who were in relationships that lasted from three to thirty-eight years and who are now living violence-free lives. At the time I conducted interviews, the women had been out of their abusive relationships for at least five years, though the range in time varied from five to forty-three years. I also explore how gender and power shaped their understandings of their experiences with social support and their use of the criminal justice system. Using a multimethods approach that included participant observation at the monthly meetings of a survivors' organization and in-depth semistructured interviews with both women in this organization and another sample of survivors who were not part of any formal survivors' organization, I found that the women showed enormous perseverance and growth—despite the pain they had experienced in their abusive relationships and the challenges they faced negotiating the paths to where they were at the time of my study. Though trauma and recovery shaped their lives, these women demonstrated that the victimization was not the centerpiece of their identities (see Anderson, Renner, and Danis 2012; Saakvitne, Tennen, and Affleck 1998). Women in the first group of survivors chose a more public recognition of their experiences as members of a statewide group that led public efforts to increase awareness about IPV/A. Their commitment to collective efficacy was maintained even as some women moved from the group to other activist-minded efforts. Women in the second group were long-term survivors who were not connected to specific IPV/A organizations or movements against violence against women, yet were no less resolute in their quests to eliminate abuse and violence. Despite some differences between these groups, the women showed many similarities that speak to central issues related to resilience, strategic negotiations, coping, and thriving. My aim was not to directly compare these two groups, but I was interested in how their paths to resilience might differ, and I discuss these circumstances when relevant.

This issue of long-term survivorship merits serious attention. Although there is a lot of research on crisis and short-term needs, we know very little about how long-term survivors transform or incorporate their "victim" identities and lives while encountering what sociologists refer to as social structural constraints (such as poverty or lack of resources that may affect help-seeking behavior, as well as housing and employment options) and legal and criminal justice obstacles. The challenges abound even for those victims/survivors most likely to have a strong sense of personal agency,[3] as well as access to a range of emotional and instrumental support from service providers, family, and friends. Moving from being controlled by an abusive partner or ex-partner toward a life where one is in control is an accomplishment from which other abused women can learn and find inspiration. Understanding more about this process from the women themselves will assist victim service providers as well as policy makers to incorporate a deeper contextual analysis of survivor resilience and growth.

"Making lemonade from sour lemons" is how one woman I interviewed described how the very worst aspects of her life became the impetus for her becoming a strong, tenacious fighter and survivor. This movement captures the essence of how trauma can challenge one's core assumptions and lead to growth in its aftermath. In the psychological literature, *post-traumatic growth* refers to adaptive resources that trauma victims utilize when confronted with highly stressful events, resulting in positive psychological change (Tedeschi and Calhoun 2004). Trauma is profoundly distressful, and if the circumstances are severe and long-lasting, negative physical and emotional responses are common, including disbelief, anxiety, fear, sadness, depression, numbness, guilt, and anger (Tedeschi and Calhoun 2004; Wortman and Silver 2001). Post-traumatic growth is not inevitable and can co-occur with personal distress. However, a long tradition reveals that suffering and trauma can also be a source of positive change (Tedeschi and Calhoun 1995). Some of these early ideas emerge from Hindu, Buddhist, Islamic, and Christian teachings (see Tedeschi and Calhoun 1995). More scholarly exploration of post-traumatic growth has emerged across a wide variety of people and across circumstances including bereavement, coping with children's medical problems, HIV, cancer, sexual assault and sexual abuse, combat, and refugee experiences (see Tedeschi and Calhoun 2004, 3). Indeed, the women in my resilience project discussed the positive benefits of their traumatic experiences of IPV/A and how they drew strength from adversity. It was a process, however, that combined their coping skills with social structural supports and key people in their lives, culminating in their ability to reinterpret their hellish experiences and incorporate them into a position of flourishing. My point, as illustrated by the women's narratives in subsequent chapters, is that resilience is not a linear process and that the women underwent much soul-searching and help seeking before they were firmly established in a position of growth and well-being.

I have always been concerned about portrayals of battered women as passive or disempowered because I know from my own work in battered women's shelters that victims are active resisters of the deep pain (emotional, physical, sexual) and other injustices they experience in violent relationships. Often victims live in bleak environments without the financial means or social connections necessary to escape. They develop protective strategies to keep themselves and their children safe, while waiting for the opportunity to end and leave the relationship. The women in my study were utterly depleted by the relentless attacks on their self and the abuse, while at the same time yearning for a better future and exhibiting positivity amid the chaos. Many scholars document the constraints a battered woman faces, including the abuser's efforts to maintain power and control over her with threats and violent behavior, financial obstacles that limit her ability to find a place to live, lack of health care for herself and her children, lack of funds to seek counseling, or employers who do not allow her time off to access resources. Institutional obstacles are evident as well, such as limited shelter residency, lack of access to child care or transportation when one needs to appear in court, and limited ability to hire an attorney (see Hamby 2014). A woman may also encounter a chilly reception to divorce from her family or religious community, which can also jeopardize a source of financial and emotional support if she ends the relationship. Of course, these complications are exacerbated for women who are immigrants, lesbian, elderly, pregnant, disabled, or facing other life complexities.

Many women *do* leave these horrific situations and work to transform their lives by challenging individual and collective barriers, engaging with social and legal institutions and people for help, and pursuing other strategies to reinforce resistance and resilience. Yet with a few exceptions (see

Anderson, Renner, and Danis 2012; Crann and Barata 2016; Humphreys 2003; Flasch, Murray, and Crowe 2017), these women's voices are missing from the literature. We rightly focus on immediate crises and safety issues but lose sight of the long and often perilous journeys undertaken by many victims to survive and even thrive years after their abusive relationships end. To better convey the context of their journeys, chapter 1 provides an overview of research exploring women's agency and resistance within the social structural constraints and opportunities faced by long-term survivors of intimate partner violence and abuse and reveals how their courage and strength emerge in the shadow of the enduring effects of trauma. I use the term *long-term survivors* to characterize women who were victims of IPV/A but had terminated the relationship and had been living as survivors without violence in their intimate relationships for at least five years. This linguistic choice is not without controversy, as I describe more fully in chapter 1. Suffice it to say, I alternate between using *victims* and *survivors* and most frequently use the term *victims/survivors* to be as true as I can be to the words of the women I spent so much time listening to and learning from.

Chapter 1 also explores the pushes and pulls that women experience in relationships characterized by IPV/A and what we understand women to need in the short term and long term after the dissolution of a violent relationship. Drawing on the literature, I raise issues related to safety, access to services, social support, legal assistance, children, faith, housing, employment, and economic justice. For instance, we know a lot about the help-seeking behavior of women in crisis. We know what social structural factors and institutions have been identified by them as helpful, such as peer support, victim services, and faith communities (see Belknap et al. 2009; Hamby 2014). However, many studies do not conduct long-term follow-ups of the women after their stay in the shelter ends. Leaving the relationship does not usually end the abuse. Stalking escalates, as do the threat and use of more serious violence (Tjaden and Thoennes 2000). Chapter 1 also incorporates a discussion of key thematic concepts such as growth, healing from trauma, individual agency and collective efficacy, identity, and meaning making. I challenge the false, or incomplete, assumption that there is some kind of closure for women after leaving a violent relationship. Though that relationship is no longer the "master status," triggers and connections to this time recur and fade. Many women describe this state as being one of liminality, or "betwixt and between"—no longer under the abuser's control but not fully on the other side. As research with women in shelters demonstrates (Humphreys 2003), resilience and distress are not necessarily opposite. In one of the few studies that explores the recovery process for women who have left violent relationships, Anderson, Renner, and Danis (2012) found that social and spiritual support can help victims make meaning of the suffering they have experienced in a way that fosters their resilience. Therefore, to establish a sense of well-being, women need to be able to access that support.

Chapter 1 also looks at what it means to be "resilient." Resilience has been primarily studied by psychologists, who have explored how people, particularly children and aging adults, find strength in the face of adversity when confronted with profound challenges (O'Leary 1998), such as cancer (Molina et al. 2014), bereavement (Bonanno et al. 2002; see also M. Stroebe and Stroebe 1983; W. Stroebe and Stroebe 1993), and post-traumatic stress disorder (especially among war veterans; Eisen et al. 2014). Psychologists also consider how people can move beyond mere functioning or recovering to flourishing (see O'Leary and Ickovics 1995) and have shown that success in confronting challenges and moving beyond them can be transformative. From a sociological standpoint, however, transformation cannot be achieved in a vacuum—abused women, including the ones that I interviewed, often talk about the myriad resources, agencies, and social relationships with people who have facilitated their resolve to live violence-free lives. Support mobilization, however, seems most successful for women who are going through the challenge of dissolving the abusive relationship, staying in battered women's shelters, receiving counseling during this time in victim support groups, and navigating through their early court procedures or obtaining protection orders. Given that the women in this book had left IPV/A behind for at least five years, their connection with support from crisis centers, shelters, or victim advocacy groups had decreased. Yet years later, many of the women sought a connection with other women who had endured similar experiences and had been drawn to activism through a sense of collective efficacy. I explore why some women joined a survivors' group or were drawn to working as professionals in the field of domestic violence with battered women, while others revealed their past only to a few individuals who might be in danger or made no explicit connections in their present lives to their past experiences with IPV/A. The rest of chapter 1 explores in further detail some of the key theoretical and empirical literature guiding my research.

In chapter 2 I describe how I located and connected with interviewees and gained access to the organization where I did much of my research. I forged connections both with a statewide survivors' activist organization that I call WIND (a pseudonym that stands for "**W**omen **in N**on**violent Domains**," which captures the essence of the group's real name and its mission to work against violence in any kind of connection or relationship) and with survivors who were not formally affiliated with an anti-IPV/A activist organization. Long-term survivors of IPV/A were in some ways a hidden group. Many survivors have placed their past abusive relationships at the periphery of their lives, to be acknowledged when relevant and if the circumstances seem safe, but otherwise consider them to be merely one piece of a larger self-identity and life. For other survivors, victimization experiences still feature as central to their identity, propelling them to publicly disclose their arduous journeys to survivorship. All of these women are courageous; they just have taken different paths in their long-term journeys of resilience. The methods section details how my fieldwork and my in-depth interviews were conducted and provides an introduction to WIND and to the women who participated in this project.

The last section of chapter 2 explores how the women I interviewed described themselves in relation to "victim" and "survivor" labels and images. The difficulty in describing oneself as one or the other is emblematic of larger struggles with identity construction. As discussed in chapter 1, social institutions and actors within those systems, such as social service providers and criminal justice system personnel, and supportive family and friendship networks, utilize different images to reinforce guiding perceptions about victims and victimization. *Victim* is a loaded term, evoking often negative portrayals of fragility, passivity, and blame. Yet being labeled a victim can also facilitate access to sympathy and resources. Many women I interviewed chafed at the negativity of being seen unidimensionally as a victim, yet knew their opportunity to garner support could be influenced by such a presentation. Many moved over time to rejecting their victim status and embracing a survivor status. They explained that the strength, resistance, and resilience associated with surviving were better reflections of themselves. But they did not express "victim" and "survivor" as an either/ or dichotomy; rather, for them these identities existed on a continuum. The narratives of moving from being a victim to being a survivor helped women to look beyond their immediate grim circumstances and to hope for a better future. Chapter 2 ends with the women's thoughtful insights on this point.

Chapters 3, 4, and 5 delve more deeply into the specific themes and issues that emerged from the women's narratives during interviews and my fieldwork with the activist organization WIND. More specifically, chapter 3 situates the women in their former abusive relationships, asking them to think retrospectively about the dynamics that had encouraged involvement with the abuser, obscured early warning signs, numbed them to highly dangerous living conditions, and discouraged them from leaving.

Women actively resisted, even under incredible constraints; they endured much abuse, but many of their subtle strategies of resistance helped them achieve long-term growth, understanding, and recovery. In particular, this chapter reveals how—despite vulnerability and diminishing self-worth—the women transcended abuse and used their survivor skills to gain eventual well-being. Although many abused women shared certain vulnerabilities, such as naive assumptions about romance and what constituted healthy and unhealthy relationships, differences in coping strategies emerged in the interviews. A personal belief in God or in the role of faith or religion could sustain some women in pain, provide inner strength, or connect women to a religious institution or community for help. For other women, however, seeking help from faith-based communities or religious leaders reinforced their internalized victim blaming, causing them to question their faith. Chapter 3 exposes the multiple and complex factors that bound the women to their relationships, from physical threats that included the use of lethal weapons, to economic abuse, to concerns for their children. Despite these obstacles, the women's narratives reflect their dogged determination to move forward from their traumatic experiences.

Chapter 4 looks more closely at the ways long-term survivors construct meaning from their experiences. A good deal of psychological literature demonstrates how adversity can promote personal meaning and growth; this chapter, however, uses a sociological lens to explore meaning making and post-traumatic growth. When trauma occurs, people restructure their assumptive worlds and reestablish their equilibrium (Janoff-Bulman 1992). Leaving an abusive relationship does not mean leaving all of the abuse behind, since often financial, legal, custody, and other issues continue. The women's narratives describe how they were able to confront their fears and ongoing entanglements with the abusers and exert their own agency to secure long-term peace. These accomplishments were not linear, as the women worked to negotiate ongoing strife in their lives, especially in interaction with parenting and family issues. Women exhibited both individual and collective efficacy when they challenged the assumptions and limitations of their past and shifted to a quest for long-term well-being. The chapter also explores how women seek meaning in their situations through efforts to make other women's lives better, whether through private conversations or public campaigns, and whether through faith-based or secular organizations.

Chapter 5 continues to explore women's efforts to establish long-term security and well-being, with a specific focus on informal and formal support networks and structural challenges. Many women described their help-seeking behavior and the positive responses and empathy they received from supportive people in their lives and from social service providers. But too many women also experienced a dearth of support; a prominent theme was how women responded to the perceived betrayal of putative allies, such as religious counselors and members of the criminal justice system (e.g., police, prosecutors, judges), when these people failed to dignify the women's stories with understanding and instrumental help. While many people did provide women with assistance, long-term survivors often received less attention and help once they were out of a crisis and had fewer options or people to turn to for help as time went on. On the one hand, this facilitated their continued growth in resistance strategies and resilience; on the other hand, the women felt profoundly alone when challenging paternalistic family courts, avoidant or victim-blaming religious communities, or police who arrested them for defending themselves. Race and class positions complicated many women's access to help from various branches of the criminal justice system.

The final chapter addresses the broader impact and significance of this work. In particular, chapter 6 explores the meaning of long-term recovery, growth, and resilience by recognizing the multiple pathways to survivor-ship. The women's personal narratives—powerful in their description and insight—combine with my analysis of the women's experiences in their many years of living violence-free lives to offer suggestions to programs in developing long-term support for survivors and to serve as inspiration to battered women still immersed in violent and abusive relationships. By listening to the experiences of long-term survivors of IPV/A and analyzing common themes and highlighting significant issues they face, we have derived practical recommendations for victims/survivors, criminal justice and social service professionals, and policy makers. This project helps us to better understand resistance and agency, given the obstacles as well as the opportunities faced by long-term survivors of IPV/A: women who have been resolute in their efforts to overcome fear and victimization and to live lives of dignity, positivity, and peace.

1. Framing the Issues

In 2002, fourteen-year-old Elizabeth Smart of Salt Lake City, Utah, was kidnapped from her bedroom by a religious fanatic and kept chained, raped repeatedly, and threatened that her family would be murdered if she tried to escape (Smart 2013). Today she is an activist and president of the Elizabeth Smart Foundation, which works to promote awareness about abduction; she has also worked with the Department of Justice and other recovered young adults in creating a survivors' guide, *You're Not Alone: The Journey from Abduction to Empowerment,* to encourage children who have gone through similar experiences to not give up and to know that there is life after tragic events. Her foundation has merged with Operation Underground Railroad to combine efforts in the fight against human trafficking (see https://elizabethsmartfoundation.org).

In the beginning of his freshman year at Rutgers University, Tyler Clementi's roommate filmed an intimate act with Tyler and another man through a webcam set up to spy on him. The roommate uploaded the video online, and Tyler discovered through his roommate's Twitter feed that he was widely ridiculed and that his roommate was planning a second filming. Tyler committed suicide several days later, a victim of cyber bullying. Tyler's parents cofounded the Tyler Clementi Foundation to promote safe, inclusive, and respectful social environments in homes, schools, campuses, churches, and the digital world for vulnerable youth, LGBT youth, and their allies; to honor their son and brother; and to address the needs of vulnerable populations, especially LGBT people and other victims of hostile social environments (see https://tylerclementifoundation.org).

On December 14, 2012, a disturbed twenty-year-old man opened fire on children and teachers at Newtown, Connecticut's Sandy Hook Elementary School, killing twenty first graders and six educators and community members. In response, several family members established a foundation called Sandy Hook Promise that supports solutions to protect children and prevent gun violence with the intent to honor all victims of gun violence by turning their personal tragedy into a moment of transformation (see www .sandyhookpromise.org/), and other Sandy Hook parents founded an organization devoted to educating and empowering school communities to improve school safety (www.safeandsoundschools.org/).

What do these people have in common? How could they emerge from such suffering to lead profoundly courageous lives of hope, resistance, and transformation? What comes to mind is the word *resilience,* which suggests that, despite violence or pain or suffering, something internal or external sustains and gives hope to people who experience trauma. The literature offers little insight on how resilience develops over time—if we tap into it in times of need and how a resilient spirit or coping strategies or support from others may assist in survivorship. The social psychological literature tends to approach this issue more individually, whereas the victimology literature in sociology and criminology generally adopts a more structural analysis. Overall, however, not enough sociological attention has been paid to the resilience and long-term survivorship of women who have experienced IPV/A and have ended their abusive relationships (for some exceptions, see Anderson, Renner, and Danis 2012; Crann and Barata 2016).

This book explores resilience by focusing on women who have experienced intimate partner abuse of all sorts, and the ways in which they have been able to regain a sense of mastery or control over their lives, reclaiming themselves and forging new paths over many years following the end of the relationship. While many of the chapters analyze the themes and issues that emerged from interviews with the victims/survivors, this chapter first addresses the cultural and political milieus in which the battered women's movement and the women's narratives are embedded.

FRAMING VICTIMIZATION

In 1992, Tamar Lewin, writing in the *New York Times,* cautioned scholars and activists about overemphasizing the "victim" label for battered women. Specifically, she wondered if women became "victims of their victim status." During the infancy of the movement, use of the term *battered woman* was necessary to evoke sympathy and to better explain why women stay in abusive relationships or have such a difficult time leaving. But although the term is well intended, it perpetuates stereotypes of women who have experienced IPV/A as helpless, passive victims—a strategy that backfires when women diverge from these scripts, perhaps by fighting back in self-defense. The feminist legal scholar Elizabeth Schneider explains, "Women don't identify with the term 'battered woman,' even if they arrive bleeding at a shelter, because no one feels that her totality is being a victim" (quoted in Lewin 1992).

Assumptions of what a "real" victim looks like perpetuate the problem in research, the criminal justice system's response, and social service provision and programming. Presenting IPV/A as a problem that is widely shared (i.e., promoting messages like "Battering affects every woman" and "It could happen to anyone") is important, but it blurs the differences between individual women's experiences and presenting one kind of victim—typically the most readily sympathetic—as emblematic of all victims. In doing so, it tends to portray all battered women as blameless "good women" who are passive, nonviolent, and visibly afraid of the abuser (Berns 2004; Lamb 1999a; Loseke 1992). This lays the foundation for viewing women as "bad victims" or even "offenders" when their actions and/or situations deviate from this characterization (Creek and Dunn 2011; Dunn 2004, 2008). As early IPV/A researchers Walker and Browne (1985) found, women who violate feminine norms of passivity, submissiveness, politeness, and helpfulness are more vulnerable to victimization's social penalties. Consequently this strategy of advocacy has repercussions for social service providers' assistance and the criminal justice system's actions. It also ignores the structural issues that complicate women's positions, such as the special liabilities and challenges of poor women of color, who are "most likely to be in both dangerous intimate relationships and dangerous social positions" (Richie 2000, 1136).

Advocacy groups' stories and photos of the iconic battered woman represent only the most extreme, dramatic, and sensational images and narratives. Lost are the "in-betweens" and nuances of the complex and varied context of IPV/A. This is claims-making in action. In leaving little room for victims who do not fit the stereotype, it can backfire against victims. For example, when battered women actively fight back, they can no longer be characterized as passive docile feminine victims (Chesney-Lind 2002, 2004; Chesney-Lind and Eliason 2006; Chesney-Lind and Irwin 2008; Davidson and Chesney-Lind 2009; Irwin and Chesney-Lind 2008; Lamb 1999a) and they increasingly are arrested for using violence against their abusers (Larance and Miller 2016; S. Miller 2005). Also, parading an image of a black-and-blue bruised battered woman negates or hides other more insidious abuses—sexual, emotional, and financial—and more covert elements of coercive control that are present in IPV/A. The sociologist Evan Stark

(2007, 228–29) describes coercion as entailing "the use of force or threats to compel or dispel a particular response" but points out that "in addition to causing immediate pain, injury, fear, or death, coercion can have long-term physical, behavioral, or psychological consequences. . . . Control is comprised of structural forms of deprivation, exploitation, and command that compel obedience indirectly by monopolizing vital resources, dictating preferred choices, microregulating a partner's behavior, limiting her options, and depriving her of supports needed to exercise independent judgment." And recent work by Crossman, Hardesty, and Raffaelli (2016) reveals that women who experience nonphysical abuse feel as afraid during their marriage as women who experience physical abuse, and even more afraid after separation.

The battered women's movement in the 1970s and 1980s achieved some early success in shifting from a pathological focus on women's personality traits (such as masochism) to a focus on the constraints that explain why women stay in abusive relationships (Walker 1979; Goodmark 2012). Expert witnesses could deploy the concepts of "battered women' syndrome" and "learned helplessness" in court to counter the assertion that abused women could leave whenever they chose or to explain why some women, failing other options, were justified in killing their abusers (Walker 1984). But today these notions, and their incorporation of the cycle-of-violence theory (cyclical phases of tension building, violent episode, and remorse/ honeymoon that trap women in the relationship psychologically), have lost their cultural currency. They are critiqued for reinforcing pervasive sexist stereotypes of meek, passive, and disempowered women and for creating "little more than a more compassionate and gender sensitive version of the traditional psychiatric view of women as 'irrational' or even 'insane,' except that this version incorporates a recognition that the women's alleged 'irrationality' or psychological incapacity results from the infliction of abuse upon her by a male intimate" (Randall 2004, 124). Yet the dissonance between an assumption of passivity in victims and stories of victims' aggression against their abuser continues to complicate the message to the general public (Goodmark 2012); my own work in this area with ninety-five women arrested for use of force against an intimate partner or ex-partner revealed that 95 percent of these women used violence in reaction to a partner's violence, to protect themselves or their children, or to prevent an imminent attack (S. Miller 2005).

Nicola Gavey's (1999) work on rape similarly explores how the politically important strategy of defining a "common experience" to raise awareness ultimately backfires when a particular kind of rape case or rape victim is universalized. Gavey also notes that society's definitions of certain acts in a legal sense do not always align with how victims experience them: how should we respond to a woman who describes an incident of forced, unwanted sexual intercourse but says she was not raped? Being defined as a rape victim means taking on the "negative social value" and the "obligations" of the victim role (see early work by Burt and Estep 1981). The feminist movement succeeded in expanding the continuum of sexual victimization to include forms of coercion from unwanted kissing and touching to rape. However, some women who have experienced unwanted sexual victimization do not view themselves as victims and reject legal and scholarly definitions; instead they tell stories of empowerment and triumph in which they thwart rape or limit the scale of a sexual assault (Gavey 1999, 72). Gavey even states that "not all women are traumatized by rape," while adding that this does not trivialize rape or its brutality. She contends that "it may be possible to experience rape and suffer no lasting devastating psychological effects" but that such a possibility is "less often articulated than is the discourse of harm" (70). Of course, this view does not come without complications: we do not want victims who do not fight back (because of fear, being overpowered, or other reasons) to internalize any self-blame.

We can extend this perspective on rape to think about IPV/A. The portrait of a "battered woman" was crafted as a political tool by the battered women's movement in the 1970s to heighten awareness of a pervasive hidden problem. In this way, it served its purpose.[1] But there are many different narratives of victimization (Gavey 1999). One such narrative is the refusal to see oneself as a victim or battered woman or to label the experience as one of victimization, even though the descriptions of the abuse endured meet normative understandings of IPV/A. As one of my participants, Jazzy, described her abuse, "It just was. That was life. Nothing to be done about it."

Jazzy's experience is complicated by her social location—she experienced her initial relationship violence in her first marriage, about forty years ago. Though the term *battered women* was politicized around the same time (the 1970s), the language of white, upper-middle-class activists was little known in her working-class African American milieu. Her community accepted "hitting" in relationships, and she herself talked about the normalcy of it. She described her retaliatory violence as restoring her dignity and commented that she egged on her husband in order to have some degree of control over when he hit her, since she knew the violence was inevitable and did not want it to interfere with her ability to get to work.

Gavey (1999, 76) suggests that in the arena of attempted sexual assaults women can be seen as fighters and survivors, warriors and heroes. The same imagery can apply to battered women who resist in ways that may be sub-tle and invisible to outsiders yet succeed in salvaging some self-esteem and self-efficacy. This is not to suggest that the framework that has been so suc-cessful in politicizing IPV/A be abandoned; the issue is that there is room for alternative ways of thinking about victimization and space for those who have other legitimate stories to tell (see also Waldrop and Resick's 2004 work for a way to examine coping strategies of battered women using a psychological lens).

TRAUMA-INFORMED PRACTICES

The emerging focus on trauma-informed, gender-responsive practice (Bloom, Owen, and Covington 2004) acknowledges survivorship histories in ways useful for practitioners and researchers. When practices are trauma informed, there is an acknowledgment of how a traumatic incident can lead to behaviors related to the pain and lack of power over the incident. Practitioners must take into account these effects and ensure the safety of the individuals, have transparency in their connections with professionals, provide support, and assist survivors in finding their voice and becoming empowered to choose what they want. This approach is very appealing because it validates how early childhood or adolescent trauma can have a long-lasting impact and helps us understand why adults may have fright-ening flashbacks and fears. A trauma framework can also embrace many forms of violence, which helps in drawing parallels with and connections between those forms. Gender-responsive practices create "an environment . . . that reflects an understanding of the realities of women's lives and addresses the issues of the women" (Bloom and Covington 2000, 11). Most gender-responsive practices incorporate the understanding of other differ-ences too, such as race/ethnicity, social class, (dis)ability, and sexuality.

In counseling, women are often open to using a trauma framework for understanding their pain and suffering and some of the frightening afteref-fects of victimization (flashbacks, nightmares). It is more empowering for women who have experienced intimate partner violence or sexual violence to have a scientifically sound explanation that recognizes they did not bring it on themselves than to receive the earlier victim-blaming alternative explanations offered by traditional psychoanalytical perspectives (Gilfus 1999). Finally, trauma research has facilitated treatment interventions that offer relief from symptoms and are very helpful for victims because of this compassionate and holistic approach and the efforts made to keep from retraumatizing victims/survivors. Victims can get insurance coverage for treatment, but being labeled a trauma victim can also stigmatize them or even be used against them by abusers in court decisions over custody issues (for instance, see Saunders, Faller, and Tolman 2012 on how women and perceptions of their mental health are interpreted by court professionals in IPV/A custody cases).

Despite its popularity, the trauma framework is not without critics and has its limitations. If trauma is understood as an individual psychological response, it can conflate cause and effect and be seen as a "psychological condition caused by exposure to violence/extreme stress, leading to the assumption that all types of traumatic events are precursors of psychological symptomatology, unless the victim is exceptionally resilient" (Gilfus 1999, 1241). It can be used to frame IPV/A as a crime arising only from individual-level pathology; to ignore the victim's agency; and to excuse men's violence if they themselves have experienced trauma (Gilfus 1999). If we focus too much on childhood traumatic experiences, we risk ignoring structural factors, including racism, poverty, and other forms of oppression that can be just as traumatic. By focusing on the trauma victim, we also ignore the offender. A trauma framework risks our losing sight of the social and political context and the gendered nature of the inequalities of power within which IPV/A occurs (Larance and Miller 2015).

Moreover, the trauma paradigm has become increasingly medicalized; it seeks to explain and treat the psychological aftermath, which also contributes to rendering trauma an individual psychological response, separate from social-structural correlates (Gilfus 1999). A trauma diagnosis effectively erases the real source of the problem—the individual and collective perpetrators of violence, shored up by a broad range of structural conditions and societal mechanisms that allow men to control and disempower women. A checklist of standardized symptoms or experiences is devoid of social or political context about the gendered nature of the inequalities of power relations that give rise not only to IPV/A but to other forms of privatized violence, such as child sexual abuse or marital rape. These narrow measures also do not recognize the injuries of racism, colonialism, homophobia, and other pains of inequality. Moreover, trauma is not random; it happens to specific groups of people more than others and is perpetrated by some groups of people more than others.

Finally, by focusing on individual trauma, we miss not only potential sources of injury but also potential sources of strength: coping and survival skills and strategies that victims employ against insurmountable odds and despite the constriction of their choices by considerations for the safety and welfare of others, such as the victim's children. Many psychologists now contend that resilience in the face of acute distress or trauma is more common than often believed and that there are multiple pathways to resilience (Bonanno 2004). Battered women use myriad invisible coping strategies on a daily, ongoing basis. Using only a trauma paradigm underestimates, ignores, or invalidates women's varying courses of action and prevents a true accounting of their strengths. This feeds into a deficit-focused paradigm versus a strength-based one. Psychologist Sherry Hamby (2014, 161) constructs a list of 144 strategies that women use to keep themselves safe while in a relationship characterized by IPV/A. Hamby is convinced that the battered women's movement has been guided by forty years of bad advice and has done victims a disservice in focusing solely on getting women out of relationships and failing to recognize that for some women that is not the optimal outcome. Leaving is not always the safest strategy, given what we know about stalking, serious injury, and death. Greater attention is now paid to separation violence, since more than half of attempted homicides of intimate partners are precipitated by the victim's leaving (see M. Johnson, Leone, and Xu 2014). For victims, a strength-based approach is far less stigmatizing than a deficit-focused approach and far more validating. It acknowledges that many women choose to stay and that in doing so they actively engage in a rational calculus, weighing the pros and cons of this decision.

Lack of safety in staying was highlighted in the early years of the battered women's political movement in order to capture national attention and achieve public recognition that violence against women was a significant, widely occurring social problem that everyone should be concerned about. Thus advocacy campaigns emphasized the very visible signs of physical abuse and the need to develop shelters and services so that victims of abuse could end the relationship and get out safely.

Women's difficulties in leaving, however, are not entirely due to fears of the batterer's violence (Hamby 2014). Economic (in)justice plays a major part (see Sanders 2015). It is critical for women to have financial access and savvy or money saved—a theme you will hear echoed in later chapters of this book. In some states, financial empowerment projects provide financial literacy training or matched-savings programs for survivors. These encourage women to save for a first month's rent, for a used car or car insurance, for a computer, or for legal representation; there is a 1:1 savings match (see, e.g., Sanders 2010). For some women with no other financial means, this kind of support is crucial for getting out. Also, women's range of choices is often limited by their desire to protect others (Hamby 2014); thus women's efforts to protect pets, children, other family members, and friends are a huge part of the equation. These concerns can stall or prevent a decision to terminate the relationship, but they should not be misperceived as examples of women's inertia or avoidance—they are part of women's calculated assessments of risk. In this same vein, Hamby asserts that choosing not to disclose one's abuse to others, while often interpreted as springing from denial or some other cognitive distortion, can instead be a way to finesse impression management or minimize social stigma. Avoiding a problem or leaving a violent confrontation can be coping strategies (as can hitting back). The assumption is that women leave and go to a shelter (which also assumes that shelters welcome children of all ages and both sexes and have space) and that this is the safest strategy. But we know from the research that most women turn first to family and friends and that there is a larger range of protective strategies than just seeking safe shelter.

SURVIVOR-CENTERED ANALYSES

Any trauma approach that is overly individualized takes our attention away from the social-structural context in which violence and abuse occur (Gilfus 1999, 1239). We are better informed by what we have learned from and about survivors, such as Hamby's (2014) list of 144 help-seeking/protective strategies that illustrate women's agency. Survivor-centered analysis recognizes strengths *and* injuries, is culturally inclusive, is informed by feminism, builds on the wisdom of victimization and survival that is part of women's lives, and widens the lens of trauma theory to include racism, poverty, and other forms of oppression as potential sources of traumatic injury.

As criticism mounted against the theories of a battered women's syndrome and learned helplessness to explain women's attachment to abusive relationships, the sociologists Gondolf and Fisher (1988) introduced an alternative paradigm to better explain why women stayed. Instead of casting women as immobilized or passive, their "survivor theory" portrayed women as actively seeking social support and resources to assist them in getting out of abusive relationships. But, again, it is not so simple (Goodmark 2012, 63): survivor theory still focuses on why women stay, as if leaving is every woman's ultimate goal; women who make active choices to stay in a violent relationship may be mistakenly interpreted as passive by outsiders. The psychologist Sharon Lamb (1999a, 126) warns that "if the culture overemphasizes the helpless victim, and if victims overemphasize the survivor victim, we are caught between two stereotypes that preclude a range of experiences and the unifying awareness that victimization is too frequently a part of every woman's life." Even when women stay in abusive relationships and do little things that promote safety and exert control in their daily lives, they are more likely to identify as "survivors" than as "victims." As bell hooks (2000, 46) asserts: "Women who are exploited and oppressed daily cannot afford to relinquish the belief that they exercise some measure of control, however relative, over their lives. They cannot afford to see themselves solely as 'victims' because their survival depends on continued exercise of whatever personal powers they possess. It would be psychologically demoralizing for these women to bond with other women on the basis of shared victimization." Moreover, legal scholar Leigh Goodmark (2012, 63) cautions us that although survivor theory's contribution has been useful for advocates and abused women, it has failed to exert much influence over the legal system's enduring notions of the "paradigmatic victim" as a white, straight woman who is compliant, passive, and defenseless.

IDENTITY CONSTRUCTION AND SEMANTICS

Given the discussion above, I have faced an issue of semantics both in the literature and in my own writing of this book: What to call women who have experienced victimization but have moved forward to live free of violence? Most state coalitions against domestic violence refer to battered women as victims or survivors, depending on their position in the process. For task forces in a coalition, the common nomenclature is to describe the women as survivors. The activist organization WIND that I investigate in this book uses "Survivors' Task Force" as its descriptor.

I find it useful to think about this issue in terms of how women self-identify. Sometimes women themselves describe a transition from victim to survivor, like one woman I interviewed who stated that at this point in her life she could tell the story of her abuse to others "without feeling revictimized, since I've got so much distance from it, which in my mind is a key marker of difference between victims and survivors." In any case, women may not want to be defined by their worst incidents of victimization. The sociologist Erving Goffman (1963), who has written extensively about identity, relies on the term *master status* to describe a social position that, more than any other position a person occupies, constitutes the core of that person's social identity and influences his or her roles and behaviors. Often, one's occupation is a master status because of its salience to one's identity, to one's other roles, such as family roles, to friendships, to where one lives, and so forth. Gender, sexual identity, age, and race are also common master statuses. Some women reject the label of "victim" as a stigmatizing master status. Goffman (1963), in theorizing about spoiled identities, notes that people try to hide their stigma if possible or limit its social impact on their identity. Coping strategies include withdrawing from social interaction so as not to draw attention to the stigma or forming or joining a social movement to combat the negative stereotypes associated with a stigmatized status.

Language is significant in that words become the lens through which a person is judged. Several researchers working in the field of IPV/A have been sensitive to this point. Hamby (2014, 11) deliberately uses the phrases "women who have been victimized" or "women who have experienced domestic violence," much as researchers and activists have redefined an "AIDS patient" to a "person with AIDS" so that the person is first and their experience or condition second. She also states, and I concur, that "'survivor' is an insider word. Some feminists and advocates use it, but few others do" (10). The psychologist Mary Koss (2014, 1626), in her groundbreaking work on sexual violence and restorative justice, uses *survivor victim* to retain "the empowerment conveyed by the word survivor and the outrage implied by the word victim."

Perhaps the most thorough exploration of the implications of terminology around IPV/A is that of the linguist Julia Penelope (1990). She argues that language is a form of social power; it is not neutral and can reduce women's stature and agency (see also Caputi 1977; Spender 1980). Thus, for instance, she notes that

> euphemisms abound for male violence. . . . Men have created a plethora of euphemisms to downplay their violence and hide their sexual exploitation of women and children. . . . Men beat their wives, but the media talk about *spouse abuse, battered spouses,* and *domestic violence.* In the last phrase, *domestic* hides male agency and focuses our attention on the places where men beat their wives and children, dwellings, disguising violent acts as well as erasing the male agents. Men rape children, but we talk about *incest, sexual abuse* and *molestation,* making the men who commit crimes of violence against women invisible. (1990, 209, italics in original)

Euphemistic language, by drawing our attention away from men's violence and power, permits men to deny their responsibility for their harmful behavior to women and allows women to "pretend that they don't know what men are doing. If we remain 'unaware' of male violence, we don't have to challenge them and, in this way, avoid the possibility of yet more male violence" (210).

Penelope also discusses the complex connotations of *victim* and *survivor,* arguing that both terms are necessary "to remind us of our pain, our anger, and the strengths that enable us to survive" (217). With these two words we distinguish between those who survive their victimization and those who do not. A victim "merges past and present contexts and interprets events and actions in the present only on the basis of her past experiences. A 'survivor,' in contrast, is aware of how her past influences her behavior in the present and consciously attempts not to confuse it with present situations"; in other words, her past is still part of her, but it does not control her (216).

Women make agentic, conscious choices to free themselves from abuse. Even if they decide to stay in their relationship while refusing to accept abuse, they take active steps to achieve this result (Eisikovitz, Buchbinder, and Mor 1998). It is crucial to let go of the dichotomy of staying versus leaving, especially since 50 percent of women stay with or return to abusers after leaving or getting help (Lesser 1990) and since the National Domestic Violence Hotline (2013) reports that it takes a victim seven times of leaving before she stays away for good. Active resistance can still occur within an abusive relationship, though it is often difficult for service providers or members of women's informal support systems to know what to do. Should they help her leave or respect her choice to stay and support her in developing ways to better cope or defend herself? Above all, women are actively creating meaning and consciously negotiating their situation. When they decide what they will or will not tolerate anymore, this involves a need to break with their personal meaning systems; it is not sudden, but rather a culmination of a lengthy process "in which women actively negotiate, plan, and experiment with the idea that violence must be stopped—a process that is associated with a series of personal and interpersonal losses" (Eisikovitz, Buchbinder, and Mor 1998, 415).

It is important to situate the construction of the "victims/survivors" discourse in a larger effort to have public conversations about crime—responses to it and control of it—and about the expanding role of the mental health profession in treating victims (Best 1997). Early theories in the discipline of victimology focused on victim blame and responsibility (see Karmen 2013) but were later challenged by the second-wave feminist movement that involved battered women's advocates and feminist activists (Pleck 1987; Schechter 1982). I have noted that the image of the battered woman as passive and blameless that emerged from this movement is misleading because it fails to take into account the issues and struggles women encounter both within the relationship and outside of it: greater attention must be paid to women's multiple oppressions shaped by race, sexuality, poverty, religion, and so forth if we are to better understand women's reactions to abuse. Berns (2004, 55) adds that a "victim empowerment" model that stresses efforts to increase self-esteem and "take control of your life" and "refuse to be a victim" continues to hold women responsible for solving the abuse in their lives.

The sociologist Amy Leisenring (2006, 312) has looked at the survivorship discourse, seeing it as "the other side of being a victim." She states that in contrast to the negative connotations associated with the word *victim*, the word *survivor* is associated with "agency, coping, resistance, decision making, recovery, and survival" (see also Crann and Barata 2016; Dunn 2005; McLeer 1998; Meloy and Miller 2011). The reconceptualization of victims as survivors reduces the stigma that attaches to a victim identity, yet it can still reinforce a dichotomy instead of considering the continuum of victimization and empowerment that most victims experience. While victims of IPV/A encounter all of these perceptions of their abusive situation in their interactions with other people (such as friends, family, and victim advocates), in other places (like shelters or the criminal justice system), and in the media, Leisenring (2006) is most concerned with how women construct their own meanings and interpretations. Her work with forty battered women reveals that they both claimed and rejected a victim identity. Leisenring (2006, 307) identifies four common ways of perceiving a victim identity that represent the women's constructions of the concept, all of them viewed negatively by the women: one who suffers a harm over which she has no control; one who deserves sympathy and/or requires some type of action be taken against the accused; one who is to blame for her experiences; and one who is powerless and weak.

The women interviewed by Leisenring (2006) stated that they were victims to convey the trauma and harm they suffered and had no control over and to demonstrate their worthiness of sympathy and support, but they also distanced themselves from a victim identity because they did not feel they were culpable for the abuse they endured. Missing from the women's understandings of the dominant meanings of the "victim" concept were the themes of empowerment and survivorship—underscoring the importance of listening to how women articulate their experiences and construct meaning. While half of the sample took some responsibility for the role they played in their abusive relationships, for instance by not standing up to their partner or by remaining in the relationship, they did not feel they caused or deserved the abuse. Profit (1996, 29) conceptualizes a survivor identity to highlight both victimization and agency: "The conceptualization of 'battered women' as 'survivors' acknowledges their tremendous strengths and coping skills in surviving violence as well as their victimization, pain, and loss." Some women explicitly embraced a survivor identity that focused on strength and resilience, but others felt that even after they left their abusive relationships they remained victims of the abuser's stalking and harassment through the courts, a situation that created some dissonance with being a survivor. Leisenring's interactionist framework helps explain why women struggle with identity stigma and the methods they use to combat cultural stereotypes associated with the victim label. She points to legal scholar Martha Minow's (1993) description of victimhood as a "cramped identity" and argues for the broadening of victim discourses to recognize that neither "victim" nor "survivor" is a static category; rather, victim discourses "appear to both enable and constrain battered women's processes of self-construction and self-representation" (Leisenring 2006, 327).

In this book I have made every effort to avoid drawing any linguistic distinctions between women who did the "right" thing versus those who made what could be judged as the "wrong" choice. The word *survivor* connotes a positive reclamation of one's experience but sets up a distinction between "good" victims and "bad" victims (who cannot just move on, get over it, and so forth). At the same time, however, we do not always have the luxury to choose our own words; words take on very specific policy connotations and importance. Victim or survivor identities cannot fully account for the nuances and complexities of women's daily living situations, and I believe in letting the women's narratives speak for themselves. In my work, I let the women choose, knowing that while *survivor* sounds more positive and empowering, it ignores the victimization and violence (Dragiewicz 2011; Hamby 2014) and can also create more distancing from and diminishment of the experience of violence and abuse. In this book, I primarily use the term *victims/survivors* because it best reflects how the women characterized themselves. We will hear more from the women about where they see themselves in this conversation in chapter 2.

RESILIENCE, GROWTH, AND RECOVERY

Without necessarily saying the word *resilience,* the women I interviewed talked both about a process of moving forward in a positive way and regaining strength and self-esteem and about specific actions they took to keep themselves (and their children in many cases) safe and to facilitate their well-being. That is one way to think about resilience. Growth and resilience, for these women, ebbed and flowed, much as grief does in the bereaved. One minute they could be doing fine, but then a memory or some kind of reminder like a familiar smell or strain of music could come flooding in, uninvited, and challenge their hard-won equilibrium. Though we understand a lot about the deleterious effects of IPV/A, until very recently the sociological literature restricted discussion of these effects to PTSD and was more focused on crisis needs for victims, problems with gaining social support, and dealings with police, courts, and other institutions.

Definitions of resilience and views on its meaning vary across disciplines, reflecting the lack of a conceptual framework to guide this work. As the psychologist Ann Masten (2007, 924) states: "There is a long history of controversy about the meaning of resilience and how to operationalize it . . . including debates about whether resilience is best defined as a trait, a process, an outcome, a pattern of life course development, narrow or broad, multifaceted or unidimensional, short- or long-term, and whether resilience should encompass recovery as well as resistance, internal as well as external adaptive functioning, and external as well as internal resources." Indeed, in my study, resilience manifested in a multifaceted way, with the women's actions and behaviors vacillating between many of these meanings, reflecting resilience as a process. It was not a trait; rather, it emerged from their experiences, though the women connected it to aspects of their personalities such as strength, stubbornness, and fighting spirit.

Since the 1970s, psychological research on resilience has focused primarily on the impact of adversity on children—what helps their chances of getting through childhood trauma relatively unscathed—and the elderly (Williams 2002). Psychologists have wanted to know why some children are more successful in overcoming challenges, and their research has measured competence (the presence of good outcomes based on life tasks that can be measured) and attempted to identify the qualities that could protect someone against future adversity (Williams 2002, 200). They have noted that resilience cannot be mistaken for individual ruggedness or willpower (Blundo 2002); it is not just about "bucking up." When people succeed in overcoming adversity, they do so within the context of many other circumstances and caring individuals; again, it is not a trait but a process. This kind of conceptualization makes sense for looking at resilience in relation to IPV/A as well.

Not until the 1990s did psychologists move away from vulnerability/ deficit models of the adverse circumstances that many people faced to look at cases of success in adversity, reflecting a discipline-specific paradigmatic shift from illness to health (O'Leary 1998). However, resilience is not just a shift from the negative to the positive pole on the risk continuum. O'Leary and Ickovics (1995) suggest that people faced with challenge can succumb or respond by *surviving* (continuing to function but in an impaired fashion), *recovering* (returning to a previous, baseline level of functioning); or *thriving* (going beyond the original level of psychosocial functioning, growing vigorously, flourishing). They believe that thriving is transformative, since it rests on experiencing a fundamental cognitive shift in response to a challenge:

> Challenge provides the opportunity for change because it forces individuals to confront personal priorities and to reexamine their sense of self. It can alter social roles, resulting in the acquisition of a new role (e.g., role of patient), loss of an old role (e.g., parenthood, after the death of a child), or a reordering of role priorities (e.g., recognition that it is more important to focus on interpersonal relationships than career success). . . . For such a transformation to occur, the challenge must be profound, an event such as facing a fatal illness, a severe traumatic accident or victimization, a great loss, or an existential crisis—events that shake the foundation of one's life, calling into question one's sense of purpose, meaning, or identity. (O'Leary 1998, 430)

Snodgrass's (1998, 431) reports this kind of transformation in a breast cancer survivor who is thriving and who "attributes some of her growth to spirituality, a belief that everything she encounters, positive or negative, provides an opportunity for growth."

Thus the psychology literature acknowledges both individual and social resources as key factors undergirding resilience and thriving. In particular, the individual's mobilization of social support is associated with health and well-being, particularly for women, so it is important to examine the role of social relationships as central to women's resilience. We know that many battered women in relationships are isolated or prevented by their abuser from reaching out to significant others in social networks—or that the abuser has destroyed their networks—so understanding how ending the relationship affects support mobilization and social support is crucial for understanding long-term survivorship and resilience. A sociological framework adds to these factors by examining how social structure and social institutions contribute to survivors' resilience and growth.

Psychologists have mostly explored individuals' resilience using quantitative measures, but there is disagreement on both how to define resilience and how to measure it. Crann and Barata (2016) identify salient theoretical and methodological concerns raised in the psychology literature, including assumptions that resilience is consistent over time and populations; the varying conceptualizations of resilience as a trait, an outcome, or a process, depending on the researcher (see broader discussion including critiques in Luthar, Cicchetti, and Becker 2000; Roisman 2005); the possible lack of a meaningful distinction between different measures of resilience because results depend on the types of questions used, the longevity of the stressor, and who is being studied (Macini and Bonanno 2006); and the failure to consider how contextual and environmental factors, such as the criminal justice system and family courts, influence women's response to IPV/A. Thus Crann and Barata (2016) and others critique the bulk of the resilience research for being too narrow and reducing resilience to an essentialist construct (see also Massey et al. 1998; Ungar 2004). In this vein, Ungar (2004, 345) contends that quantitative approaches are "unable to accommodate the plurality of meanings individuals negotiate in their self-construction as resilience."

Another limitation of the research is that definitions of resilience may explicitly require the absence of diagnosed mental health issues, such as PTSD (see, e.g., Crann and Barata's [2016, 854] summary of psychosocial indicators of resilience). Other researchers who have looked more holistically at women's lives note that individuals can have a diagnosis yet still be able to function well in other areas (work, school, and so forth; see Luthar, Cicchetti, and Becker 2000). Bonanno (2005), for example, claims that resilience is a common response to trauma, that it can wax and wane, and that there are multiple ways to be resilient. Many sociologists (and criminologists) who have studied victimization take this perspective, finding that even when victims are embedded in situations with intense stressors they can exhibit resilience. Indeed, Saakvitne, Tennen, and Affleck (1998) have argued that "standing alongside the entire range of debilitating effects of trauma, most survivors display a stunning capacity for survival and perseverance. Growth and pain, therefore, are not necessarily mutually exclusive, but instead are inextricably linked in recovery from trauma" (quoted in Anderson, Renner, and Danis 2012, 1280). Anderson, Renner, and Danis's (2012) study of women who had experienced IPV/A but had not been in an abusive relationship in the past year and Humphrey's (2003) study of battered women living in a domestic violence shelter report that although the women were still experiencing distress and trauma they were at the same time demonstrating resilience; such findings buttress Anderson and colleagues' conclusion that "resilience and impairment are not necessarily opposites, but instead appear to be different aspects of the overall experience of coping and adjustment for survivors of domestic violence" (2012, 1294).

Some researchers have distinguished between resilience or recovery and post-traumatic growth, a psychological concept that implies a significant positive reconfiguration in emotional and cognitive functioning (see Tedeschi and Calhoun 2003). O'Leary and Ickovics (1995, 122) similarly distinguish thriving, or "the effective mobilization of individual and social resources in response to risk or threat," from mere coping or resilience because, as an "adaptive response to challenge," thriving "represents something more than a return to equilibrium." Other psychologists do not make such distinctions (see, e.g., Bonanno 2004). Crann and Barata (2016, 855) conclude that concepts related to positive functioning after trauma, such as growth, adaptation, coping, recovery, and thriving, are typically not well defined and are often used interchangeably across studies. A multimethods approach can better clarify our understanding of paths of recovery and resilience and the distinctions between them.

RESEARCH APPROACHES TO RESILIENCE

Some IPV/A researchers use quantitative methods to test models of resilience in specific populations such as women in battered women's shelters (Humphreys 2003) or African American women (Meadows et al. 2005). As noted above, resilience is typically measured by the absence of PTSD (Wright, Perez, and Johnson 2010), or the absence or low levels of anxiety, depression, and suicide attempts (see Carlson et al. 2002; Crann and Barata 2016; Meadows et al. 2005). Results from these quantitative studies suggest that protective factors for building resilience include social support, self-esteem, positive health, religion and spirituality, hope, self-efficacy, effectiveness of obtaining resources, and coping and empowerment (Bradley, Schwartz, and Kaslow 2005; Carlson et al. 2002; Coker et al. 2005; Meadows et al. 2005; Wright, Perez, and Johnson 2010).

Quantitative studies do not acknowledge the diversity of responses to IPV/A and the complexity of women's experiences and understanding of resilience. Qualitative approaches tend to better recognize how much women's experiences vary and are influenced by particular social and cultural contexts (see Anderson, Renner, and Danis 2012; Crann and Barata 2016; Young 2007). Other work that explores how women describe their experiences of leaving the abuser sheds some light on the issue of growth and resilience in IPV/A survivors (see Crawford, Liebling-Kalifani, and Hill 2009; R. Davis 2002; Hamby 2014; Kangagaratnam et al. 2012). But there is still a need for more work on women's lived experience and women's own constructions of resilience (Weiss 2008). Although some qualitative studies have sought to identify individual and institutional factors that aid recovery and resilience during a set period of time following abuse, I have sought to go beyond this frame and look at the process of resilience as a journey *throughout* the relationship, not just after the relationship ends, and to explore how resilience emerges and is maintained over time. My work builds on Crann and Barata's (2016) phenomenological work and offers a lens through which women describe their process of resilience during their relationship and as their life apart from the abusers continues.

SOCIOLOGICAL FRAMEWORKS

I favor an understanding of resilience that is more sociological or holistic than anything that can be conveyed by a quantitatively measurable construct or scale. My in-depth interviews with victims/survivors reveal a process of resilience that ebbs and flows, depending on the buffers and support the women receive and other contextual factors. These women are able to navigate parts of their life with impressive competence while they simultaneously lack efficacy in other areas. Yet overall they are growing and rebounding and showing resilience.

While the early research on "thriving" has a psychological focus on individual issues such as developing self-esteem, finding new meaning in life, and overcoming depression, some sociologists such as Blankenship (1998) urge us to look at thriving within a feminist sociological frame that takes into account race, class, and gender. Such an approach explores factors that influence thriving or predict its likelihood and uses communities, institutions, and organizations as units of analyses. This approach also acknowledges that individuals can respond to crisis not just in psychological ways but also in social ways, by devoting themselves to a cause or to social change.[2] Thus a sociological perspective turns our attention to "social structures of power and influence rather than the characteristics of individuals" (Blankenship 1998, 395). Many of the women I interviewed engaged in a commitment to community advocacy, such as activism in WIND, while other women performed activist work within their circle of friends, acquaintances, and coworkers. As public speakers or volunteers drawn to speaking up against IPV/A, the women behaved similarly to the recovering drug addicts that Blankenship discusses, who sought jobs as outreach workers or substance abuse counselors, or became political activists, as a way to repay society or express gratitude to those who had assisted in their recovery. So one pathway to thriving, or resilience, is survivors' politicization, a sociological outcome.

Feminist theory conceptualizes social context as involving the intersections of race, class, and gender to form a complex system of domination and meaning (see Blankenship 1998, 396; Andersen and Collins 1995; Crenshaw 1991), operating simultaneously (not additively) to organize social life in general and women's lives in particular (C. West and Fenstermaker 1995). Many researchers have asserted that IPV/A survivors who can mobilize resources are more likely to thrive, but if we look at resource mobilization in terms of intersectionality, individual and social resources are not easily disentangled or randomly distributed. Some individuals' more marginalized position, lack of resources, and lack of access to resources such as social services or the criminal justice system can adversely affect or wholly preclude thriving and can increase their likelihood of becoming victimized in the first place.

The other crucial argument in Blankenship's work is that some challenges are extraordinary while others are routine and that defining which is which may depend on where one is situated in the social hierarchy: "What is profound and extraordinary in one context may be routine and ordinary in another" (1988, 399). In particular, she explores urban violence through the life histories of women who witnessed or experienced violence, none of whom characterized the challenges of their lives as extraordinary. It is hard to view individuals who have undergone IPV/A in a before-and-after framework when challenges are part and parcel of their everyday life. For many of the women I interviewed, experience of IPV/A was not an isolated traumatic event but one in a series of long-term cumulative traumas. Blankenship's distinction between extraordinary and routine violence helps us understand the dissonance felt by some of the WIND women, many of whom occupied more marginalized social positions, because of race, class, and education, than other members of the community-based group.

MEANING MAKING

Another way to look at resilience is to explore how people make sense of change through the process of "meaning making," further discussed in chapter 4. Some social psychological work looks at how survivors reconstruct their assumptive world following trauma: over time, survivors can perceive events in a new way that gives them a sense of purpose and value (see Tedeschi and Calhoun 2004). This change in meaning rests on Janoff-Bulman's (1992, 2006) work on world assumptions theory, which asserts that people have inherently positive core assumptions about the benevolence of the world and meaningfulness and their own self-worth; an event such as interpersonal trauma shakes their assumptive world to its foundations and thus may offer opportunity for profound growth (see Lilly, Valdez, and Graham-Bermann 2011). For instance, Elizabeth Smart attributes her greater empathy and understanding for others and her activism to the traumatic experience she endured. She explains: "Because of the things I have lived through, I can help other people now. I can reach out to other victims and help them to learn to be happy. Because I have actually lived through these experiences, I am able to be a voice for change. If I hadn't lived through these experiences, I am not sure that I would have cared enough about these issues to become involved" (2013, 303). Valdez and Lilly (2015) were the first to examine longitudinal changes in IPV/A survivors' assumptive worlds with post-traumatic growth They asked a sample of twenty-three women who had experienced IPV/A to complete self-reports at two time periods, about a year apart. They found that if the women were not revictimized in the year following the initial self-report, they reported greater post-traumatic growth (87 percent of their sample). Just before the women I interviewed left their abusers for good, they often experienced an epiphany much like the one characterized in Valdez and Lilly's (2015, 225) research: "In a world that is not comprehensible, controllable, or predictable, survivors are confronted with the fact that living can no longer be taken for granted and human life appreciates in value. In response, survivors embrace life and create a meaningful existence through goals (interpersonal, spiritual, altruistic), commitments (to friends, family, and community), and self-determination that serve to provide a sense of meaning and purpose."

But we still lack knowledge on what helps women achieve and sustain new meaning in their lives long term (Goodman et al. 2003). Dutton and Greene (2010) explore resilience in relation to crime victimization, guided by the fact that many people rebound and adjust quite well in the aftermath of adversity and trauma (see also Ai and Park 2005). Their interest, similar to my own, was to see how knowledge of resilience could enhance the development of resources used by the criminal justice and health care systems to help victims navigate their exposure to adverse events. Reviewing all studies they could locate that measured resilience in some way in the aftermath of crime victimization, they looked at resilience as defined in three ways: as protective factors existing prior to the victimization (for example, individual characteristics and community and social network characteristics); as adaptive processes occurring in response to the victimization; and as positive outcomes after victimization (220). Five of the studies they found were on the resilience of women exposed to IPV/A specifically and used psychological scales and checklists such as Wagnild and Young's (1993) Resilience Scale (a twenty-five-item self-report measure using two factors, personal competence, and acceptance of self and life), and Derogatis's (1994) Symptom Checklist-90. The most salient of these findings in relationship to meaning making is from a study of sixty IPV/A survivors living in a shelter, reporting that ending the relationship and having a role model (i.e., knowing another person who experienced positive change after terminating an abusive relationship) predicted overall post-traumatic growth (Cobb et al. 2006).

In one of the first studies to use both psychological measures of post-traumatic stress and resilience and qualitative interviews, Anderson et al. (2012) looked at thirty-seven women who had not been in an abusive relationship in the past year to determine what factors help women recover from IPV/A relationships and how they achieve long-term success, finding that social and spiritual support were instrumental factors. They queried women about their use of informal and formal support systems in addition to discovering what other personal qualities and social conditions influenced their lives after their abusive relationships ended. Recovery outcomes were also measured, with results indicating that the women in their study were largely asymptomatic for PTSD (1286) and had high scores of overall resilience in psychosocial and spiritual domains.[3] In particular, the women's highest-scoring single item was "I have at least one close and secure relationship which helps me when I am stressed" (1287). Using grounded-theory methods to account for categories and patterns related to recovery and resilience, Anderson and colleagues found that women's determination was strengthened by spiritual and religious beliefs and by the acceptance of informal and formal support from other people in their lives. Not all of them found spiritual support from their faith communities; some had crises of faith during their recovery or found that their faith communities failed to provide any emotional comfort or practical assistance with pressing financial or housing needs. But in the aftermath of their trauma, many of the women, whether in tandem with organized religion or not, relied on a sense of meaning and purpose that they derived from their faith and a belief that the source of their strength was a Higher Power or God (1289). They also tended to see the adversity they had suffered as a catalyst for growth, claiming, like many of the women I interviewed, that "what doesn't kill you always makes you stronger" (1290).[4] Women in Anderson's study also emphasized the crucial role that friends, family, and employers played in their lives. Sometimes informal social support networks, such as family of origin, played a more significant part during their recovery than they had during the abusive relationship (because family and friends might not have known about the violence or wanted to interfere) (1292). Such support is especially valuable in helping victim/survivors make meaning of what they have experienced.

Another more recent study explored the "recovery process" for 123 women survivors of IPV/A by using an online survey method that permitted open-ended responses (Flasch, Murray, and Crowe 2017). They identified intrapersonal and interpersonal processes involved in recovery, with participants echoing the women in my project in their descriptions of resilience as a journey with ups and downs (3390).

Such research is important in our quest to understand victims/survivors' perceptions of what helps them make sense of their chaos in the aftermath of their abusive relationships, and my work adds to it by increasing the ethnic, racial, and sexual diversity of my sample and looking at the process of resilience in two different groups of women—those who are public activists associated with an organized group embedded in a state coalition against domestic violence and those who are unaffiliated with a formal survivors' group.

Moving away from a deficit-based analysis of IPV/A to a strength-based, survivor-identified one is a major development in our understanding of how women make sense of the complexities and contradictions of their lives. This chapter outlined how the social movement advocating for "battered women" has both helped and curtailed efficacious responses. Abused women, as experts of their own situation, can tell us how IPV/A affects their daily lives, what made it possible for them to end their relationship, what their short-term, crisis-driven needs are, and how they are making their longer-term journeys to well-being. A trauma framework can provide a broader range of women's responses to IPV/A and of the paths women take in repudiating such violence and abuse.

Both sociological and psychological research provide a window into the construction of meaning making and identity reformulation following adverse life circumstances. People show more resilience in recovering from trauma than was once believed, and negative life events do not need to be the cornerstone of one's identity. Rebuilding shattered assumptions entails both personal understanding of one's experiences and inner strengths and interaction with social others and institutions. Survivors construct their own meanings and interpretations of their identities, and their conceptualizations interact with responses by significant people and social institutions. Scholarship on post-traumatic growth attests to the possible transformative effect of cognitive shifts following adversity. These opportunities for change are not a given but can be part of a process that connects growth with other factors such as support mobilization and faith. A sociological approach to survivors' resilience joins micro-level factors identified in the psychological literature to more macro-level factors such as social structure and social institutions and, with the addition of qualitative research, can go beyond psychometric measurements and gain more insight from in-depth interview methods. The discussions of trauma, identity construction, victimhood and survivorship, resilience, and meaning making presented in this chapter provide a theoretical framework that will help inform the analysis in the subsequent chapters.

2. Situating the Research Project

This chapter has two sections. The first section describes my research methods and my approach to data collection with victims/survivors. It provides a demographic snapshot of my interviewees and introduces and provides background on the organization where I did my fieldwork. The second section lays the groundwork for the subsequent chapters' exploration of themes that emerged from my interviews by describing how the women in my sample understood themselves in relation to their abuse and to the concepts of victimhood and survivorhood. Many of the women drew strength from seeing themselves as survivors. Yet this identification was not as clear-cut as one might think, even though they had been away from their abusive relationships for at least five years. Their lives reflected experiences as both victims and survivors. Seeing themselves as resilient, capable, and hardy survivors did not erase the fear and trauma associated with victimization, and some women struggled with finding a way to balance honoring their past and appreciating their future. When I asked the women how they characterized themselves, their dissonance underscored the complexity of identity construction, incorporating the many layers of both individual perceptions and the effect of social institutions in shaping presentations of their experiences.

METHODS

The aim of my research project was to understand, from victims/survivors of IPV/A themselves, their process of resilience: how they became and stayed free of abusive relationships and the factors that helped or impeded that process. Because of my interest in hearing the women's own stories, I employed a multimethods strategy. I did fieldwork as a participant observer at the meetings of an activist organization of IPV/A survivors (here called WIND, or Women in Nonviolent Domains) that was housed within their state's Coalition against Domestic Violence; I supplemented this with content analysis of the organization's written materials; and I conducted in-depth semistructured qualitative interviews with survivors. I also conducted in-depth qualitative interviews with state coalition members and service directors who worked with survivor groups, though these interviews merely helped me to frame questions; they are not quoted here and are only indirectly featured in my analysis.

Fieldwork

Beginning in January 2012 I spent approximately thirty months attending monthly meetings of WIND in order to better understand the women's approach in tackling IPV/A issues. This contact offered me an up-close view of the factors that helped shape women's resilience and the multidimensional nature of the resilience process. My exposure to the women's challenges, triumphs, and struggles for almost three years provided me with a great deal of insider information about their lives, which in turn would enrich the creation of my in-depth interview questions for survivors.

I sought permission to do fieldwork at WIND by presenting my research ideas to WIND's chair, who agreed to bring a written description to the meeting to present to members; I received consent from the members that they would like to participate in the interviews and would also welcome my presence in the monthly meetings. I was invited to talk more about the project at their next meeting, and the women were eager to sign up for interviews.

Through my fieldwork I became fully immersed in WIND's culture. I took notes on group dynamics and discussions at every monthly WIND task force meeting I could attend. These field notes (approximately 180 pages) were later typed up in greater detail and augmented with WIND material (meeting agendas, minutes, handouts, and so forth). For the few times I could not be there, I had process observation notes taken by the coalition staff member liaison to WIND. I was also able to check in with WIND members, in addition to the liaison staff member and various coalition members (the executive director, the media specialist, and so forth), to receive clarification on issues I did not fully understand. Most members attended a light buffet dinner before each meeting, so I always came early enough to have the opportunity to chat informally with members during the meal. Anywhere from six to twelve members (plus a coalition staff member) attended meetings. Women's attendance varied depending on what else was going on their lives. Race/ethnicity varied among the participants. Of the three elected positions, at least one was held by an African American woman during the years of my fieldwork.

The continuity of my involvement with WIND allowed me to follow conversations, understand allusions to past events or issues, and stay connected to members. It facilitated members' ease and familiarity with me, thus establishing an informal rapport when I conducted individual in-depth interviews later. I became "one of the group" in some ways—included in in-jokes (to some extent) and confidences, while still being able to provide feedback or resources that I had at my disposal, given my academic job, when asked.[1]

WIND is described as a "domestic violence survivors' task force" of the state's Coalition against Domestic Violence.[2] Its purpose is to use members' survivor knowledge to inform the public, including social services and criminal justice system professionals, about IPV/A. WIND's pamphlet, readily available for public distribution, says that its members view domestic violence as one part of a larger foundation of oppression that shores up violence against women. Some of WIND's frequent activities include public speaking in order to inform the public about what abusive relationships look like, how to understand the warning signs, and how to help someone in an abusive relationship; these speaking events often occur in town libraries, and WIND members regularly talk to residents at battered women's shelters in order to show them that they were able to get out of their abusive relationships and inspire them to believe in themselves. Annually, WIND coordinates a drive that collects clothing, linen, toiletries, and household items needed for women and children residing in and leaving shelters. During Domestic Violence Awareness Month, WIND designs displays for public libraries. WIND is often sought out by the state coalition or other service providers and professionals to weigh in on policy issues and criminal justice or legal practices.

Thus, first and foremost, WIND is a task force with an activist agenda—not a support group, though in the meetings I observed members were always willing to suspend an agenda to console or problem-solve with a group member. Potential members are screened by the chair to ensure they understand the mission and goals of the task force and that they do not seek a therapeutic group structured for victim support. In other research projects, I've attended victim support groups, and the tenor of the WIND meetings was different because the women were very engaged with local and national efforts to address survivorship issues. Members contributed a lot of shared knowledge and a valuable perspective, despite the private fears and uncertainties they sometimes revealed in their individual interviews with me away from the group. Though any physical abuse was no longer ongoing, and all of the women had been separated or divorced from their abuser for at least five years, it was clear that some abusers continued to use tactics designed to intimidate or harass the women.

As a group, the WIND members emboldened each other and strove to utilize their combined enthusiasm, experiences, and varied skills to affect social change. What struck me each month was the women's energy. Consistent at the meetings I attended was organization members' warmth and good humor. Though there was talk about ex-partners/spouses if relevant, as in the case of the women who were still involved in messy child custody battles, conversations mainly revolved around present-day circumstances—who was finishing a degree, whose birthday was coming up, who was changing jobs, who was becoming a grandmother or was pregnant. The women exchanged high-fives and support, and laughter filled the air.

My fieldwork revealed that women in WIND showed and developed their resilience by exercising their voice and agency within a structure where the larger state coalition had most of the power. As stated earlier, WIND is part of the much larger umbrella organization, the state Coalition against Domestic Violence. The interdependence is visible and offers both benefits and disadvantages for each entity. The coalition provides staff support for WIND, as well as resources for printing brochures and money for purchasing materials for WIND's projects, publicity, and ongoing efforts to shore up sustainability. It is important for the coalition to recognize survivors and their voices, and the executive director and other staff actively seek supporters' input in domestic violence–related issues.[3] For most of the years that I attended WIND meetings, at least one and often two WIND members served on the coalition's board of directors.

Many state coalitions rely on victims/survivors to tell their stories at certain events, to help with public service announcements (PSAs) during annual conferences or retreats, or to staff a table at events to highlight survivors and WIND to the community. These kinds of contributions by WIND members gave legitimacy to the coalition's mission and gave the women of WIND a feeling of "buy-in" and a sense that they were respected for their lived experiences. One of the WIND members had a beautiful voice and wrote a song about survival in order to spread hope to others. The coalition invited her several times to sing her song at large public events and sell her CD with the song on it; 50 percent of sales proceeds went to the coalition, and one of the WIND members designed the CD cover (she also planned to sell the original cover painting and donate 50 percent of the profits). When you walk through the door of the coalition's office, the front conference room is adorned with brightly painted and decorated suitcases—symbolizing the first steps of leaving an abusive relationship—created by WIND members for their Survivor Suitcase Project (two of these grace the cover of this book). WIND also provided input to the curriculum developed by the state men's anti-IPV/A group; at least five women attended their annual event and felt honored to be asked to participate and offer constructive suggestions. The coalition, when able, provides funds for at least two WIND members to attend the annual conference of the National Coalition against Domestic Violence; at the survivors' Speak Out, the WIND members who attended that year shared that every culture, sexual orientation, and race was represented and that they had never received such "honor" as victims of domestic violence. WIND is also part of the annual legislative day, when supporters of the coalition travel to the statehouse to make their presence and beliefs known at the legislative hall. Some WIND members have given speeches during the legislature's open meetings, and they also call senators and representatives (both state and federal level) about issues that concern them, such as laws that permit the carrying of concealed weapons.[4] One woman talked about the backlash effect for women who asked too many questions, however, especially in terms of custody issues and/or the civil Protection from Abuse (PFA) process, saying that the court "paints us as trouble." WIND provides the opportunity for members to learn about what is going on in the community; for instance, the VINE (Victim Information and Notification Everyday) system is supposed to contact victims when their perpetrators are released, but members fear that VINE is spending too much of its resources contacting people about outstanding traffic tickets or upcoming court dates.[5] Once the women were alerted to this practice, one of the members volunteered to pursue this concern through the appropriate channels.

This all sounds very harmonious, but strife and misunderstandings arose at times between WIND and the coalition. A bit of background is necessary. The coalition is explicitly guided by feminist principles, even though the word *feminist* is more implied than stated. Past research demonstrates that women respond better to advocacy when it avoids controlling behaviors that resemble what women experienced in abusive relationships and when it recognizes women's individual needs and the importance of their gaining control over their lives and exercising choice (see Goodman and Epstein 2008; Weisz 1999; Zweig and Burt 2007). Yet stakeholders (i.e., domestic violence organizations) may have very different agendas than the individuals they serve or work with. Patricia Martin's (2005) work on sexual assault organizations, for example, demonstrates how even when organizations are founded on feminist principles they can revictimize victims by adopting gendered policies and practices that make structural, cultural, and ideological assumptions about behaviors and perspectives associated with masculinity and femininity and tend to perpetuate inequality (see also Nichols 2011, who draws on Joan Acker's [1990] work on gendered organizations).

Part of the rift between domestic violence organizations and those they serve reflects the "successful" evolution of these organizations as they become embedded in collaborative efforts with police, the court system, and child protective services in their community-based victim advocacy (see McDermott and Garofalo 2004). The pressures of answering to multiple constituencies and funding sources often relegate feminist principles to the back burner (see, e.g., Macy et al. 2010; Murray 1988). Though domestic violence advocacy, through organizations such as domestic violence coalitions, is described as challenging the reproduction of male dominance over women in principle and practice, this aim has been compromised or deemphasized as the movement has grown to incorporate so many competing perspectives and people outside of the core IPV/A realm. Murray (1988), drawing on fieldwork at a battered women's shelter, shows how the shelter movement can become depoliticized. At the shelter she studied, staff focused more on women's psychological progress in reaching certain conclusions about their abusive situation than on the practical resources women needed to disengage from their abuser. Pressures to "fix" women can conflict with the feminist goal of empowering them. Although the shelter that Murray studied offered peer counseling as a vehicle of self-empowerment, in accordance with feminist principles, the goal of self-empowerment was undermined by the asymmetrical relationship between shelter staff and residents, in which residents could be penalized for not conforming to staff's expectations about how a woman's process of leaving the abuser was supposed to play out. Though victim advocates are well intentioned, IPV/A as a whole has become more mainstream, and that means having to work with more bureaucracy, regulations, and professionals than ever before; often the professionals outside of the coalition are not as well trained or knowledgeable about domestic violence (McDermott and Garofalo 2004). Lynne Haney (1996, 760), in her research on two state agencies, a juvenile probation department and a group home for incarcerated teen mothers, has drawn on feminist theories of the state to argue that even when state institutions are guided by female-dominated staff and challenge gendered norms, their underlying patriarchal structure makes it difficult to carry out feminist principles in practice (see also Gregory,

Nnawulezi, and Sullivan's 2017 work with shelter residents, which found that too much staff surveillance of residents and too many shelter rules negatively affected residents' well-being and empowerment).

During my own ethnographic study of WIND, I saw firsthand some of the tensions between the coalition and the survivors' task force. The coalition had concerns that some of WIND members' suggested actions or statements might jeopardize women's safety or garner bad publicity for the coalition or for WIND in particular. Though they sought WIND's input, they tempered these solicitations with strategic plans about how to include them in a way that fit into the overall mission of the coalition so as not to undo any hard-won alliances across the state. Thus they wanted to vet WIND members' ideas and written work before these went public, and it was apparent to WIND that their efforts to independently frame their organization's activities were not always well received. This created hurt feelings and some anger among WIND members, who believed that a survivor task force, composed of "experts," should not have to get permission from the coalition at every turn. Despite the good intentions of coalition staff, many WIND members felt silenced or condescended to by coalition responses and felt they were treated in ways reminiscent of their former abusers. They used words like *disempowering, paternalistic,* and *controlling* when they talked about some of the coalition's reactions to their efforts.

Such tensions were dramatically illustrated after a battered woman and her best friend who had accompanied her to court as a support person were shot outside the courthouse by a relative of the woman's batterer. This happened in the state where many of the WIND members resided, at a courthouse (housing the family court) that many of the survivors introduced in this book had visited too many times to count. WIND members were outspoken in their critique of the courthouse safety precautions, sending the coalition drafts of a letter to the editor of the state's largest newspaper and an appeal to the state chief judge to heed their suggestions for improvement based on their collective experience. But the coalition, despite its commitment to feminist advocacy, feared jeopardizing community liaisons with the police and courts and therefore told WIND not to send the letter. WIND members felt that the coalition was silencing them and reproducing patriarchal ideologies that rendered their views insignificant. On a personal level, they also felt betrayed that the coalition could engage in so much rhetoric about the strength of survivorship, yet at the same time try to micromanage their task force. Simultaneously, however, most WIND members had strong friendship or collegial ties with coalition members and spoke of the executive director and other staff members with great respect and affection. So although they were sometimes critical of the coalition as an entity they refrained from attacks on individual staff.

When strife erupted, some WIND members felt the same frustration and anger that they had experienced when their batterers tried to define their reality or control the situation, and they sometimes responded with perhaps unintended, disproportionate drama because of their determination not to be silenced or feel "less than" again. Yet although I witnessed friction during the period of field observation, I was more struck by WIND's collective efficacy. These were not the meek, submissive women, afraid to speak up for themselves, that they described themselves as being during their abusive relationships. Rather, they displayed tremendous personal growth in their ability to trust others, to assert their positions without apology or capitulation, to resist being bulldozed over by people who had positions of greater power, and to resolve conflict nonviolently, thus living the principles of healthy relationships that they had forged since terminating their abusive ones.

Interviews

Participants   My interview sample consisted of thirty-one women who had ended their relationship with their abuser and had been living free of violence from their former abuser or any new abusive partner for at least five years. A few words are necessary to explain my sample criteria. Women were included if they had ended their marriage or relationship with their abusive partner, through either a distinct breakup or a divorce (though three women had partners who died, their deaths occurred many years after their relationships ended). All of the women had lived with their partner/spouse while the abuse was ongoing, so the "violence-free for at least five years" criterion included no longer sharing a living space with the abuser. However, being "violence-free" does not mean that the abuser necessarily ceased all tactics of coercive control. Gendered power dynamics still existed if the ex-partners had minor children with the women, since they often used opportunities to manipulate the legal proceedings as a means of revenge. The women's new circumstances existed on a continuum: at one end were women whose ex-partners had died, or who shared no children with the ex-partner, or whose ex-partner had stopped abusing them through court proceedings. On the other end were women who still had some ties to their exes, who had some ongoing experiences of fear or harassment via "paper abuse" (the ex's deliberately frivolous filing of court papers to ensnarl them), or battles over custody, child support, and visitation. Often these women moved back and forth on the continuum. But regardless of the abusers' intent and actions, the women were steadfast in their determination to make better lives for themselves and their children through career achievements, home ownership, educational attainment, remarriage to a nonabusive partner, or other forms of growth and well-being, and to keep their lives and homes peaceful and free of the kind of abuse and violence they had once contained.

The overall sample included those who had experienced physical abuse and nonphysical abuse, those who were mothers and those who were not, and a broad range of racial, ethnic, and sexual identities. Of the thirty-one women, seven were African American, two were Latina, one was Asian, and twenty-one were white. Five of the women had married outside their own racial/ethnic group. Two identified as lesbian (though one was married to a man during her abusive relationship); two other women had children who were LGBTQ identified. The range in age at the time of interviews was between twenty-seven and seventy. The range of time out of the abusive relationship, at the time of the interview, was five to thirty-eight years. Two women mentioned having a disability and four mentioned having a child with a disability. At the time of interview, nineteen of the women were either remarried, engaged, or in a serious relationship. During their abusive relationships, twenty-five of the women had children and six did not; by the time I conducted interviews, three of these six women had children. Some women were very involved with the criminal and/or civil legal systems, whereas others were not. Some had an abundance of faith and sought solace in religion, while others gave little or no thought to religion or faith. Social class is always tricky to measure, given that many abusers are secretive about their financial situation. In addition, women's employment and education—essential components of social class measures—were often curtailed because of the abusers' sabotaging of such efforts. Many of the women completed educational paths or embarked on careers only after they had terminated their connections to the abusers. At the time of the interviews, educational attainment ranged from a GED to a PhD. Sixteen of the women interviewed were current WIND members, while twelve were not connected to WIND at all or to any other IPV/A activist organization; an additional three women had been to no more than three monthly meetings of WIND and had not remained part of the organization because it did not fit their current circumstances or they had moved out of state, and they were not WIND members at the time of the interview.

I divided the women into two groups: a "WIND" group, consisting of the sixteen current WIND members, and a "community-at-large" group, consisting of the twelve women who had no connection with WIND at all, as

TABLE 1 Participants' demographics

Name (pseudonym)	WIND member at time of interview	Length of abusive relationship	Length since termination (as of 2015)	Age at time of interview	Race/ethnicity	Children at time of abusive relationship	Education achieved before/during relationship	Education achieved since termination
Sandee	N	2	12	29	W	2 (not his)	HS	BA, MSW
Joan	Y	2	8	40	AA	3 (not his)	HS	BS
Abigayle	N	5	21	55	W	2 (not his)	BA	MBA
Celeste	N	3	31	50s	W	2	AA	PhD
Danielle	Y	14	5	36	W	4	BA	Online MA in process
Ellen	Y	7	6	20s	W	2 (1 his)	AA	
Elizabeth	Y	5–6	16	36	AA	1 (not his)	BS	
Florence	Y	10	10	Late 40s	W	3 (not his)	HS	
Brenda	N*	8	5	29	W	None	BA	
Julia	Y	13	7	52	W	1	BA	
Jenny	N*	15	10	35	Latina	None	PhD student	PhD
Pepper	N*	2.5	11	30	W	None	BA	
Terri	Y	5	6	29	W	1	BA	
Jayde	N	8	11	50	W	None	BA	
Katherine	N	3	35	70s	W	1 (not his)	HS	
Rosa	Y	7	34	70	Latina	3	BA	

Reeva	Y	5.5	15	40	AA	2	BA	
Jazzy	N	3 IPV relationships	23+	65	AA	3	HS	BA
Anita	Y	12+	15	54	AA	None	BA	
Amy	Y	2 IPV relationships	12	54	W	3 total	MA	
Tina	Y	10	25	64	AA	2 & step	HS	AA
Haley	Y	5	8	55	W	None	BA	
Dale	Y	17.5	8	52	W	2	HS	
Winnie	Y	16	8.5	52	W	3	MA	
Vanessa	Y	16	10	43	W	3	BA	Two MA
Sara	N	7	15	40s	AA	2	BA	MSW
Kristen	N	15+	6	40s	Asian	3	MA	EdD
Megan	N	11	20	39	W	3 (2 with him)	GED	
Casey	N	2.5	14	39	W	3 (1 with him)	BA	MA
Naomi	N	5	27	55	W	1	BA	PhD
Robyn	N	21	28	66	W	2	GED	PhD

* These women had attended a few (no more than three) meetings of WIND but had decided the organization wasn't for them; they are considered part of the community-at-large group.

well as the three women who had briefly attended WIND but had left. The women in the community-at-large group were distinct from WIND members in that they were not interested in playing an active public role in IPV/A organizations or groups or in becoming activists. Some of the women in this second group gravitated toward pursuing an education or job within the field of victim services, social work, or domestic violence, while others did not have any continued contact on a personal, volunteer, or professional level with IPV/A programs or related work.

A formal comparison between WIND members and women who did not participate in anti-IPV/A activism was not the purpose of my study. But I was interested in noting whether there could be differences between people who were drawn to joining activist organizations and publicly making statements about their history of being abused and people who shied away from the limelight and any kind of collective action but might still engage in individual advocacy and share their stories. Perhaps the members of the WIND group would have a different path to resilience, coping, and moving forward after abuse. I note these issues where relevant.

Sampling To obtain my interviewees, I used three sampling methods for the interview component of this project: purposive, convenience, and snowball. Purposive sampling specifically targets a population that fits the study's sample criteria and goal (Gay and Airasian 2003); here, I drew on the membership of WIND to obtain my "WIND" sample, introducing my project at their monthly meeting and requesting participation. However, my "community-in-large" sample was more difficult to obtain. My focus on victims/survivors of IPV/A who had been abuse-free for at least five years meant that such individuals might no longer be connected to any social service or criminal justice professionals and might not be publicly traceable at all unless they were associated with a survivors' group and were "out" as abuse victims/survivors. Consequently I also employed snowball and convenience strategies, which are often used when it is difficult to locate respondents that fit the sample criteria (Gay and Airasian 2003). Given the work I do (both scholarship and activism), I have numerous contacts with justice system professionals, victim advocates, and service providers. I asked them to contact or provide flyers about my research project to any women they knew who had left an abusive relationship years ago to inform them about my research project and to keep a stack of flyers on their tables at statewide meetings or trainings. I had flyers distributed at events of the state Coalition against Domestic Violence and I posted an ad on the coalition's website. I also relied on personal connections with victims/survivors who had learned about my research or the subject of IPV/A through my university teaching and other activities and who shared past abuse stories with me. Using this combination of strategies, I obtained my community-at-large sample of women.

Interview Protocol When conducting all the interviews, I followed similar protocol and conventions. I met women in the social service building where WIND meetings were held, in public spaces such as coffee shops, or at other locations the women themselves selected, which could include private homes. In all, the interviews totaled sixty-seven hours, resulting in several hundred pages of transcription; interviews ranged from one hour and fifteen minutes to six hours.'

When conducting the interviews, I followed Lofland and Lofland's interview preparation guidelines (1995, 78–88). I introduced myself and provided a broad outline of the project; I adopted the language of the respondents and did my best to be sensitive to what made sense to them; I structured the questions around general clusters and topics; I tried to build trust and rapport by demonstrating any personal knowledge about the issues they talked about; and I developed probes that addressed what the respondents mentioned and what they did not mention. Although for consistency I followed an overall checklist with each interview, I let flexibility rule, remaining open to pursuing other lines of inquiry. Respondents knew that they could skip answering questions and could challenge my questions or direction (e.g., on the grounds of style or content). I tape-recorded the interviews, but the women were assured that I would turn off the recorder at any point or erase any of their comments if requested. Many of the women said they would be honored if I used their real names, but in the interest of safety and consistency all names are pseudonyms.

Storytelling and the Narrative Arc "This book might be confusing to some. But keep in mind throughout my book that this was a very confusing world I lived in. I think to truly begin to understand what it was like, you would have had to be there, and since I wish that on no one, this book is my attempt to convey the overwhelming confusion I felt during those years and to begin to unravel the damage that was done to me and my family" (Dugard 2011, viii). These words open Jaycee Dugard's memoir *A Stolen Life* that chronicles her eighteen years of captivity after being abducted by a stranger at age eleven; her words capture her difficulty in expressing the pain of remembering and describing a deeply abusive situation in a concise fashion. The women I interviewed also recounted their stories with great passion and insight but with a constant chronological back-and-forth. Their narratives were not necessarily linear, since so many of them had lives that alternated between extreme abuse and moments of abuse-free living. They often talked broadly about situations or time frames, yet other times they dwelt upon the minutest details of an incident. For instance, at the monthly WIND meetings, when the organization's chair asked the women introducing themselves to say how many years they had been out of their violent relationships, many responded with an actual date, not just the year. I felt it was important to talk to women who had been out of their abusive relationships for at least five years because it gave them the ability to look beyond their individual stories and see how larger structural issues might affect other victims/survivors. In fact, the retrospective insight of WIND members was probably why the state coalition against domestic violence so frequently asked for their input on legal and service provision issues. But for both samples of women narrative arcs were not always chronological constructions. I believe it is vital to give primacy to women's lived experiences in their daily lives and to locate these meanings in the sociocultural context that they felt was most relevant. Thus I followed and respected the sequences women took in talking about their lives, while still ensuring that the themes in the interview guide were covered (J. Smith 1995; Fontana and Frey 1994). I was encouraged in this endeavor by reading how the power of writing or telling—and then rewriting—one's personal story can lead to behavior changes and even improve happiness: as the *New York Times* columnist Tara Parker-Pope (2015) has stated, drawing on work by psychologist Timothy Wilson (2015), "We all have a personal narrative that shapes our view of the world and ourselves. But sometimes our inner voice doesn't get it completely right. Some researchers believe that by writing and then editing our own stories, we can change our perception of ourselves and identify obstacles that stand in the way of better health." As a feminist scholar, I find that this coincides with my understanding of feminist standpoint epistemology, which is grounded in a respondent's ways of knowing that are based on her various social location statuses (D. Smith 1989). Both retelling and rewriting about situations can change over time to reflect new insight and capture layered and complex meanings. It is these layered stories that the women tell.

Identification of Themes

Following grounded-theory methods, I identified themes only if they were raised in at least three of the meetings (for the ethnographic portion) or by at least three of the participants in the interviews (Lofland and Lofland

1995). There was room, however, for me to pursue issues that seemed unusual or significant, which I then added to the open-ended questions in the semistructured interviews. The data were analyzed using coding techniques described by Strauss (1987). I employed three phases of coding: open, axial, and selective. For open coding, I exhaustively read each transcript and my fieldwork notes to develop categories that constituted a working coding manual. I segmented the texts according to these initial coding concepts and developed a list of preliminary codes (Strauss and Corbin 1990). Axial coding involved my comparison of the data across transcripts to modify any codes that emerged in the data. Selective coding entailed figuring out how these fit together to best clarify the factors that influence resilience, coping, and growth among long-term survivors of IPV/A. Once no new conceptual categories were unearthed, I took theme identification to be complete (Krueger 1994). The major themes and subthemes are presented in the subsequent chapters of this book. NiVIVO, a qualitative software package, provided a double-check of the themes.

Feminist Research Design

My study employed a feminist approach with respect to four major areas: topic selection, methodology, interruption of power and control hierarchies, and acknowledgment of researcher subjectivity (Flavin 2001; Gelsthorpe 1990). My topic selection was guided by the gap in knowledge about resilience and women's experiences in long-term longevity of violence-free lives; it is particularly relevant to women, since they are disproportionately the targets of IPV/A. Though feminist research does not have to be solely about women (see Cain 1990), it does involve looking at relationships between and across people and arenas, exploring any gendered patterns or phenomena. In addition, research findings tend to speak to audiences beyond academia, and I believe my analysis will be useful to people outside the university, including law enforcement, court, IPV/A advocates, and social services and treatment personnel as well as to women currently or previously in an abusive relationship and the people who care about them. I have drawn on the findings to suggest efficacious policy recommendations.

Methodologically, I chose a qualitative research design (interviews and fieldwork) in order to fully capture the women's narratives and perceptions in a way that could be masked in quantitative studies. To honor the women's insight, I phrased my questions so as to convey respect for their "expert" status and to indicate my belief in the existence of multiple truths rather than a single objective "truth." This recognition is a hallmark of feminist research (Gelsthorpe 1990).

In terms of communication style, feminist researchers strive for an interactive approach that avoids a hierarchical relationship between the interviewer and interviewee. This means being fully cognizant of the role of gender, race, social class, education, and sexual identity when engaging with respondents, understanding that we both occupy many social positions, and seeing respondents in their full contexts—in this study, seeing them as more than just long-term survivors of IPV/A or key stakeholders. It also means I am intensely involved in the conversation, reflecting my knowledge and experience, all the while probing issues raised by respondents as well as soliciting their interpretation of other aspects of the data in an ongoing exchange.

The final theme involves research subjectivity, and I acknowledge that no research is ever value-free, since it is conducted through the interpretations of the researcher. As I wrote in an earlier publication: "As Flavin [2001] contends, in any kind of research endeavor, subjectivity is unavoidable, but it could also serve as strength: learning from respondents can help researchers better understand and appreciate the respondents' experiences. Moreover, as Dubois [1983] asserts: 'A rejection of the notion of 'objectivity' does not mean a rejection of a concern for being accurate'" (S. Miller 2005, 49). In sum, while exploring my research questions—What affects IPV/A victims/survivors long after their abusive relationship ends? What are the survivors' long-term journeys like, and what do their paths tell us about resilience? How can this knowledge help us develop better support and policies?—I listened to the knowledge, perceptions, and experiences of women who directly grapple with these questions, and I let their narratives construct meaning and make sense of their world.

Reflexivity

Since my graduate school days at the University of Maryland in the late 1980s and early 1990s, I have worked in the movement against violence against women—as a shelter volunteer in two states, as a hotline crisis counselor, as a court advocate for victims, as a board member in my state's Coalition against Domestic Violence, and as a teacher and researcher. I have seen up close the struggles, the injustices, the challenges— and, yes, the joys and validation—experienced by survivors. This has reinforced my sense of the vital importance of context for understanding the meaning of these events in the women's lives and the choices they make.

Did my presence at WIND change any dynamics? I was often hugged hello and always warmly greeted before the meetings began. I was respectfully quiet in the groups, but sometimes the women would ask for my opinion based on my academic work. If I felt there was some information that related to the discussion at hand (and felt as if I had some credibility based on my experience), I did speak up. Whenever I knew all the members present, I was not even reintroduced; people just accepted my presence.

THE SELF-IDENTITIES OF VICTIMS/SURVIVORS

I believe it is important, before I dig more deeply into the themes that emerged from my in-depth interviews, to anchor the women's understandings of themselves and showcase the complexity and nuance of their self-awareness. As understood from an interactionist perspective, social identities are subjective, and individuals can move between victim and survivor identities. In my interviews, the women actively engaged in identity work, with all of them believing that the term *survivor* resonated with their self-perceptions currently, though when providing retrospective accounts of their abusive relationships they tended to use the word *victim* to describe themselves.

Amy Leisenring's (2006) work with battered women in shelters or immediately following their court appearances shows that the word *victim* is rife with negative connotations of being weak and powerless and even blameworthy (see Best 1997; Lamb 1999a; Holstein and Miller 1997). The abused women in Leisenring's work, who had recently left their abusers, struggled with a victim identity, since it excluded attributes more culturally valued, such as strength and agency (see Dunn 2005). Leisenring's sample was heavily influenced by a victim discourse that holds victims somewhat responsible for their situation if they stay in the relationship. Yet the word also suggests suffering a harm that is out of one's control and being deserving of sympathy. Leisenring (2006, 326) points out that "a victim identity is not solely a discredited identity, but in some contexts can be necessary and even beneficial to claim" (see also Goffman 1963).

The women I talked with vacillated more between victim and survivor discourses than Leisenring's sample did, but they ultimately rejected the victim discourse as too narrow, failing to take into account social structural and institutional factors. They noted that although they had been victimized and still might have some fear of their abuser or their abuser's actions, they were good people, good parents, and good employees— thus countering the negative connotations associated with a victim identity—and they tended to embrace a survivor identity that would highlight their strength, choice, coping skills, and power. Perhaps this was because many of the women had been out of their abusive relationship for almost a decade or more and had gained some distance from the period during which they had lived with their abuser. At the same time, however, they demonstrated political savvy in knowing when to acknowledge their victimization, such as when they needed the "receipt of sympathy and assistance" (Leisenring 2006, 309). They recognized that they needed to present as credible victims when interacting with the criminal justice system and in civil cases concerning continued financial, visitation, and custody issues around children. Given the prevailing social constructions of victims, when women present a survivor identity, they risk losing access to services or other protections (Dunn 2001; Loseke 1992, 2003; Schneider 1993). My interviews show multiple and layered meanings underlying their self-conceptions, typically with clear movement away from feeling like a victim to gaining a more nuanced and complex understanding of their identities and the foundations on which they now rested.

Women's identifications were shaped by popular images of the socially constructed abused victim—someone who is bruised and *physically* injured. Those women who experienced primarily emotional abuse were apologetic about calling themselves victims or even survivors. Despite everything the research reveals about psychological abuse leaving a far more lasting and devastating mark on victims (Crossman, Hardesty, and Raffaelli 2016; Stark 2007), and despite research showing that even without physical violence women who experienced patterned coercive and controlling behaviors from their partners feel terror (Velonis 2016), the women I interviewed echoed popular stereotypes about the violence being "not that bad" if they had not been beaten up or threatened with a gun or otherwise seriously injured. If they had experienced their relationships as abusive and terrifying despite an absence of physical violence, they were confused by cultural images of relationship abuse that featured primarily physically battered victims. For instance, when one woman, Brenda, first reached out to join WIND, the organization's chair (who screened initial interest calls) asked her if she was a victim. This confused Brenda: "I wasn't sure, so I asked, what do you define as a victim? I had heard of other stories where women had to go to shelters because their life was in danger." Brenda did not feel as though she fit those characterizations, but the chair assured her that "abuse included verbal, physical, whatever the case, any kind. There are extremes, there's all different kinds of cases." The chair convinced her to give it a try. A survivors' group appealed to Brenda. She liked that there were

> things you can talk about and share things and not be looked at like you're odd. I would talk about it to my friends and they are just like, what? They don't really know what to say, and they would say, "Well,

that's too bad." For people that haven't been through it, I don't think they can really understand the toll it takes on your body . . . the toxicity of it and just the patterns of up and downs.

Her friends thought she had a "picture-perfect marriage." So WIND was a good fit for Brenda:

> I have been going and I think it's really great. It's not really like you sit around and everyone tells you their problems. It's just a joined group of people that have had similar situations and they want to help others, and that's what I really want to do. But it makes it nice that the group has all been through some aspect of it so it's easier to just help.

Another woman, Amy, also was initially unsure if the emotional abuse was "enough" to "qualify" her as a victim needing protection: "I had been praying, 'God, this is sick; is this domestic violence? Is it?' Because I couldn't even tell; he is not punching me in the nose, so it is unclear to me. And I am praying, 'Is this domestic violence?. . . Make it clear to me and I will call the police if it is.'" By the time Amy joined WIND, many years had passed; she no longer questioned whether or not she was victimized, and she had moved to thinking of herself as a survivor, with great pride.

Vanessa had been hospitalized in critical condition after her husband viciously attacked her with a hammer, but she too was uncertain if she could be considered a "bona-fide" IPV/A victim:

> I listen to other women's stories, and I'm like, "Oh my God!"—they went through so much, and I don't think of myself as like being a domestic violence victim, because I wasn't beaten unconscious. . . . When I hear people talk about, like, the violence that they have lived and things that they have been through, I'm like blown away because to me my hell is so small and insignificant compared to what they have gone through.

Winnie's husband was violent and destructive and there were a number of times that she thought he might kill her. Still, she and her husband did not fit the social construction of victim and offender because both had master's degrees and high-paying jobs and lived in a very nice house. These accouterments seemed to belie the fact that she could be as trapped in an abusive relationship as "real" victims. She stated,

> That's why my story is a little different. Sometimes I don't really get the kind of support I'm seeking because people say—she's educated, she'll figure this out, or she's educated and she's bullshitting me, or he really didn't put a gun to her head, he really didn't run her over, he didn't strangle her, she didn't have broken bones, it's not that bad, she doesn't have a bad case of it.

Winnie left him so that her three kids could live without violence, and declared herself (at the time of the interview) a survivor.

Celeste, who had endured sustained terror and really horrific violence in her relationship, recognized the tendency of other survivors to believe that their own experiences were not bad enough to deserve the name of abuse:

> Having worked in the battered women's movement—much later on— in many ways, my relationship and the trajectory of the violence and the phases—because there were honeymoon phases in the marriage, in many ways, it's the typical story. But in some ways, it's very atypical because of the relentless severity and I'm careful about sharing it with other survivors because I don't want them to say, "Oh well, then I wasn't abused because mine was nothing like that."

Many women spoke of how their self-identity had changed over time. Megan initially felt very distant from seeing herself as a victim. Years after her abuse, when she went to college, she took a class about domestic violence and realized that others would see her as a victim.[6] The label, she felt, did not fit her: "I never did see myself as a victim because I saw my mom as a battered woman; my dad was just a tyrant and I never saw my mom fight back. I *always* fought back . . . so I didn't identify myself as battered; I was going to give as good as I got." Over time, however, her self-perception became more complex:

> But my mom—we both ended up the same way. We both got the worse end of it and basically powerless. Now I see that I was kind of a victim a couple of times in my marriage with my first husband. He ultimately did have the power, like he kept all the keys to the car. He made the most money. I always believed he could take my kids, and to me, that meant life was over. So I have learned to kind of identify with being a victim. But I don't like it. I don't like thinking of myself as a victim because in our society, everyone wants to be powerful and it's a negative word. Even women like to have a little power.

Elizabeth associated feeling like a victim with being trapped in the past:

> [It] kept making me re-live the past and be present in the past and I missed out on my *now* . . . and in this now moment I am a survivor. . . . My focus now is that the past is dead and has no life and it's already been done. The only way it resurrects itself is if I talk about it. . . . I always tell myself I was a younger girl then. . . . I was young and really alone. So it's like I didn't have power over certain situations like being molested and getting older and getting raped, but I always put myself in my adult situation now. I have options and I have rights, and the right to happiness is the only one I'm choosing. Anything or anybody that doesn't add to my own happiness doesn't belong with me.

It was difficult for some of the women to incorporate both feeling that they had not had a lot of control over their abusive relationship and feeling that they were actively resisting the abuse and making choices to protect themselves. This difficulty echoes Minow's (1993) notion of victimhood as a "cramped identity" that cannot adequately contain abused women's experiences, where they are traumatized but also survivors. For instance, Pepper wavered about seeing herself as a victim or survivor. Most of the time, she saw herself as a victim, but not a domestic violence victim; rather, her identity was that of a victim of a gun crime or a violent act. Her boyfriend almost killed her with the gunshots to her head, but while the surgeons were trying to save her life that night in the emergency room, he killed himself. In the months following the incident, Pepper wondered if she would have gone back to him. She still was not at the point where she could imagine an autonomous life free of his threats and violence. By the time five years had passed, she described herself as stronger and felt that she would never put herself in that position anymore or be attracted to him, since the years had made her more mature and she had a professional job. However, Pepper realized she had evolved because her boyfriend's death meant that he was not there anymore (to define the relationship), so she felt still stuck wondering at times.

Pepper attended WIND for only a few months and was uncertain if she fit in with the organization:

> I don't think that I'm benefiting from it, though it's good for me and my well-being to get out, but also I don't talk about my story much anymore. . . . Talking to these folks, it brings it back that I'm so thankful that I'm not in a situation like this anymore. . . . It kinda keeps it in more visible, but I'm past it and other people are still living with violence. So if I can help somebody else, I can. Like talking to teens about dating and warning signs. What to watch out for. So I can be part of the group to help others.

Julia also spent about half a year attending WIND meetings. She stated:

> It is hard, because you get to a point where you don't want to be a victim. You want to be a survivor. And you don't want everything in your life around the fact that you have been victimized. You want to let go of that. You get sick of it, because anytime something bad happens, you go back into that feeling like a victim, then you are giving the power back to him. . . . WIND was important because I heard other people's stories and I have seen other people who are survivors. It was not a victims' group. It was a survivors' group, and that's where I was mentally. By year 5 [after leaving her abuser], after being dragged in and out of court . . . I was determined not to let him upset me, or be

upset for any amount of time; I was more about taking back more
control of my life.

Julia's words suggest that reconstructing identity is a process that evolves over time, and many other women echoed this realization.

Some women created their own words to describe themselves. Jenny, for instance, called herself as a "winner" because "I went through several situations and came out completely different, stronger and able to live a full life. Because I don't have to live with him, I don't have to hear his voice for the rest of my life. That makes me a winner." Haley introduced another word: "Not a victim, but victorious. A victor! You know, like, I got through it. . . . I see myself as definitely a survivor, but I think *victor* fits well because I'm out there helping others, speaking up against it, and even in my job—I work with people who really like to bully—I speak up there as well." Haley worked with a group of advocates and attorneys to get a bill passed to better protect IPV/A victims, and her name was published on the front page of the state's newspaper as a survivor of domestic violence. Her employer found out and required her to talk to the human resources personnel. She found out that her company did not have a policy against domestic violence, but after raising awareness the company decided to help sponsor a 5K run to raise money for the cause.

For Katherine, the self-reflection involved in our two-hour interview led her to change her perception of her identity. Initially she said, "I haven't given that much thought, but I guess I see myself more as a victim than I do as a survivor because I was so shocked that I got myself in that situation. I was in disbelief." In the 1970s, down south, little help or resources existed for battered women. There were no shelters in her county, and she did not know anyone who talked about domestic violence. But by the end of our conversation, as Katherine reflected on her experiences, she described herself as moving away from being a victim:

> Being able to be that strong and sustain that, even through the
> emotional, real pain of losing what we had—now that I think of it, I am a
> survivor. . . . I sometimes wonder how well I could have pushed through
> it had I not had the support that I have and had, but nonetheless, I put a
> stop to it. . . . It took a great deal to persevere and get out. . . . I guess
> *resilient* is a good word. I came out on the other side of this and I was
> able to function beautifully in life, and continue a great career and rear
> an amazing child and be happy for decades after going through that very
> shallow and limiting and fearful situation. So I guess I am a hero.

Dale's husband left her for dead after he ran her over. This shaped her feeling of being a victim until she was interviewed for a story on workplace violence:

By telling my story, I started feeling more like a survivor than a victim anymore 'cause I feel like I am doing something good, and being able to help other people, so that kind of helped me. I didn't feel like a survivor at first because of so many things happening, I was just so tired of all the court appearances, the trailer falling apart, the new job, the stress, the kids . . . and I didn't have any money, or any job or place to live. . . . When I went back to work I was still on crutches and bandaged up. . . . It was just nonstop and I was beat. And then I was going crazy, imagining seeing my ex everywhere—in the backyard, when I was walking my dog, even in the back seat of my car when driving, out of fear, because I was sure he'd try to kill me again.

After time passed, Dale found a stronger support system and more help from service providers and the criminal justice system, leading her to think more optimistically about her position and seeing herself as moving out of victimhood. Several other women talked about how their interactions with social structural institutions, like the justice system, could reinforce the survivor discourse, not just the victim discourse.

Tina also credited her support system for giving her an understanding of her situation that moved beyond internalized victim blaming.

I'm a survivor! I didn't even know I was a domestic violence victim until I started reaching out for help. Women need to know that no matter what they have been through previously, even as a child, that nobody has a right to do that to them. And even if you are not ready, you need to have an advocate to confide in, and so you don't continue to blame yourself. When you talk about it . . . it sounds differently when you verbalize than what you are feeling inside and what you don't verbalize. When you hear it echo back in your ears, it's a totally different picture. It's important to know—I don't care what he is, what kind of house you live in, car you drive, nothing, how much he makes— he still doesn't have the right to hit you or abuse you in any way. Nobody does.

Once Jenny finally obtained a divorce, she severed all ties with her abusive husband. In some ways, this was easy for her since she landed a terrific job and moved across the country. They did not share any real estate, and they had no children together. She was interested in meeting other women who had left abusive relationships and heard about WIND. But "when I went to the WIND meeting, I just felt a little bit of bitterness. Why I don't know, but I went three times. They're all very nice and friendly, but they were angry. . . . They seemed stuck in anger and I just didn't want to be around that." Part of what she described further was that a lot of the women present at the meetings did not experience the clean break that Jenny did;

they had children with their exes and felt manipulated by the abusers and the court system as they kept getting hauled back into court about child support, custody, visitation, and so forth. She suggested, "Sometimes being an activist means you need to hold on to some of the anger. So that could also motivate the women to take on the system." Ultimately, Jenny was seeking more of a victim support group than an activist group—even though she saw herself as a survivor. Since she had kept her abuse a secret for so long, she wanted to talk more about her personal experiences than what the WIND activist organization welcomes.

Rosa believed she was a survivor because she did not follow Latina cultural traditions and uphold her marriage vows no matter what. As she declared,

> Latinas more than any other groups stay in abusive relationships because of religion, because the women don't work, and because of the culture. One of the things my ex said was, "You'll never leave me because you're Catholic." . . . He thought I would never get a divorce. He obviously didn't know me! . . . I'm a survivor economically and emotionally. All the things you have to go through. These are women who want to stay because they want to stay in their house. . . . I would rather live in a cardboard box. To me, material things don't mean a thing. . . . Nothing means anything more than my freedom. Who I am means more. . . . I feel that when you stay for the material things, you are selling yourself. You are paying a high price and so are your kids.

Sara focused on the word *victim* to explore how her personality had lent itself to being victimized:

> I think I'm a victim because of my niceness, or because I want to see everybody happy. . . . I need to be really vigilant because people take advantage of kindness. And I think because of the way I grew up, I didn't want any problems because it was always crazy when my parents would argue or have a fight. Then they would separate, get back together, separate, get back together, separate. So as I kid, I just wanted everything to be okay. . . . And then I carried that over into adulthood. . . . I sometimes am naive and mistake kindness, and people take advantage of that. Even men. . . . But I also see myself as a survivor because there are many times when I could have been in harm's way. Like fatally . . . I just never thought about the gun he could have killed me with until today when I was talking with you.

Jazzy was definite in her self-assessment: "I have been a victim, but I'm definitely a survivor because I didn't allow myself to even fall into the pattern and stay there. I fought back. And now I'm out, and I didn't and don't plan on going back in." Anita felt the same way. Casey was ambivalent about seeing herself as a victim or a survivor and relied instead on her own ability to make choices with help from God. She believed that "women who take on a victim mentality do themselves a disservice . . . because you then live in that cycle of 'I'm a victim, I'm a victim,' and you're never going to have freedom." She stated that

> God gives us free will. He puts choices in front of you, and whether you believe in God or not . . . you have this free will to choose whether or not to stay in an abusive relationship. . . . So, I guess I just see myself as fortunate to have been able to make the right choices to be free from it and that God truly was able to release me from all of it.

Celeste's marriage had ended almost two decades previously, giving her a lot of perspective about the victim-survivor continuum.

> It's not just that there's a lot of distance from events in my life, it's that it's a different life. It doesn't even connect to me the way that other people's histories might. There's just a huge divide there. . . . I know that at some point I reached some kind of analysis saturation and was able to push it aside. Once you do that, then you can have room in your head for other stuff that's more pressing, or equally important, or that's connected to a future as opposed to just your past.

Naomi's musings about her identity led her to think about how many abusers had victimization or trauma in their past; now that her husband had died, her fear of him had evaporated, and she admitted that she could see him with more sympathy because of the abuse he had suffered as a child:

> I know that gets politicized in certain ways. People don't want to claim victim. I think it's both and there are ways that he's a victim also. I say that not to take away his responsibility. . . . He was blind in one eye because his father assaulted him, and he ended up with glass in his eye and they couldn't treat it. His mother took his father back about a week later. That marks you in so many ways, not that it excuses any of his behavior towards me and my son. But poverty, and racism, and abuse, and all of those things that he experienced as a child growing up in the inner city, had all of these ramifications for me and for my relationship. . . . I guess this far out I identify certainly more as a survivor and that's a process. Being a survivor is a process, just like being a victim is a process.

Apparent in most of the women's identity constructions was how profoundly they had been influenced by social visions of victimhood and how these shaped their interpretations of who they were, how they reacted to abuse, and how they would be seen by other people and institutions in their lives. Women recalled at length the fortitude they had had to summon up just to persevere when interacting with social agents who demanded proof of victimization: they wanted desperately to retain a semblance of self-control and pride in their own resistance, yet they knew that in doing so they might be cast as undeserving of assistance. The women's self-perceptions cannot be viewed in isolation from the social factors and institutions that both oppress and empower women, such as their community and social support, the health care system, religious institutions, and the criminal and civil justice systems. With this backdrop of identity construction and meaning making, the broader themes that emerged from the women's narratives and my analyses are presented in the next three chapters.

3. "Leaving the Horrible for the Not-So-Horrible"

This chapter title quotes a woman I interviewed who was describing what it was like to leave her abusive and violent relationship. Leaving enabled women to secure at least provisional safety without the relentless intimidation and abuse that was part and parcel of daily living with their abuser, but it still meant dealing with their abuser's machinations, struggling with hardships that their abuser had foisted upon them, and taking on the difficult task of rebuilding their lives. The process of separating from the abuser and developing resilience was often nonlinear, complicated by lingering fears, challenging new living conditions, and often ongoing negotiations in court with the offender, which could drag on for many years, over child custody, parental visitation, legal issues, and finances.

To give a sense of the challenges involved in this transition, I begin by providing retrospective accounts of women's early vulnerabilities that their abusers capitalized on in their efforts to exert dominance and control in the relationship. What often preceded IPV/A was the women's lack of prior dating experiences, a prior history of violence in their family of origin, and for some women, having a disability or having family members with a disability. Many of the women's daily circumstances, such as economic abuse and the presence of weapons in the home, contributed to routine horrors as well as to a long-lasting impact on their ability to end their relationships. Despite these obstacles, women developed survival skills. Most of the women had left their abuser at least once and often many more times before the final termination and had reunited out of concerns about finances or children, hope that the abuser had changed, or fear of his retaliation. They talked about "the straw that broke the camel's back"—an epiphany of some sort—that gave them the final push to challenge the abuse and end the relationship once and for all.

Anderson, Renner, and Danis (2012, 1279) discuss how women experience the transition from "being controlled to being in control while coping with the costs of a domestic life filled with fear, terror, and devastation." This accomplishment is no small feat, as leaving does not guarantee a safe or stress-free time. Many of these women would be considered at high risk of imminent harm, if not death, because of their abusers' continued abuse and violence after the separation. But even when the abuser was no longer in the picture, fear could linger. One woman lived with a gun set out prominently on her living room coffee table, even though her abuser had committed suicide after shooting her and her best friend at a dance club. Safer circumstances could also change: one woman who had had full custody of her children for nine years and had felt relief about not having to battle her ex-husband in court, as so many women do following the end of an abusive relationship, suddenly faced a motion for joint custody from him. Another woman, who slept clutching a hatchet, found that her ex-husband had just been released from prison, where he had served time for attempting to murder her, and feared that he would break into her house and "take care of her," as he had vowed to do. Despite her success in finding stability and peace in other aspects of her life, she repeatedly prefaced her comments to me in our interview with "when he kills me" or "after I'm dead." Yet simultaneously she publicly told her story—how her ex-husband had abused her, stalked her, and attempted to kill her in the parking lot after she finished work one afternoon—as part of a national public service announcement aimed at drawing attention to workplace violence.

In the first part of this chapter, I explore the warning signs and vulnerabilities experienced by the women in their early courtship and relationships and the effects these factors had after the relationships ended; I also examine psychological manipulation, weapons, and economic abuse. Despite these constellations of control, women developed survival strategies and long-term hopes and plans in their determination to live violence-free.

VULNERABILITIES

Regardless of race, educational achievement, membership in WIND, or age at time of interview, the women described similar vulnerabilities that have been identified as risk factors associated with intimate partner abuse. It was common for them to have had little dating experience prior to meeting their partner, and they described being swept away and flattered by his attention and interest. Often there was a significant age difference between the two, which meant not only that he had much more relationship experience but also that she—perhaps unconsciously—assigned a more "mature" status to him and deferred to his judgment. In addition, some young women went straight from their parents' homes to life with their abuser, whether they were rebelling against their parents' overprotectiveness or desperate to get away from abuse and dysfunction in their family of origin. Ellen grew up in an abusive household where violent outbursts were excused; she was happy to meet someone who could "take her away from the chaos." He was ten years her senior. Within six months she had fallen in love with him and started making long-term plans. Terri was intrigued when a man fifteen years older started showering her with attention: "I used to be very shy and I never dated at all in high school, didn't go to the prom, so I had little experience with guys, and I was naive about a lot of things." Her overprotective parents did not allow Terri to participate in sleepovers with friends, so her "rebellion" was to attend a college that was four hours' drive away to force herself to get out of her shell. She met her abuser almost immediately and felt comforted that he was from her hometown. He took her to a bar even though she was not twenty-one yet, and Terri felt older and special: "I was looking for someone who really loved me. He said he did and I really believed him. I was so excited. I didn't realize that people could say that but still abuse you." Terri and her boyfriend quickly began living together, curtailing opportunities for her to have friends her own age and isolating her from involvement in college life.

Young girls are particularly vulnerable to male attention when they are adolescents; research has shown that they tend to highlight desirability as a central aspect of their self-image, to depend on boys' approval for a sense of self-worth and lovability, and to lose self-esteem and belief in their own abilities (Orenstein 1994; Levy 1991; D. DuBois et al. 1998). Girls and women often embrace romanticized versions of dating and love and are socialized through parents, media, school, and peers to conform to gendered expectations about becoming wives and mothers. Pioneering work on girls' psychological development has revealed that young women silence themselves rather than speak their true feelings, being careful to suppress unruliness or disagreement with male peers so they will be viewed as virtuous, nice, and kind (see Brown and Gilligan 1992). All these features of feminine socialization can increase young women's vulnerability to intimate partner abuse (Levy 1991). As Lamb (1999b, 39) explains, "Attitudes that have been traditionally associated with women in our culture and have traditionally benefited men (the desire to preserve relationships, trust, compassion, and the ability to take another's perspective) are all qualities that can incapacitate a woman when faced by a perpetrator of abuse."

Reeva's story illustrates her youthful susceptibility to her boyfriend's obsessive attentions: when he pursued her relentlessly from a different home state with phone calls, letters, and visits she thought it demonstrated his devotion.

> He knew all the right things to say to my parents and was involved with the church, he won everybody over. . . . I was so flattered with this older, accomplished, white-collar guy . . . with a profession?! All my girlfriends were impressed, and that piqued my interest in him even more. He proposed; my father grilled him about our age difference and that I was still in college, and he assured my parents that I could complete school, and he'd treat me like a queen.

Many women got involved with their abuser very quickly. Although Haley was older and had extensive dating experience, she began living with her abuser soon after they met. She described meeting him, literally, on the street after he had yelled out a crude sexual innuendo: she went over to dress him down verbally but found herself attracted to his big blue eyes and "bad boy" looks. Three women married their husbands when they were under eighteen. Megan married her abusive husband when she was sixteen (he was eighteen), and they had a child right away: "I grew up in a very rural community in Appalachia, and it wasn't a big deal to get married and have a child when you are sixteen. I dropped out of school and had two children by the time I was eighteen."

Part of the women's rush to get involved was their awe at the overwhelming intensity of the abusers' romantic gestures—many women used the words that they were simply "swept off their feet." Though the research suggests this is a calculated move by abusers—with a concomitant tactic of moving the woman quickly away from her support network of family members and friends—the women (mis)interpreted it as indicative of heartfelt loving commitment. Joan described "a whirlwind romance" in which everything was perfect and her abuser was "Prince Charming"; she married him after only two months because "I didn't want to live in sin, and he felt that same guilt." She even moved from another state to be with him, trusting him because they were introduced by people she knew from church. Joan's children from a previous relationship were ages seven, ten, and thirteen, and she hoped this new man would fulfill a lot of dreams. "I had a long list of broken relationships, brokenness in the home, and my dream was always to have a father for my kids." But soon after they married, he began to control Joan and her children.

Jayde, a lesbian, described a similarly rapid involvement with her ex-partner, whom she met through an online dating website. Jayde was still grieving from three recent deaths in her family and poured her heart out to this woman in e-mail exchanges and over many hours of phone conversations (and one in-person meeting); the new girlfriend became her solace. Within three months, Jayde moved from the East to the West Coast, leaving all family and friends behind. "It was one of those magical things." The abuser had a college degree and was just starting her law enforcement career, so Jayde considered her to be very stable and was keen to begin a happier time in her life.

Some women spoke of religious and other cultural pressures on them to marry soon after meeting their abuser. After Rosa turned thirty and was still unmarried, she followed her father's advice: "Don't date a guy for years, because you really don't know him until you're married. . . . You'll be wasting your time if you just date." Also, she said, "In the Latino culture, if you hit thirty and you aren't married, any children would come out deformed because you waited too long." So when she met a man who was in college and was Catholic, "He proposed to me and I got married. . . . I didn't find out until later that he had substance abuse in his family."

Abusers could on little acquaintance present a good front—a good job, good manners, religious beliefs—that led the women they courted to assume they were stable and trustworthy. Dale was in her late twenties when she met her ex-husband and felt that she had enough experience to know she wanted someone who was gainfully employed and ready to settle down and start a family. She had never pursued education past high school, so she liked that he was a "good provider." But in retrospect, she realized,

> I made a mistake. . . . I didn't date him long enough. I was older, and I figured he seemed like a good guy—had a job, no drinking, no drugs, good Catholic boy. But he hid the bad stuff, like his bad family history. And then I found out he was a gambler, which he had hid very well; he would go out every night around 7 p.m. and call a bookie to make a bet. He was real controlling and didn't like me having friends or a close relationship with my family, especially my twin brother—he was always putting wedges in that. . . . Then it got easier to isolate myself because I didn't want them to know he beat me up. By the time the neighbors called the cops when he beat me up, strangled me, tripped me in front of the kids, he had convinced me not to report it because he would lose his job.

Winnie, who got engaged and married to her abuser after the first year of dating (a time line she considered "quick" because she had been more hesitant with other men) was similarly drawn to a man who, at first, looked good: she found it refreshing that, unlike many thirty-year-old men, he had no prior marriages, no kids, a master's degree, and parents who were still married. But looking back, Winnie recalled signs of his aggression and bad temper even in the first week she met him when she observed how disproportionately mad he got at his dog. They had their first child two years after the wedding, and he was violent and verbally abusive during her first pregnancy; he threw a shovel at her: "I left and drove to a McDonalds. I just laid out on the seat and cried, 'Oh, my God, I'm pregnant, this guy's a lunatic, and I sold my home to build this one. What have I gotten into?'" But by then "I was so cut off from who I really was. I didn't see my friends because I was too nervous about his anger. It had gone on so long that I had lost myself."

Amy's story of how she got married to the second of her two abusive ex-husbands showed a common abuser pattern of pushing for commitment early on. After the end of her first abusive marriage, she did not trust her instincts about men and stopped dating. She met her second husband while working at a company in which she handled phone orders.

> I speak fluent Spanish, he was in Mexico City and I worked in the US many miles away (but I didn't let him know that I spoke Spanish). . . .
> He started making phone calls to me and not ordering parts . . . and with each phone call, he would ask a personal question. It didn't occur to me that was a little desperate. When he switched jobs, he asked if we could write letters. A Mexican pen pal, that's what I thought. So we write a few letters. I hadn't gone on a date in six years. I wrote to him that "I am finally ready to go out to dinner with somebody if they were to ask me." So he wrote me an eighteen-page marriage proposal, all in English, sent it Federal Express. Again, a little desperate, but I didn't see this. *No* red flags for me. . . . He was so romantic.

Once he moved to the United States, the romance flourished: "He's a flower man. I never had a man bring me flowers in my whole life. . . . We traveled all over. . . . He swept me completely off my feet. I didn't have a loving father, and I needed that love, probably more than a healthy person needed love. Whatever crumb he gave me, I was just like a starving person."

Although a number of the women had been involved in prior relationships that had failed, at least half of the women had never dated before or, if they had, not seriously. This gave the women no point of comparison—especially if their home life did not offer examples of healthy partnerships. Sandee had not been in any serious relationships before: "I was like every typical girl wanting a boyfriend especially because I ached to be wanted, and also since I had no stability at home." Danielle recalled: "He pursued me relentlessly—he was from a town about forty-five minutes away, so he seemed new and exotic. I was flattered and inexperienced. I had never had a boyfriend." This vulnerability led her to ignore and explain away what she would later recognize were warning signs:

> They were red flags, looking back. He was very aggressive with his driving and had a lot of accidents. He didn't like to work; everybody was out to get him. . . . He got mad at my dog and hit her with a frying pan when I was pregnant right after we were married, but I needed health insurance and thought maybe he was just immature.

They were married after knowing each other six months.

For Brenda, the abuser was her first serious boyfriend. They met during their freshman year in a college several hours from her home. "He was the man of my dreams; he was gorgeous." Jenny also described how her boyfriend captivated her when she was nineteen and in school with him (he was twenty-one): "I was very young and he was my first love. . . . He was abusive about six months into the relationship." Naomi, who began living with her boyfriend after landing her first job following college graduation, recalled that "even though I was twenty-two and had a bachelor's degree, which made it more possible for me to leave in the end, I was very young, and I never really had a long-term relationship." Before she knew it, she was increasingly entangled with him and was separated from her friends and family when they moved to a new city about a thousand miles away.

> Sometimes people don't understand when women get into these abusive relationships. It's not like it starts abusive. The controlling behaviors started fairly early, before we got married, and then it got worse especially after my son was born. . . . I got pregnant before we got married, although we had talked about marriage before I got pregnant. Once I was pregnant, I felt like I had to get married.

Isolation and early pregnancy restricted the options of many of the women. Sara initially saw marriage as a way out of an unpleasant living situation with her step-parents. She had met her ex-husband right out of college through mutual friends. Although he lived in an adjoining state, he was in the military and soon transferred to her state.

> I thought I was all grown up and here's this guy with a college degree and my parents will like that. Then I ended up getting pregnant by him, and so he said, "Well, we were gonna end up getting married anyway, so let's just do this." So all in the same year, I got pregnant, got married, built a house with him, and I moved, but I had never been away from home before. My mom was living in a southern state far away.

Once they moved to where he was transferred,

> I was depressed after having the baby because I had no friends, no
> family here, and he was so engrossed in his job and achieving success.
> So he worked long hours and I had a very sick newborn. . . . He was
> having an affair. Two different women called the house, and when I
> addressed it, he tried to strangle me.

Abusers who wanted to isolate women from their families did not have
to distance them geographically; psychological means could be just as effective. For example, one woman in a mixed-race relationship, Naomi, recalled
how her husband told her that "both of our families are racist" as a way of
separating her from them.

When parents had disapproved of the woman's choice, it was especially
easy for an abuser to isolate her from her family—sometimes under the
guise of protecting her from hurtful family members—and to reinforce
that he was the one who really mattered. Robyn's mother signed the documents that allowed Robyn to marry at age sixteen but warned her, "'Don't
you come to me in five years and tell me you've met someone you really
love and you deserve to be happy." Later those words would linger in
Robyn's mind and contribute to her sense of having no escape from her
abusive relationship.

Shame at having made a mistake and reluctance to let anyone know
could further reinforce the abuser's control and the woman's vulnerability.
This is acutely captured by Joan's description of her experience: about a
week before the wedding, red flags appeared but she was too embarrassed
to seek help. He started controlling her freedom, first by selling his car so
they would have one car, then by putting the car only in his name so he
could make all the decisions about who got dropped off or picked up first for
work. Joan recalled, "I never said anything. I was so ashamed. I had this
long list of broken relationships. I didn't want to prove anybody right. . . .
Everyone thought we were crazy for marrying after such a short period of
dating." Sara similarly described how ashamed she felt after it became generally known at the military base where she and her husband were living
that he was abusing her. "I had to deal with the embarrassment where I
now lived and telling my parents." Like many of the other women I interviewed, Sara internalized the blame rather than holding the abuser accountable for his actions, and implicitly expected her parents to judge her as well.

And in fact many women described how their parents had been judgmental or were otherwise unsupportive when they disclosed what was
going on in their relationship. Danielle's mother told her, "'Marriage is
hard, you need to go work it out, and no, you're not coming back.' So, at

that point, I'm nineteen and I made my bed so I have to lie in it." When Haley met her abuser, she made more money and owned her own house, but she had just ended a relationship with a man who had been cheating on her, so her self-esteem had plummeted. It did not help that when Haley told her mother about the abuse her mother was "very judgmental," telling her things like "'You weren't raised this way; I don't understand why you're with him.' Then he would use my mother's words against me.... 'Your family doesn't care about you because they don't do anything with me hitting you.' So he would play on that; my self-esteem was on the floor."

Some women said they knew their families would be unsupportive because of their religious and other cultural beliefs that discouraged divorce. Rosa kept her husband's abuse from her parents and siblings, explaining, "Latinos have this thing. You make your bed, you lie in it. That's the way I was raised. In my mind, I got into this and I can get out of it. I'm not gonna go to my mother's house or to my brother with three kids. I just couldn't." Vanessa similarly described how her family had "strict religious values, like, women can't wear makeup, or jewelry, must wear their hair in a bun, wear dresses always, submit to your husband, and he could do anything he wanted to but get divorced."

Even women who came from families that did not sweepingly condemn divorce could still feel that getting divorced would mean that they had "failed." Anita stated, "My mother and father are now divorced. My father beat my mother up all the time, and I swore I would not get into that kind of relationship." Yet it was very difficult for Anita to contemplate leaving him: "I didn't want to be looked upon as a failure, plus I was scared of him." African American women that Richie (1996) studied were especially likely to conceal their abuse, not only because they did not want to be complicit in exposing black men to the grave dangers and inequities of the criminal justice system (a concern shared by the African American women I interviewed; see chapter 5), but also because their disclosure of abuse would reinforce racial stereotypes and damage their community in the eyes of others. Middle-class black women in particular bore a "symbolic burden" to preserve their marriage and uphold the ideal of a perfect nuclear family— again, concerns consistent with those of the middle-class African American women in my own project.

Research demonstrates that a prior history of violence or substance abuse in either the victim's or the offender's family of origin has profound effects on risks for one's own IPV/A (Hotaling and Sugarman 1986); this marker increases men's tendencies to be violent with their own partners and interferes with women's ability to detect early warning signs of violence.

In my own interviews it showed up frequently when women described their or their former partners' families of origin and childhood environments. For example, Celeste had alcoholic and dysfunctional parents and liked to party and do drugs. When she dropped out of high school and ran away, she became susceptible to her abuser's attention. Her self-esteem was virtually absent: since she was a high school dropout, she believed that he was smarter than she was and that she might as well get used to being a wife and mother. She recalled, "I thought I can't outdo him in any way. The only thing I can do better than him is nurse a baby, deliver a baby, and cook him a meal." He moved them hundreds of miles from her family to be near his own family in a very rural, isolated part of the country. He was a police officer, and had many other guns and hunting weapons. His family was dysfunctional and alcoholic, and no one challenged his abusiveness or any violence by other family members.

It cannot be emphasized enough that exposure to childhood violence in the home "normalized" the abusers' violent behavior and controlling dynamics (Lichter and McCloskey 2004; Markowitz 2001; Yount and Li 2009). Sandee's family life was very chaotic, since her bipolar father often skipped his medication. Joan endured tremendous childhood trauma; she was raped at age ten and later became pregnant, was forced to abort, and was put into foster care at age thirteen. Her mother committed suicide when she was age sixteen. Elizabeth was molested and raped as a young teenager in her childhood home and felt abandoned and neglected by her family. She left home at age sixteen when she told her mother about the rape and her mother did not believe her. She ended up meeting a man who seemed sympathetic and moving in with him and his mother. She finished high school, but the day after graduating discovered she was pregnant. When her boyfriend became violently jealous, Elizabeth felt betrayed and stuck:

> I had confided in this guy all my secrets. He had his way of showing me that he cared and understood, so I didn't want to see the incidents as a pattern. I grew up seeing my mom with a man who would get mad and he would hit her. But when I was an eighteen-year-old, all I had was this guy and his family. This was my second pregnancy and I wanted someone to love me and I felt that I was hurt by the first miscarriage and this one I truly wanted. All I had was this family I had created.

Elizabeth had a second miscarriage, probably on account of the abuse. She would go on to be in two more violent relationships.

When she was twenty years old and living with an aunt, Pepper was drawn to a small-town drug dealer who provided drugs and a good time.

Later he became physically violent, but Pepper dismissed his actions, since she was used to conflating violence with love:

> My mother abused me. We were always in and out of court, 'cause my dad would try to get custody. . . . My mom used to hit me, and I would land against the wall. When she was disciplining us children, she would kick me down on the floor. . . . I remember when I was with my (ex) boyfriend, thinking in my head that when he hits me, he really does love me because my mom loves me. You don't think your own parents don't love you just because they abuse you—they just have a bad temper that they can't control.

Megan also experienced a violent childhood. Her grandmother was beaten to death by her grandfather: "She was horribly physically abused and then the last beating he gave her, she suffered brain damage. . . . My mother's response to the violence was to get a dog to beat up." Megan thought that violence occurred only in her own family—"When I was growing up, I really thought that I was the only one afraid; I'd be sitting in my little desk at school, scared to death to go home." Many families have unwritten rules about what you talk about and what is off limits. Megan was warned that "if you go to the door and talk to a person from a social service agency, you'll get hauled away into foster care. There was always that threat, so no one said anything."[1]

Tina witnessed her mother being brutally abused by two husbands. Further, Tina was sexually molested by her father, something she realized later in life. "I just knew I didn't like my father. I never called him dad or anything. I would just cling to my mother. Nobody ever questioned why I was so hateful about him." Tina was twenty-five years old when she met her husband, who was eight years older than her; even during the dating phase he was very controlling and always unfaithful.

> He dictated how I wore my hair, how I dressed. . . . I had a designer leather coat and he told me it was ugly, so I just stopped wearing it. He bought me a cloth coat, and I wore that ugly thing instead. I was so insecure that I would always be available. He was living with someone else, so I jumped whenever he called. I wasn't eating regularly, and I remember passing out in the car . . . and ending up in the hospital. . . . I was living on hotdogs, tasty cakes—anything I could eat on the run just so I was available.

Even when a family of origin was not violent, it could prepare the woman to accept being treated badly. Robyn said of her abuser:

> I had noticed when we were dating, how inconsiderate he was with my feelings and my time and my ideas. He was consistently late and he

sometimes didn't show up, but he was also very charming, and he had a very good job. About a month after we were married, he had started to see other women. . . . That was the first year and I was pregnant; it never occurred to me to leave him.

After all, being neglected seemed familiar to her: "It wasn't very different from the way my mother treated me. Not that she was violent, but my mother always assumed that I could take care of myself and my siblings."

Women's experiences of abuse in their relationships seemed normal not only because they had already experienced and witnessed abuse in their families of origin but also because they often knew nothing about IPV/A as an issue. Time after time, the women mentioned that when IPV/A first manifested in their relationship they had absolutely no understanding of the phenomenon in their current life or in their family history. Although Sandee graduated college in 1996, dating violence was never mentioned in her high school classes or by her peers. Women also mentioned a lack of knowledge among their relatives. Jenny stated that although she was aware that her family did not like her boyfriend, they never raised any concerns with her about him because they felt sorry for him since he seemed unhappy and needy. Her friends and family "did see that he was bossy and that he isolated me so quickly and that was just routine. I lost all of my friends. I was really dependent on him emotionally. Now I know that these were the typical signs." Jazzy, in her midsixties now, recalled:

> I wasn't young when I got married. I was in my midtwenties. But nobody ever heard about domestic violence being something wrong, thirty, forty years ago. . . . When I learned later about DV and was able to put a name to it, it surprised me that it applied to me. I don't remember anybody ever saying the words *DV* or *abuse*. So I didn't see a need to tell anybody that he hit me. Maybe in conversation with somebody else who had gotten hit, we might compare our notes, but other than that, no. . . . Later I started looking at my family and who in my family has ever been hit and it's everybody—my sister, my nieces, my daughter, my cousin, but nobody would ever think to name it DV.

Women's lack of awareness about IPV/A was compounded by a lack of awareness of resources that might help them. Katherine, who encountered abuse in her second marriage, spoke of how she had not known anything about shelters or about laws to help victims of IPV/A. Of course, some women encountered IPV/A at a time or in a place where such resources were not available. Megan spoke about how when she was young it had been "too hard to leave": "Try packing up your life in a bag and hauling the kids to a shelter— not that there were shelters back then or in the hick town where we lived."

Single mothers were an especially vulnerable group. After an unhappy first marriage to an emotionally distant, unfaithful man, Katherine was a lonely single mother with a four-year-old child, working hard to make ends meet: "I was very eager and I met this man who had a very strong leadership personality. I was so in love. I was being rescued from this life of having to manage everything myself and I thought, 'This was it' and we really would live happily ever after." She had moved to a southern state without family close by. Once the abuse began, she was mortified even to tell her parents that her second marriage also failed, let alone that she was being abused. Abigayle talked about her yearning for something better for her children after her divorce; moving in with her longtime boyfriend meant that her son could have his own bedroom instead of sleeping in the walk-in closet in their small apartment. She explained,

> Living in a nice house in that high-end part of town, that's what I wanted for me and for the kids. I couldn't afford it on my own and that's what really held me back from leaving . . . I didn't want to disrupt their school or friendship groups by moving. I thought that I was providing a good home for the kids, where in reality it was not so good.

Having a disability or having children with a disability can increase vulnerability even more (Hahn et al. 2014). Ellen's son was thirteen years old when she met her abuser. He looked up to her new boyfriend, following him all over the house. Her son had special needs, and his biological father was uninvolved in his life, so having help was attractive, even though her abuser was only sporadically employed at a garage and also sold drugs on the side. When she realized she was pregnant, she felt hopeless and stuck: "What am I going to do? I don't believe in abortion for me." Florence was herself disabled and had three children from a prior marriage. Her husband not only pelted her with constant verbal abuse about her disability but also often left her with no means of getting help by hiding her cell phone or turning off the electricity. Florence used a wheelchair to get around, and she believed that her limited mobility gave him the excuse to be "in charge," since he could drive a car, withhold money, and isolate her from the rest of her family. His favorite pastime was taunting her about other women he would meet while she was abandoned at home. "I worried all the time about a bill not being paid, or having him sneak around and shut the electricity, phone, or heat off." He would also undo her cleaning and hide or break her wheelchair. She was afraid to report him; he still had possession of a gun that he was supposed to have surrendered when she obtained a civil protection order. With her own disability and three children, two of whom had cognitive disabilities, Florence felt overwhelmed and defeated. These abusive tactics are commonplace for IPV/A victims with disabilities (see Gilson, DePoy, and Cramer 2001; Lund 2011).

Once a relationship was under way, abusers' manipulativeness and relentless verbal abuse kept women second-guessing themselves and eroded their sense of self-efficacy. As Naomi described this process, "You deserve to have your own life the way you want it . . . but abuse happens so gradually. You don't realize you're giving things up. . . . You get into a smaller and smaller cube until you're contained in this one tiny square cube. . . . You are cut off from your friends but you need allies to leave. . . . Abuse makes you not confident in your own voice, so you second-guess everything you do." According to social psychologist Sharon Lamb (1999b, 35), "Perpetrators will tell their victims that they are worthless, or sluts, or seductresses, or manipulating bitches, and because of the perpetrator's relationship to the victim, the consistency and sheer repetition of such remarks, these words can be both deafening and defining. In addition, the perpetrator will sometimes blame the victim outright by pointing out ways in which a wife could have avoided getting hit ('If only you had . . .')"—reinforcing her self-blame (see J. Herman 1992). Sandee described how her high school boyfriend threw out her clothes because he thought she dressed like a hooker and how he broke up with her often, leaving her desperate for any of his attention. The women talked about how the outside world saw a very different picture of the men that left their younger selves wondering what they did to not deserve such charm. As Brenda declared, "No one believed it was so bad because they saw a respectful man who seemed in love, not his possessiveness or verbal abuse. . . . I thought I was going crazy because he would tell me things and I would have never said them, or he would just twist stories." Tina's husband outright called her crazy: "He told me if I didn't stop being so dramatic he was going to take me to the state mental hospital. And he started driving in that direction like he was going to; I was begging—please don't do that, don't take me there. . . . He had me thinking that there was something wrong with me." Such "gaslighting" tactics caused the women to question their own reality and increased their dependency on the abuser.

RELIGION AS CONTROL

Religion and faith can be double-edged swords. While we will see later that religion can be a source of strength for women healing from an abusive relationship, it can also facilitate the agenda of the abuser. Abusers often displayed an ostentatious religiosity during courtship, as in the case of

Joan's husband, who made a big show of praying before meals. She met him in church, a setting that gave him instant credibility. Danielle similarly met her husband at church and described how her church's doctrine that God "sends" the person he plans for you encouraged her to rush into marriage:

> I was taught that God's gonna send the right person to you. He lived with a family from the church and attended the church I grew up in. He was twenty-three. We were young. We didn't have any money. It was just one of those things where we wanted to do what God wanted us to do. We did youth group stuff at church. . . . We went to premarital counseling and thought we were ready. It was a big fast thing, but the big push is when God chose for you who it is, then you should get married. I only knew him for six months before marriage.

For Reeva, a "preacher's kid" (both her parents were ministers), the conviction that "God gave me you" led her to hasten a marriage with a man who was in her church. She left college in the middle of the semester, overriding the objections of both her parents and ignoring the red flags that manifested early on: after the couple announced the engagement to their church assembly, "my mother was approached by trusted friends that knew women that he had been sleeping with in the church. But I gave him the benefit of the doubt." They moved down south—a decision that isolated Reeva from her family—and Reeva got pregnant right away. Her husband was not happy about it and began physically abusing her during the pregnancy. Following the birth of her first son, she had two miscarriages, which she attributed to his abuse, and then gave birth to another son who was profoundly handicapped.

Abusers also manipulated religious doctrine to encourage women's initial involvement in a relationship, to justify controlling behavior, and to make the women stay committed to the relationship. Women who had been raised by religious parents were less likely to question abusive behavior if their suitors claimed religiosity. Scholars have documented how abusers use religious beliefs and doctrines to exert control (Giesbrecht and Sevcik 2000; Nash 2006; Nason-Clark 1997). They invoke religious prohibitions against divorce, make their wives feel guilty for even thinking of divorce as an option (Sharp 2009), and employ the Christian doctrine of wifely submission as a way to control their partners (Sharp 2014).[2] Anita described this pattern of manipulation when she said of her third husband that he "claimed to be a very spiritual man, but I called him a demon. There's a way people can use the Bible against you, and that's what he did."

Such religious coercive control can be very difficult to counter. Recent research demonstrates that abused women who succeed in resisting abusers' use of the Christian doctrine of submission to rationalize abuse (Giesbrecht and Sevcik 2000; Nash 2006) need both knowledge and mastery of their religious culture, in addition to possessing confidence in their ability to provide an alternative framing of the scripture used by their abuser (Sharp 2014).[3] For IPV/A victims/survivors who have low self-esteem that has been whittled down even further by their abusers, the confidence to interpret scripture independently can be impossible to obtain. Indeed, Sharp (2014, 1410) argues that when abusers turn religious doctrine into a weapon, it puts "victims between the rock of managing their faith in their religious beliefs, values, and doctrines, and the hard place of having these beliefs, values, and doctrines used against them in a coercive way." Thus Amy looked in vain for help from the Bible; rather than finding solace in its words, she felt admonished for considering leaving her husband, notwithstanding his abuse. Clergy who support victims'/survivors' readings of scripture that challenge the doctrine of wifely submission or writings against divorce can help interrupt abusers' religious control. This issue will be explored further in chapter 4.

WEAPONS

Given men's larger physical size and strength, on average, fear and intimidation can be part of a victim/survivor's daily experience, with or without actual "hardware" like knives or guns (Stark 2007). But according to a 2014 national survey (T. Smith and Son 2015), about one in three Americans owns a firearm or lives with someone who does. Even if weapons are not brandished or used, if one exists, a victim knows the threat is real and ever-present. Research reveals an increased risk of lethal injury or death from IPV/A when firearms are present in the relationship (J. Campbell et al. 2007; Gwinn 2006; Sorenson and Wiebe 2004). Firearms account for approximately 60 percent of homicides annually that are committed by a current or former spouse (Vidgor and Mercy 2006). One study found that households where chronic violence occurs are 20 percent more likely to own firearms than the general population, entailing a greater risk for IPV/A victims (Sorenson and Wiebe 2004).

Both state and federal laws and amendments have been developed to address this increased danger and lethality, with the goal of restricting violent offenders' access to firearms (Fleury-Steiner, Miller, and Carcirieri 2017). The federal Violence against Women Act of 1994 banned individuals from firearm possession if they were subject to a protection order. The 1996 Lautenberg Amendment to the Gun Control Act of 1968 banned access to firearms for those convicted of misdemeanor domestic violence. Yet early research results suggest that the laws designed to disarm abusers have been poorly implemented; for instance, among the victims in one study (Webster et al. 2010), judges required offenders to surrender their firearms in only 26 percent of cases, and law enforcement routinely failed to notify victims when the firearms were relinquished. In a more recent study, the firearms prohibition was not mentioned by judges in more than 25 percent of the court cases (Fleury-Steiner et al. 2016), a finding that does little to ensure the safety of the victim and any children who could be in harm's way.

The women I interviewed tended not to mention weapons until directly asked and were nonchalant about the abuser's possession of them. Weapons were just there, in the background of their lives. And after all, national polls indicate that 15.4 percent of US households have hunting guns (T. Smith and Son 2015). Many of the women discussed their partners/spouses owning guns and other weapons for hunting, not security, purposes, with the exception of five women whose abusers owned firearms—sometimes in addition to hunting weapons—because they were in the military or law enforcement. Danielle casually mentioned her husband's hunting bow and arrow and guns: "I grew up in a rural area so it was for hunting. I wasn't afraid at first, but when he stared acting whacko, I did get afraid." Winnie described a similar nonchalance at first regarding her husband's multiple weapons:

> WINNIE: He's an avid hunter. He had rifles, shot guns, bow and arrows, handgun.
>
> INTERVIEWER: Were you afraid of those?
>
> WINNIE: No. I was so numb. Once he said, "How much life insurance do we have on you anyway?" I said, "I don't know. I can check." . . . I'm thinking, it's the first day of the New Year, he's reviewing our finances. He said, "Well, you know what my New Year's resolution is. don't you?" He said, "It's to kill you. I'm gonna kill you." I didn't say anything. . . . I think I was going to be a hunting accident.

Winnie now feared that something could happen and no one would ever know. Their home was surrounded by many acres of forest, so even the closest neighbors could not see or hear anything.

The women did bring up weapons when describing incidents where the abuser used a weapon to threaten or hurt them. Dale described how her husband had used a gun to scare her not only about the possibility of his shooting her but also about the possibility of shooting himself: "So many times in our marriage he would act like he was going to kill himself; he would leave with a loaded gun and be gone for hours, or a day or two," leaving her petrified, waiting for a phone call from the hospital or for him to appear on her doorstep with a gunshot wound. Joan's husband, a hunter, had a shotgun at the house that was not registered in his name. He would not only point it at her but also rape her with it. "He told me he would kill me when I was asleep. I now know how to sleep with one eye open. It was ridiculous—I would go to work to sleep." The restraining order she filed did not cover the gun because it was not registered in his name, and his cousin came over and took it, so he still had easy access to it. Although Abigayle's boyfriend never fired his gun, he had one in the house. Once he chased her around the house with it but maintained that he was going to kill himself with it. The next time he brandished a gun she was the target, although he stuck to taunting her by saying, "I should have killed you the last time when I had the chance."

Pepper's boyfriend, a well-known drug dealer in their town, owned a number of guns and knives. He stalked her to a nightclub, shot her in the head, and also shot her best friend, leaving them for dead. Then he locked himself in their house and eventually killed himself hours later. Miraculously, Pepper (and her best friend) survived, though she endured many, many months of intensive therapy. Pepper, who had never owned a gun before this, now kept a loaded gun within easy reach in the living room, visibly present as we conducted the interview.

Amy's first husband was a drug dealer and addict who was very violent and who cheated on her with many women:

> The final straw, when I finally got it through my head that it is time to go—in the middle of one of these very violent arguments, he went to look for his .35mm. I had hidden it before he came home that night. Two weeks later, he kept saying, "Where's the gun?" But I had turned it in to the police because I was afraid to throw it away but I could see that if it stayed in the house something bad was going to happen. Finally I told him, "I turned it into the police." He had a fit. He got an ax and he started chopping furniture. . . . The only way out of the house was past him through the front door. . . . I couldn't go out the back door, he nailed it shut. So I stood in the doorway and I hid my kids under the kitchen table and I said if I live through this—I am done. Two weeks later I found a place to move out. . . . That was marriage 1.

The women identified much slackness in the policies on relinquishing weapons. Although Danielle turned in the weapons she could find when she filed and received a restraining order, she remained convinced that her abuser had access to other weapons. Florence reported that her husband had a gun that he was supposed to surrender when she obtained a restraining order but that he had refused. When Julia's husband was arrested the first time, the police took his many guns away that night but then brought the guns back. Her husband also retaliated for the temporary removal of his guns by spraying her huge rose arbor with poison; every rosebush was burned black within two hours. After his third arrest, when his guns were confiscated again, he went to the police department and picked up all of his guns and returned to the house with them. Similarly, Anita mentioned how the police never took her ex-husband's gun or ammunition because he stored it at his brother's house and even used his brother's weapons to threaten her and their son when he was drunk. A couple of years after their divorce, Anita took a self-defense course at the town library because she wanted to feel more able to protect herself.

Women faced a quandary if their abusers needed their weapons as part of their jobs. For instance, Jayde's lesbian partner, a police officer, had a police department–issued gun and other weapons, including six personal guns in the house they shared. The final violent incident that Jayde endured involved her abusive partner and two of her female officer friends; they broke down the door to their apartment, tearing it off the hinges, hand-cuffed Jayde, pepper-sprayed her, broke her wrist, and beat her. In the hospital emergency room, the attending doctor counted twenty-eight to thirty large bruises on Jayde's body. At first, other officers wanted to arrest Jayde for being combative and assaulting a police officer, since she had thrown a lamp at them in self-defense, but eventually the truth prevailed and she obtained a restraining order (though the officers did not get into trouble).

Guns were not the only cause for concern. Elizabeth, who had received gruesome physical beatings, was worried that her abuser had access to knives. Jenny described mostly verbal abuse and beatings, but her abuser did threaten her with a knife. Haley had vivid memories of a knife her boy-friend had held to her throat.

Some of the women, like Naomi, reported that their abusers did not possess any weapons—or threaten to use them—until the impending end of the relationship made them desperate. Naomi recounted: "He threatened me a couple of times; that [last] summer he said that he had a gun, although he never showed it to me, and told me that he thought of killing the three of us. . . . That made it very clear that I had to get my son and myself out of the situation." Robyn also recalled her husband's desperation at the end of their marriage (although she did not mention any firearms until I explicitly asked her):

ROBYN: When I left him, I had to hide because he was furious and embarrassed; he told everyone when he was drinking that he's gonna blow my fucking head off. I called the police, and they told me that I needed to stay away.

INTERVIEWER: It sounds like, being with the military, he had access to weapons?

ROBYN: He was in the navy. They didn't do weapons. As far as hunting, he had a lot of shotguns and knives.

As Vanessa's husband got more hooked on cocaine and paranoid about her leaving him, he applied for a permit to carry a concealed deadly weapon. She found out about this because he told her over the phone to open up his mail, knowing the permit was in the pile of envelopes:

> He starts laughing, an evil laugh. . . . I opened it up. At the top, I read it out loud, Permit to Carry a Concealed Deadly Weapon. I didn't fully understand what I was reading. . . . He said, "It's your eviction notice to life, bitch. You're gonna die soon," and he hangs up. He had filled out the Gun Permit Application, waited for it to come, immediately purchased a handgun, and then brought it home and told me he was going to kill me. He assured me that he would not shoot me in the head so my kids could see me for the last time in an open casket funeral. . . . And that he would never shoot me on a Tuesday or a Thursday, because it was inconvenient those days. So I could take a deep breath and relax on those two days every week. The other thing was, the O.J. Simpson trial had just ended. . . . He told me, "If a 'n-word' person can get away with killing a white bitch, I can get away with killing you."

Another time, he used a knife to scare Vanessa. He "cut up my kitchen counter, all the while threatening to grab me by the throat, threatening to slit my throat. But it was out of the blue these would happen." Aberrant episodes like this could be even more terrifying.

ECONOMIC ABUSE

While economic justice for IPV/A victims/survivors has only recently become a national policy issue, as evidenced by webinars, trainings, and reports on this topic from the National Institute of Justice and the Centers for Disease Control, economic abuse has long been a central tactic of IPV/A. Economic abuse is calculated behavior carried out to keep a victim economically dependent and unable to achieve economic self-sufficiency to leave the relationship. The more dependent victims are on their abusers, the greater their risk of mistreatment and exploitation and the less likely they are to leave (Postmus et al. 2012). Trapped in abusive situations that harm their psychological well-being, they can focus only on basic daily survival (see Raphael 2000). Economic abuse has been less explored in the IPV/A literature than physical violence and psychological abuse, yet victims often describe it as the tactic that most prevents them from leaving. It includes withholding/controlling income, sabotaging employment efforts, squandering a partner's finances, causing lost productivity from injuries and premature death, and causing medical and mental health expenditures (Max et al. 2004; Sanders 2015). Adams et al.'s (2008) Scale of Economic Abuse (SEA) provides the most inclusive and detailed definition, distinguishing dimensions of economic control, economic exploitation, and employment sabotage. Economic control and exploitation include controlling money the victim earns or inherits or doing anything that results in her being unable to feed, clothe, or provide for herself or her children; taking paychecks, tax refunds, disability payments, or other kinds of payments such as child support or public assistance; putting assets or deeds or mortgages all in his name only; accruing gambling debts or other debts for extravagant purchases in her name; forcing the victim to not work at a job; being intrusive or abusive at the victim's workplace so that she is fired; withholding money in retaliation for not complying with the abuser's demands; making the victim ask for money; making all big financial decisions without her input; and lying about shared assets or withholding information for education grants or financial aid (see Adams et al. 2008; Belknap 2015, 392–93; Moe and Bell 2004). Employment sabotage includes deterring her from accessing education and training or thwarting her efforts to get to work by such tactics as sabotaging cars, restraining her, not following through with child care, hiding car keys, not providing transportation to work, tampering with the alarm clock or work clothes, preventing sleep, withholding medication, harassing her during the workday with excessive monitoring phone calls to her and/or coworkers—essentially anything that prevents her from getting or keeping a job (Adams et al. 2008; Anderberg and Rainier 2013).

Dale's story captures many of these manifestations, so I retell it here. Dale's husband had left their seventeen-year marriage, which had been characterized by his frequent emotional abuse, his threats to kill her, and several strangulation attempts. He had lost a lot of money gambling during their marriage, and when he walked out—two days after their son was diagnosed with a rare cancer—he closed out their checking and savings accounts, leaving her with nothing but the five dollars in her pocket.

Fortunately Dale was employed (at a major national retail chain), but she worried about her own safety and that of their two children. Her ex-husband was using his friends to break into her car and to drive by to check her whereabouts in an unrecognizable car, a phenomenon known as "proxy stalking" (Melton 2007). Overcoming her embarrassment and concerns for privacy and keeping her job, Dale informed her company about her fears; a copy of her restraining order against him was put on file in the security office along with a photograph of her ex-husband. Dale encountered some reluctance from the security director, who questioned the reasonableness of her fears, implying that addressing her protection would be inconvenient and time consuming, and her supervisor admonished her against scaring her coworkers by talking about her fears.

A year after the couple's separation, Dale's husband, who had been used to curtailing her access to money back when they were together, was particularly upset and angry about a recent divorce hearing where the court awarded Dale more money than she had asked for. After weeks of preparation and planning, including renting an unrecognizable car, Dale's husband waited in the parking lot of her workplace. As soon as he saw her, he gunned the motor and floored it, hitting Dale so hard she flew through the air, careening off four parked cars. She was hospitalized and unable to return to work for six weeks, so she lost work income and incurred medical bills she could not pay. He was later charged with attempted criminal homicide and fleeing as a fugitive from justice and was convicted of attempted manslaughter; a six-year sentence was imposed.

Miraculously, Dale recovered from the attempted murder and returned to work. This time, the company installed a surveillance camera in her office and in the parking lot and secured a special lock on her office door. Her husband served only three years of the six-year sentence. Terrified, Dale reported his early release to her boss; he responded by cutting her hours since she was seen as a safety risk. But her part-time hours did not pay enough to cover her bills. Eventually, probably because of media attention to her story, the company reinstated her hours, gave her a walkie-talkie, allowed her to work varying shifts and use a different door into the workplace, and gave her a security escort to and from her car. She also felt safer knowing that her ex-husband was monitored with an ankle bracelet. Dale's situation was used to raise awareness company-wide about dealing with domestic violence in the workplace, but without her knowledge and consent—something companies must be aware of especially if the victim's work location is included in the story. Dale also worked at another part-time job where she had to ask that her name and address not appear on distribution lists or any Internet documents and that no one call her by her last name. At the time of interview her ex-husband no longer wore an ankle bracelet, so Dale felt even more vulnerable now that his whereabouts were not monitored by the criminal justice system.

Dale's situation is unfortunately not unique. "Nearly a quarter of employed women report that domestic violence has affected their work performance at some point in their lives. Each year, an estimated eight million days of paid work is lost in the U.S. because of domestic violence. Domestic violence costs $8.3 billion in expenses annually: a combination of higher medical costs ($5.8 billion) and lost productivity ($2.5 billion)" (Pearl 2013; see also National Center for Injury Prevention and Control 2003; Max et al. 2004; Sanders 2015). Empirical research documents the pervasiveness of economic abuse during the relationship and after separation (Jaffe, Lemon, and Poisson 2003; Sev'er 1997; Toews and Bermea 2017; Varcoe and Irwin 2004). A 2012 study by Postmus and colleagues with a convenience sample of 120 women drawn from IPV/A providers revealed that 94.2 percent experienced some kind of economic abuse. Moe and Bell (2004) found that regardless of employment or educational status, women's ability to find or keep their jobs was seriously compromised by their fear, anxiety, physical injuries, emotional trauma, and experiences of stalking. Adams et al. (2008) interviewed 103 female survivors of domestic abuse who resided temporarily in a battered women's shelter and found that 99 percent experienced some form of economic abuse, reinforcing their dependence on their abusers and creating obstacles for those attempting to leave. Economic abuse also destabilizes women's daily survival and curtails their longer-term opportunities for getting employment or education or establishing credit (see Melbin, Sullivan, and Cain 2003; Sanders 2015); they often end up on public assistance or living in poverty, which exacerbates their poor physical and psychological health. Adams and her colleagues found that women tended to blame themselves for their economic situation and to be relieved to learn about economic abuse, which validated for them the enormous obstacles to economic self-sufficiency that their abusers had created for them.[4]

The topic of economic abuse came up again and again among the women in my study. They talked about it with the certainty that their employment or interest in bettering themselves ran counter to their abuser's goals of achieving control because it gave them more power and potentially independence. The heterosexual women noted that men felt threatened by a woman who brought home a paycheck and thereby decreased the inequities between them. Abusers felt less challenged by partners who were unemployed and dependent—though they still sabotaged any efforts to improve women's employability.

Some abusers forbade their partners to work outside the home, Even though some of the women in this situation might appear to be "living the dream," as one woman with an upper-middle-class lifestyle described it, the abuse meant they were basically living in a gilded prison. Reeva reported, "I had a gorgeous home, three thousand square feet. Beautiful home, beautiful acreage, the whole nine yards. But I lived pure hell." Her husband kept her trapped at home, surveilled by cameras, as she took care of their disabled child. Some women acquiesced to the abusers' demands to stay at home as a way to placate them, but doing so only further compounded their isolation and hindered any ability to reach out to coworkers or other people.

Many women did have jobs, but their partners commandeered paychecks, sometimes doling out portions of the money to be used for groceries. Some of the women "allowed" this. Though Julia had a master's degree and a great job, she felt her husband should control all the earnings because she believed in Evangelical Christian teachings that the husband should be in charge. Amy similarly signed her paycheck over to her (second) husband, even though she was the only one working at times, and added him to all of her credit cards. She recalled having the trusting attitude that marriage meant sharing everything: "I am a person that if I get married . . . in a fairy tale life, everything is mine is yours is mine."

Tina reported being forced to give her husband her paycheck: "I could cash the check but I would bring the envelope home, put it on the bureau, and he would determine how much I got. . . . He controlled the finances, the kids, and the house."

Men took control not only of women's paychecks but also of their other financial resources. Reeva reported that her husband controlled their money and that she had no access to any financial matters since everything was in his name alone. Although she had provided the down payment for their house through a settlement she had received before she met him, her name was not on their paperwork. At the closing, she was getting some snacks for her kids, and he never called for her signature.

Other women told stories of abusers' stealing child support checks (from prior relationships), disability checks, and educational financial aid checks. Once Terri started living with her boyfriend at college, her parents stopped paying for college or helping with anything financially; she became the sole support of herself and her husband, using student loans and scholarships— and then of her daughter, for she became pregnant, and their daughter was born during her senior year of college. Danielle used her Pell grants to support her kids once her husband stopped providing for them. Abusers often tried to keep women from getting such alternative forms of income. Joan was forced to stop getting child support from the father of her children because her new husband was going to "be in charge," but he ended up not covering their needs.

Several women reported that their abuser neglected their own needs or the needs of their children while siphoning off money into gambling, paying child support to a previously undisclosed family, spending on affairs, racking up thousands of dollars of credit card debt by purchasing nonessential recreational items, or losing assets through bad financial decisions and nonpayment of bills. Julia was one of the several women who found out after the wedding that her husband owed back child support—in her case $30,000. Her husband had told her that his ex-wife had abandoned him and moved across the country, but after Julia's own divorce she found out it was her husband who had done the abandoning. Julia was bitter about the years and money spent fighting that situation in court: "The whole time I wanted kids, but because of money (according to my ex-husband) we could not." Reeva recalled how several years into her marriage, when she had stopped working to take care of their disabled son, "The Lord prompted me to look at the accounts and I realized that bills were overdue. I had thought the mortgage was being paid." She intercepted the mail when he was away and discovered the bank was ready to foreclose on their house. She realized then that he had spent much of their money on other women.

Indeed, almost all of the women shared stories about when their abusers controlled but mismanaged their finances and lied about paying bills, leaving them in the dark, only to discover later that their credit was ruined. Amy said of her husband, "He bounced checks and then accused me of overdrawing the accounts, even though I no longer had access to my earnings or credit cards. He wanted to sell my house . . . so we sell it and he buys a mobile home. Houses appreciate, mobile homes depreciate, so I lost my investment. Then he ran up $27,000 worth of credit card debt."

Facing financial ruin, Amy got a job.

Here I was with two little kids, and he brought in another woman to live in our house. I had to get a job. Because of his party life, he stopped bringing money home. I had traditional family beliefs, including that you stay home with the children. Moms don't work. I tried to stay home, but when I realized that we had no food and he was not interested in feeding us, if I didn't work we would lose the house. We had no heat, no electricity, no phone, no car. I thought, "Wait, I've got a college degree." I am thinking, "We are going to starve to death while I am waiting around to be provided for." So I got a secretarial job in a law office. It paid the rent.

Yet this prompted more abuse, with her husband insisting she was not a good mother since her hours at work meant that she neglected the family.

If the women worked outside the home for part or all of their relationship, abusers asserted their control in the domain of their work. Celeste was prevented from going back to school or taking training courses to increase her employability because her abuser deemed her stupid and said it would be a waste of money. When Winnie worked at home on the computer, her husband changed her passwords at night. Although he liked their lifestyle made possible by her paycheck, he felt threatened by her access to interact with other people. Many abusers relied on emotional abuse to degrade their partners, making them feel discouraged or unqualified to get a job. Abusers would stalk or monitor their partner at work, keeping an eye on both her and her coworkers and accusing her later of flirting with male coworkers. A number of the women lost their jobs after their abusers' stalking and calling became obsessive and interfered with the workday. Abusers would also shirk child care duties, tamper with alarm clocks to make the women late, or injure their partner so she would be forced to call in sick, in attempts to try to get the women fired. Women were also terrified to leave their children in the abuser's care while they were at work, believing he would neglect them or turn them against their mothers.

Beyond the immediate chaos created by economic abuse, long-term consequences surfaced after women left their abusers. A number of the women encountered problems when they found savings and retirement accounts changed or frozen. Landlords were often reluctant to forgive for damaged or destroyed property, which affected reference checks later; for instance, although one woman decided to explain to a future landlord what led her to have a bad referral, the prospective landlord feared for future problems with her ex-husband, and she believed she did not get the apartment because of this concern.

Reeva recounted how after her relationship with her husband had ended he kept coming around the house to stalk her. But because all the money and assets were in his name she could not afford the alarm system that would keep her safe:

> I even called the burglary alarm people and explained the situation because the alarm had been cut off. I had booby-trapped the house because I was so afraid he would break in. I had cans along the garage door so if he tried to open it, the noise would warn me. I told the alarm company, "I have two kids and I'm fearful"—and God bless them, they said, "We'll give you free coverage." They said, "As long as you're in this situation, just let us know." I cried with gratitude and relief.

Back when Vanessa and her husband were together, she had contributed financially to the mortgage and to the expenses of the children and the household (whenever she was working outside the home). But she had not wanted her name connected with her husband, so when they bought a house, she saw it as a source of pride that she did not allow him to add her name to the deed. Later, when their relationship ended, what she had done initially as a point of pride ended up hurting her. She had naively believed that their assets would be jointly divided upon divorce, but her husband sold the house and kept all the proceeds, while she had custody of their three children and nowhere else to live.

After the relationships ended, several abusers used their limited child care experiences to demonstrate that they should obtain custody. The women believed that the men thought they would slip out of paying any child support if they had custody, another economic worry.

Spotty work records caused by the abuser's interference complicated women's efforts later to get a job. Future employment also could be affected if women were arrested for an IPV/A charge. For instance, when police arrested Abigayle for giving her abuser a bloody nose the charges were later dropped. However,

> although they dismissed it, it stayed on my record, which came back and bit me, because in my career I have security licenses. I work in a bank, so everybody is fingerprinted for bank records, the FBI,—we have our own regulatory agency. So when I changed jobs, they did a background check. I just assumed things would be fine because it had been dismissed, but it wasn't, and that was very embarrassing for me. My new boss told me he found this Assault third on my record. I since then got it expunged, but I had to give a written statement about what had happened and why it was there.

Related stories about women's arrests are provided in chapter 5.

After the relationship ended, or when a woman took the first steps toward asserting herself, the abuser often escalated the economic abuse out of sheer vindictiveness. When Winnie's husband was arrested,

> He wiped out all the bank accounts that night. He had plenty of money to go to get a hotel. But he stayed at my sister's house, which was empty while she was in Florida, for free, used up all her computer paper, all her ink, printing off our accounts, changing passwords, changing the mailing addresses, wiping out all the accounts.

Tina decided to buy a used car after her husband stole hers in the middle of the night (the police could not do anything about it since her car was in his name). But following her purchase, he took her to court for child support "because he thought that if I had enough money to buy a car I could give him some money since he had taken the kids. I was working three jobs and he was only working one."

The women's experiences vividly demonstrate how economic abuse compounds the terror and pains of IPV/A. Though constrained by violence, intimidation, and control, women mustered considerable courage and coping skills to retain some semblance of dignity. Their resourcefulness, despite limited autonomy, is described in the next section.

WOMEN'S STRATEGIES OF RESISTANCE

Even within the most constricting circumstances, the women pursued opportunities to secure some small semblance of independence. They spoke about squirreling away money, furtively stuffing a dollar bill or some coins in an unexpected spot that their partner would not find.

Amy saw waitressing as the perfect job because

> tips put cash in my pocket, so he won't know how much I have, and I have freedom with money. I thought, if I can hold onto the job for six months then it can break that control. That was my goal. I got a job waiting tables, and I loved it because I was with people totally unrelated to religion and him. It was totally just me.

Whenever she got some bills, she would tape them behind the pictures in the house or "put money in an envelope and tape it to the bottom of the drawer." Her ex-husband didn't like her working, even though he was doing nothing to help support the family. But for Amy it meant not only that she could contribute to household expenses with her meager waitressing earnings but also that for the first time she had some of her own money and could give some of it to her children or take them out for a treat:

> I was never able to give them anything, I couldn't even take them out for a soda. If I found coins along the road, I'd hoard them. My husband had a jar of change, but I had to be careful how much I took, because he would notice the level had gone down. I would take dimes and quarters and hide them, a dollar here and a dollar there, and I could take my kids out for ice cream. The waitress job was great because all of a sudden I had sixty dollars in tips to spend.

Women also secretly subverted their abuser's surveillance and restrictions on their movements. Amy recounted, "I hid extra car keys around because he would take my car keys if he thought I was going to go someplace. I kept my driver's license in my pocket at all times." Other women spoke of hiding a cell phone, for instance in their bra.

Women drew on a variety of coping strategies to maintain their equanimity, courage, and self-respect within the relationship. A number of them, for example, used humor, particularly when their children were afraid and they needed to show a brave front. Using humor as a potential coping strategy is found in other work on IPV/A as well (Brabeck and Guzman 2008).

Haley said she read newspapers "cover to cover to know what's going on in the world so I knew there's misery everywhere. That helped me put things in perspective." A written record, in a journal or diary, helped the women gain a different kind of perspective. This practice was crucial for at least 25 percent of the women, both during their relationship and in the years that followed. In fact, those who wrote about their thoughts and experiences after the relationships ended described the process as "lifesaving" and "as important as breathing." Danielle wrote everything down in a little notebook, which she brought with her to our interview to verify dates.

Women talked about the need to take time alone for thinking. Winnie started doing yoga as a way to "help me have clarity and courage to and to give me some time for myself so I could relax enough to feel." Anita said, "I like to drive. I like the peace and the quiet. It gave me time to think."

Going to school, when the abuser did not make it impossible to continue, could be a source of peace and confidence. For Jenny,

> I put all my energy into studying and getting my graduate degree. That was my salvation. I know now that I was using my education as a way to block everything in my personal life; I saw it as a mental escape. I was supporting him at the time. He would convince me that I could not make the right decision in many things . . . but he also communicated to me that what I was really good at was education, saying the only thing I did well is read books. So for me, that was my saving. The world of books, what I have known all my life.

Other women's misery was allayed only by self-medicating—anesthetizing themselves with alcohol until they were numb, or to help them to fall asleep. Jazzy said, "I would drink to suppress the pain, just to deal with things." Elizabeth echoed this: "Until I learned how to build a relationship with God, I would go to work and I would come home, drink and get high, and then wake up and go to work. That was my life." Several women talked about not being social drinkers but over time beginning to drink with their husbands in order to feel the sting of the words and blows less.

Several women mentioned indirect, covert forms of resistance. One woman said she had been tempted to spit in her abuser's food while cooking dinner and that she did wrinkle his freshly ironed clothes in the closet.

Though it might appear that these women were stooping to the level of their abusers, their actions are consistent with Valli's (2007, 201) work on resistance, called "edgework," which describes battered women's intentional behavior "behind the scenes" of the relationship that is strategically meant to regain some self-respect. Over time, the women learned that responding outright with force put them in greater danger, so by engaging in these subversive acts, such as purposely sabotaging something minor, they were able to maintain some measure of control, if only from their perspective. The edgework was intended to inadvertently hurt the abuser—his work, his image, his belongings, his extended relationships—but if confronted by him, the women could easily attribute the damage to something other than their behavior (see also Larance and Miller 2016).

Three women secretly defied their abuser by having an affair. All described this action as empowering—it was the one way they received any positive attention, compliments, and respect—albeit from another man. It also was described as a way to assert some kind of control in an out-of-control situation. As Katherine confessed,

> I really did feel it was the one way I could get back at him for what he was doing to me. If he found out—I knew I'd be in fatal danger. But even though I'd be subjected to horrendous treatment if he did find out, I still did it, and in some way, I was paying him back. I didn't know how to get out of the relationship, I was too embarrassed to seek help groups, and I don't even know if they existed at that time because I'm talking the mid-1970s. . . . It was absolutely the reverse of what my principles were and what my behavior had ever been, what I believed was right, but I truly enjoyed the hell out of it because in some way I was showing him what I could do in retaliation.

The urge to regain some self-respect sometimes led women to retaliate openly against the abuser or one of his affair partners. When Sara suspected her husband of having yet another affair, with a coworker of his in the military, she went to the woman's house "to call her out about fraternizing, and to tell her what I thought of her." She saw this as a way to not be submissive (and it was not as threatening as confronting her husband). But this effort backfired, as she was arrested for making threats. Both Jazzy and Vanessa described how they would fight back, even knowing they would get more injured. "I would take a pool stick to him and hit back," recalled Jazzy. Vanessa recalled, "I never shut my damn mouth, even though it would have made it easier on me." She also set his clothes on fire when he started yelling at her that she had not finished the laundry and he had nothing to wear to work.

I had the flu, and I had ripped open my incision from just having a baby because I was vacuuming vomit off my floor because I was so sick. He starts yelling about how late he will be. . . . So I start throwing his clothes on the bathroom floor and he thinks I'm doing that so I can wash his clothes and he's screaming and cussing me out and the kids are crying. I just calmly went into the kitchen and found a matchbook. He's looking at me, I'm looking right back at him, and I strike the match and threw it on his clothes. I can still picture the look on his face because this was the first time I stood up to him.

The next month, her husband was the most violent he had ever been to her, and Vanessa kicked him out for good.

When some of the women were in the stage of contemplating leaving their husbands or partners, they started to disregard his "rules." For instance, Winnie's husband used to force her to cancel plans with friends and family, in his efforts to keep them isolated. "I started saying, if you want to stay home, fine, but the kids and I are going, or, you can stay home with the kids and I'm going to go." Once Amy realized her family's well-being rested on her getting a job, she found that being near other people, outside her husband's control, was immensely helpful in reinforcing to her that there were other ways to live. Of course, these external social connections feel threatening to abusers and often they react by strengthening their controlling tactics (Stark 2007). When Amy landed the part-time waitress job, she lasted only four weeks because of his sabotage: "He wouldn't let me go to sleep at night, keeping me up, repeating, 'You gotta quit that job, those people are wicked and evil and that restaurant is the devil, they serve alcohol there.'" Sara, as a way of asserting some of her own control—to prove to herself that she could still make some choices— gave her father $5,000 of part of an unexpected settlement from an employment class action suit, angering her husband and increasing his aggression toward her.

When the women started to envision a life without abuse or their abuser, deliberate strategizing emerged. This is not to say that women did not daily find ways to actively resist and problem-solve to protect themselves and their children before that point. They did. But leaving was often harder than staying and enduring, particularly if the abusers surveilled them or sensed something was up. Several women remarked that they could have won Academy Awards for their acting, while simultaneously trying to stay one step ahead of their abusive partner.

Several women planned their escape for six to nine months. Joan rented a storage locker and gradually moved her most important and sentimental possessions to it. Terri set up a bank account in her own name. Terri revealed she had planned her escape for six months. She would play out worst-case scenarios in her mind every day, creating many practical responses in her repertoire in case her plans to leave backfired.

Secret stashes of money now became a lifeline to escape. Many women tried to open a bank account or credit card in their own name. For some, like Joan, such attempts to leave were stymied by their abuser's excessive control and their priority of taking care of their children. Still, Joan insisted that "if I could do anything different, I would have had a secret bank account where I would have put twenty dollars every payday."

Women who openly pursued financial independence risked retaliation. For example, when Naomi set up a separate bank account, her husband realized not only that she was tired of him draining their joint account but that she was "trying to become independent from him," and his violence escalated. Thus many stories recounted the care and thought women had to put into keeping their financial strategies secret from their abuser. Terri revealed,

> I actually did a stealth move. I had him sign the paperwork to get my name off the joint checking account, but I had him sign it after he woke up from sleeping, before he was fully awake. He just signed and didn't read that I removed myself from our shared bank account, and I made sure that was kept separate.

In the year she planned to leave, she also destroyed all but one of their credit cards, preferring to incur that debt with him rather than to arouse his suspicions. She was uncomfortable about using such underhanded methods, but she maintained,

> You may have to use tactics that seem mean or things that you normally would not do to someone. But if your safety is at risk when you leave, you have to outsmart them. You would be surprised about some of the things that you will do to survive. I had to take risks for real freedom and the future I wanted because I had already left once so I knew he wouldn't have let me leave again.

Women who were strategizing leaving also often secretly collected evidence on their abuser. Florence went through her abuser's files and copied bank statements and anything else she thought she might eventually need, putting them in her own locked file cabinet. She also kept a record of his attacks. Another woman noted things, but in code so her husband would not figure out what she was doing and "punish" her for it. One woman knew that her husband's mandatory domestic violence class, which he attended following an arrest on IPV/A charges, required him to write down what he was doing wrong and how he was feeling. "He'd write it all down, like, 'I took her car keys again' or "I kicked her out of the house with only her nightgown on,' so when I left I took his workbook and gave it to the judge." She also realized that she could collect evidence to use against him; he was not allowed to get a new hunting license or get field equipment such as a long hunting knife when he was on probation, "so I made a copy of his debit card transactions, his hunting license, and I had the bag where all the trash was from his purchases and I gave all that to his probation officer."

Women also spoke of the importance of developing the psychological readiness to leave. Understanding more about how batterers could act with impunity because of societal toleration, gendered inequalities, and men's presumptive power over women helped them stop blaming themselves, freeing them to stop believing that they were doing something to cause his abuse or that they had to make the relationship work. Celeste noted the importance of "consciousness-raising,"

> the understanding of what domestic violence is and that it's not about the woman, that it's about a system of oppression that beats women down physically and metaphorically. That's important information because you'll stay where you're at if you think it's your fault, that's your life, no matter where you go or who you're with. Why bother leaving one person if you think that that's going to always happen, no matter who you're with? Women have to be able to cognitively understand that it is not them.

Celeste talked about how important it had been to read a lot about parenting and about trauma:

> I had fucked up a lot of parenting things in those early years because I was just so compromised. What helped me was understanding that what had happened, the shape I was in, was not because I was a fuck-up, that this is what happens to people who are traumatized. Somehow, that gave me permission to be hopeful. . . . It was like, if you're fucked up because something bad has happened to you, that's not really much different than being broken because of a car hitting you. So I've been hit by a metaphorical car, and it takes a while to recover from that; there's shit you have to do, there's a treatment plan, just like there's a treatment plan for other things.

Women received validation after hearing about IPV/A in general, learning that they were not alone and that their situation was not something that they had caused through some individual trait or behavior—as their abusers had repeatedly told them. Three women first heard about the prevalence and dynamics of IPV/A in a college classroom. All of a sudden, their understanding about gendered power dynamics revealed that they did not "cause" his abuse. Sandee said, "Being in a course about gender and criminal justice, talking about IPV/A—it normalized it for me so I knew I wasn't going crazy or the only one, which was huge."

An objective outsider, such as a psychologist or another kind of counselor/therapist, greatly helped validate women's feelings and supported their hopes of escape. Winnie found a therapist whom she credited as fundamental in giving her the confidence to leave: "I was so disconnected with how I was feeling because I would go crazy when he took my kids." Women talked about the value of seeing a therapist, though they often could not get out of the house or find money to pay for it or get "permission" from their partner to do so because of his fear of revealing what was going on, so therapy commenced after they left the relationship. A few women were able to maintain a closeness with a friend or family member during their relationship, confiding in him or her and often receiving help with plans to leave, but turning to or receiving support from parents was rare. Dale, for example, was adamant about not telling her parents; she did not want them to think they had done something wrong in raising their child.

Women tried to implement not only strategies of escape but also more long-term plans to gain control over their lives and to provide as best they could for their children, though often they could not carry these out until they had left their abuser. Many sought to get a job or advance in their current position by obtaining more education or training. Some women were fortunate enough, after their relationship ended, to obtain help from job-training programs that targeted single mothers or women in transition (usually from divorce, not necessarily from IPV/A situations). Educational advancement and renewal of former skills or attainment of new ones featured prominently in the women's lives not only for the financial stability they furthered but also for the women's psychological resilience. Although one woman was in graduate school during the decade of abuse, three other women achieved a PhD years after their abusive relationship ended, and they were still expressing some surprise at the time of interview that they had been able to do it after having been told repeatedly that they were stupid and lazy and unworthy human beings. Other women achieved college diplomas or excelled in their professions. The women's pride in their own successes, confirming an identity beyond that of a helpless victim, was a compelling catalyst for maintaining vigilance in new relationships and long-term resilience.

Connections that the women made with compassionate, understanding, and unbiased landlords and employers played important roles in the time following relationship termination for some of the survivors.[5] Relationships do not simply end, and this acknowledgment by landlords and employers strengthened the women's resolve and willingness to share hard personal stories in order to receive assistance. Ellen's landlords saw her working several jobs to make end meets and had an inkling about the IPV/A; they excused her late payments many times. Women—especially those who have children with their abusers, but even women who have to divide property and divorce—need time to retain and meet with lawyers, deal with banks, and go to court. Some employers who understood the situation gave women paid leave or time off that did not count against them in performance reviews. For instance, Terri's economic well-being rested on her employer's understanding:

> They let me leave to go to court without sacrificing my pay. I used all my sick leave, but then I ran out. I didn't go on vacation or take personal time off, because I spent that time going to court. I was lucky that I had a good job or I would have lost my economic ability to care for my daughter. It would be very hard if I lost my job when I was going through all of that. I was very lucky. . . . If I hadn't been paid for all that time out, I wouldn't have been able to support my daughter or myself. I wish that there was something they could do for single moms who are going through all of this so we don't have to go into court every time the abuser files something frivolous.

Many women mentioned that they yearned for opportunities to better understand financial issues, and some were able to forge connections that gave them such opportunities. Some had recourse to bank programs that were aimed at helping make women in transition more financially knowledgeable. Others made connections with individuals who gave them useful advice about their finances. Danielle had bought her and her husband's house with severance pay when their second child was born, using her own funds for the down payment but putting the property in both their names. When her husband told her that he did not want to be married anymore and moved out, a distant friend who was a real estate attorney helped her do a quit claim deed on the house and got his name off the deed. Still other women were able to find programs that offered financial help to women in IPV/A situations. Ellen talked about a state program for IPV/A victims that provided moving funds and paying first and last month's rent on an apartment. "Otherwise, I would never be able to get out. It's an awesome program. They also helped with deposits for electric, they helped tremendously." This was not a well-publicized program; Ellen stumbled onto it through the probation department. "He was on probation for a year for assaulting me. The victim advocate from the probation office got it approved for me—all because his probation officer was scared after my ex went into probation threatening me about everything, and I guess there was more stuff he said that was scary."

Some women drew on their social networks for help. Joan's godparents bought a car for her and put it in her name, and then Joan paid them back $50 each payday. They also watched her kids when she had a night class for her BA degree. Sara's mother paid the filing fees for a divorce and hired an attorney. Celeste stressed that financial assistance for legal help in obtaining a divorce was what she needed most:

> If you're poor and you're trying to leave an abuser, and you can't even get a divorce, and no shelter or organization can offer assistance, then you're fucked. . . . You're more at risk of staying longer if you have kids, if you have no money, and if you can't get divorced. Those resources would have helped me tremendously.

Once the abuser was gone, women were vigilant about remaining safe. Many abusers still retained a sense of entitlement—so they justified access to their family or residence whenever they wished. Rosa's husband would deliberately drop by when he knew she was gone and their children were home, using the pretext that he needed something that was there. "I changed the locks and he tried to break down the door, scaring my son. . . . He couldn't believe I changed the locks, even though I had kicked him out." Some women installed home alarms, while others placed objects around doors to create noise if their abusers tried to force their way in. Women also talked about alternating driving routes and not answering calls on their cells if they did not recognize the phone numbers.

EPIPHANIES

Victim/survivors often can recall some incident that broke the proverbial camel's back and hastened their decision to end their relationships. They may even recall the exact date and time of that event. Eisikovits, Buchbinder, and Mor (1998, 419) speak of a turning point that symbolizes the "collapse of a system of meaning that had kept them in the violent relationship." For some women an act of severe violence against them or their children was the final straw. Up to that point, the women had focused on using their survival skills just to keep themselves and their children alive and protected from one day to the next. As Celeste noted: "It's hard to do something about leaving when you are just trying every day not to get killed." They might, for example, try to respond to their abuser in ways that would keep him calm. As Julia pointed out, "I think what happens is that victims think that they can manage their abusers, and initially, you can. He complains that dinner is not on the table at five p.m., and you make sure that dinner is on the table. They are also more manageable when they've had sex [and are relaxed]." They also might try to explain away the abuse, accept the abuser's apologies, and interpret his jealousy as a sign of love.

Yet each woman had a breaking point. For some, the event that caused it might not necessarily seem worse than what they had already endured. Their explanations echoed those of the women in Eisikovits et al.'s (1998, 419) research, which reported that "the event was neither unique nor dramatic; rather, it was made pivotal in the process of reinterpretation and chosen as central in the reorganization of the meaning system." Jayde, for instance, who was being beaten by her police officer partner (a woman), realized that she had to rely on her own wits to be safe: "If you can't trust the police to help, since your abuser is part of the club, you have to get out." Reeva's husband chased her around the house, locking her in a room while her young children were down the hall screaming, and tried to rape her. "That was it for me; it was completely over." Sara's husband picked a fight with her when it was clear to him she intended to carry through with her plans to visit family and friends in her hometown out of state. She ended up in the hospital for a week from the punches to her face that also broke her teeth. When Sara got home, she realized, "I'm tired of this shit . . . my kids heard the whole thing. He said, 'If you call the police they will be picking up a corpse in there.' And that's when I said, 'This is over. I'm done. Leave!' . . . I was devastated, but I couldn't take anymore." Joan's decision was precipitated by his increase in violence that started to occur in public: "It was one thing to choke, slap, and kick me in our bedroom, but going out in the yard where anybody can see, and kicking me out of the car—it just went too far." In addition, "I was sick of buying makeup to cover up the scars and then told I was spending too much money. He'd want me to go back to court to get more child support from my ex-husband, and even made me pay the weekly fee for his DV classes." Celeste presented her catalyst in stark terms: "The worst assault that took place for me, physically and emotionally, was two days after my second child was born, and I was hospitalized for eleven days after that—I lost a spleen, I was damaged in unspeakable ways. [Her husband and her brother-in-law sexually assaulted her.] So thereafter, I was far more frightened. I suddenly had a real sense of my own mortality, and I believed at that point that I was going to die in that marriage, or get out." Pepper's determination to leave followed a situation that occurred less than two months before her abuser shot her in the head:

"He had held a gun to my head for about four hours and tortured me. I was terrified. . . . When I finally got away from him that time and he had calmed down (giving me the gun and crying and begging for me to shoot him), I said to myself, 'Pepper, he's gonna kill you and you just need to stop being with him.'"

Getting arrested was the last straw for several women. When Abigayle decided that she and her boyfriend needed some time apart, her boyfriend "had me up against the wall in the bathroom, trying to choke me. He went absolutely berserk. He ended up chasing me all over the house. . . . At one point, I picked up a laundry basket to put between us. . . . He snatched the laundry basket so hard that he hit himself in the face with it and got a bloody nose. So he called the police and said that I punched him in the nose." She was arrested and taken to the police station for booking. He had done some aggressive things before, but this time Abigayle felt like a target and was terrified. Megan also had an epiphany after a tug-of-war with their three-year-old son ensued when he threatened to take the kids so she would never see them again if she left. A relative called the police and both were arrested. Megan said, "I was sitting there in that cell, booked and finger-printed, thinking, what, am I nuts? And that was it. I was able to move out a week after my injury." Two of the women, Anita and Haley, talked about how they were afraid their self-defensive actions and anger at their abusive partner would ultimately land them in jail. Haley said that about six months before she decided it was truly over, he had knocked her out cold on the floor and she awoke to feel a knife at her throat. "I was trying very hard to get away from him; the last time he came at me and I went at him, that's when I knew it was done. . . . It's not who I am. And I never looked back." Anita said that when her husband put a steamy hot iron up to her face, she knew one of them would die that night if she did not leave.

For many women, the violence escalated to the point where the children were at risk of being kidnapped or killed. Up till then they had feared leaving because of the possible repercussions for their children or their custody of their children. Naomi said, "I would have left him sooner, except I couldn't figure out how I was going to arrange for my son to be cared for and safely kept away from him." Ellen similarly recalled, "I realized from the core of my soul that he would have run off with our daughter to keep me from going to the police." But sometimes a particular incident with the abuser made the repercussions of staying seem even more dire. Winnie stated, "I think when I finally had the courage to draw the line, it was when the abuse was no longer limited to me, but it included my children." Similarly for Amy, "What was the final straw for me (with my first husband), was when he went to look for his .35mm that I had hidden the night before. . . . I hid my kids under the kitchen table. and I said if I live through this, I am done." Danielle also decided it was over when her husband chased her and her three children around the house, saying he was going to kill them.

Validation from people outside the relationship sometimes provided the catalyst for women to leave. Sometimes this came from an authority figure, such as a medical doctor or a family court judge. After months of feeling disrespected, disbelieved, and not heard by a judge, the same judge asked Dale on her way out of court how she was feeling and repeated the question when she brushed him off. She stopped and turned around on her crutches and said she was better, and he told her that her ex-husband (who had tried to kill her) "really had me fooled." Dale heard that as an apology from the judge, and that vindication empowered her to continue battling her ex-husband in court. Robyn went to community college and was thriving in her coursework and exposed to different people. "Suddenly, I had just had enough. I had been back in school for a couple years and I just couldn't live with him any longer. Not that he changed, but I was less tolerant. He was spending more time drinking and out with other women." She went back to him once after that, after her son was ill, with the stipulation that he could no longer hit her, see other women, or drink while driving. Two weeks later, he was caught driving drunk in his company's work truck. That was it. "It took me and him being married twenty-two years to realize that this was not normal, not acceptable, and that he wasn't going to change and I couldn't fix it."

When Vanessa was hospitalized and admitted for the first time to her doctor that she was a victim of IPV/A, it had not been standard for the doctor to ask his patients that question. He had recently added it to his standard intake form. Vanessa's husband came to visit her and minimized her injuries, telling the doctor that Vanessa could not be so injured because she worked two jobs, organized church youth groups, taught Sunday school, and ran the household with three kids. Vanessa had never had a doctor stand up for her before, but this one doctor did. He said to her husband:

> He said, "Mr. ____, I have never met anyone like you before. You have no idea what you wife has been going through. I'm gonna put it to you in man terms. Vanessa, I really want you to close your ears right now." Then he said, "it would be like me pulling your balls up on this table, hammering them with a hammer, and strapping them to your kneecaps with a Velcro strap. That's the kind of pain your wife walks around with."

This external validation was what Vanessa needed to hear. After she returned home, she started the steps to extricate herself—it took a number of months, but she was determined. "If God can forgive me, I can forgive myself. I'm not going to hold myself accountable for a mistake I made seventeen years ago. I told him: you're not my problem anymore. I want a divorce. I'm tired of surviving; I want to live." He swore to her that he would break her, and spent the next five years trying to do just that, but he did not succeed.

Other times, women started a college program or a job, and their teachers or bosses provided some feedback, or validation, that made them think of their situation in a different way. In Sandee's case,

> All of a sudden, after hearing more and more about domestic violence in my college class, I stopped blaming myself and started changing the tape running in my head. Confiding in my professor—who had already figured it out and asked the right general questions—made me feel like someone understood me and saw some strength in me that I didn't believe in yet.

A wake-up call for a number of women was the realization that family history was repeating itself and they did not want to follow in a mother's or other relative's footsteps. When Megan was looking at a family photo album, she saw pictures of her grandmother laughing and doing adventuresome things; everyone noticed the resemblance between Megan and her grandmother. Yet her grandmother had been beaten to death by her grandfather. "She never had an opportunity, she was in the Appalachian area, and I thought, I have to take the opportunity she never had, to stop this cycle." Rosa realized she did not want to be like her mother:

> My father was a womanizer, but people don't see that as abusive. Latina women put up with that if he's a good provider as my father was. The womanizing is a cultural thing—men feel that women will take care of the family so it's okay. My husband was not a good provider, and he hadn't been a good father, so I had no reason to stay with him. . . . I became ill—the emotional bashing, the repetition, was getting on my nerves. I couldn't breathe and went to the hospital. The doctor said it's my nerves and they wanted to put me on medication. I refused, and that was when I decided to leave. No man will make me sick.

Tina's wake-up call occurred when her mother died and she discovered her stepfather in their bedroom, searching the room for her mother's pocketbook to take her money, while her mother's corpse was still in the room.

> My mother had never been a role model to me; she never had a respectful, good relationship. I realized: I am just like her, and something clicked. I thought, I am going to die the same way. I couldn't let that happen to me and have my children think it's okay to treat a

woman like that. When my mother died, my husband dared me to cry at my mom's funeral. He said she was a bitch living and a bitch dead. I went to her funeral and I didn't cry because I didn't want to get beaten up when I got home. But something clicked.

The final epiphany mentioned by a number of the women involved gazing into their future and realizing that it was too bleak to contemplate and they had to do something. Elizabeth realized she had worked too hard to let a man physically force her into a corner in her own house. She decided that although she did not want to fight a man she was going to try so "I won't have to hide in my own home, terrified." He had never been challenged before; his whole demeanor changed, and Elizabeth realized she could make choices to get him to leave. Brenda realized after her abuser escalated from emotional abuse to pushing her and punching holes in her wall, "I was like, are you kidding me? This is not the way I want my life to be. . . . I told the police not to arrest my husband, but he would destroy all my stuff and tell me that I deserved it. He alienated me from any outside contacts with friends or family. I woke up." One of Terri's fears was losing a tooth in a fight and being unable to go to work. But then he punched her in the mouth and some teeth were chipped and fell out: "He said it was an accident, but this was the final straw. I'm not sticking around anymore. He's not doing anything to improve my life. He's not working. No one likes him and I am wasting my life. I couldn't picture my next ten years. The image I had in my head was so horrible. I knew I had to leave."

Messages of validation from "decent" suitors also helped reinforce the women's growing awareness of their self-worth. For three of the women, eventually meeting and getting to know a man who was completely different from their abusers helped them realize that all men were not threatening or violent. The women remained vigilant in looking for red flags—things they had missed before with their abusers during those courtships—but the attention and respect they felt from stable, nurturing, nonabusive men helped them sever ties to their abusers.

In this chapter many of the women I interviewed describe the circumstances under which their abusers were able to gain power and control over them early in their relationships. Their reflections reveal warning signs and attendant vulnerabilities combined with naïveté and lack of access to people, institutions, and resources that could have served as an educative and preventative counterpresence. A desire to believe in romantic love, dysfunctional or abusive childhoods, economic abuse, and the threat of weapons all converged to form powerful constraints against the women's ability to leave or to hold the offenders accountable for their violent behavior. Shame, resignation over having made a "bad" choice for a partner, and a lack of familial support were some of the strong reinforcers. Yet the women ultimately did leave, despite the risks of dangerous retaliation from their abusers. Some of the women realized their own lives were mirroring other dysfunctional family relationships, and this realization propelled them to not continue the same mistakes that haunted their own childhoods. Though isolated from friends and families, many of the women eventually made some meaningful connection with outsiders who provided a "reality check" about their unhealthy relationships. Often when the women's abusive partners discovered these connections they severed them, but the glimpse of an alternative way of living persisted at the back of the women's minds, giving them some hope and contributing to their decisions to leave later on. Other powerful mechanisms of control included abusers' manipulation of religious doctrine to justify controlling behavior, often easily accomplished when women sought guidance from their faith and found little to challenge the abuser's rationale. When abuse occurred in the presence of known weapons in the house, women were on even more dangerous terrain. The male and female partners of the women I interviewed possessed a wide array of weapons, and the legal authority to own them, as evidenced by valid hunting licenses or occupational necessity (law enforcement or military). Various forms of economic abuse that limited any financial access, ability to work or keep a job, or escape kept women even more isolated, with some turning to self-medicating with alcohol to numb their pain of their partner's cruelty or their own. Even so, many women received some support from understanding employers, justice system personnel, therapists, doctors, and select friends of family members who had not abandoned hope. The chapter also looks at the women's breaking points that facilitated their decision to move forward so that abuse would no longer affect their lives or their children's lives, even though plans often took time to put in action. My interviews with the women revealed innovative ways of squirreling away money and other strategies of resistance that laid the foundation for leaving their abuser and gaining a foothold to achieving an independent life.

These broader narratives traverse some familiar terrain, but the women's retrospective accounts help fill in our contextual understanding of both how the women became entrapped and what coping skills and strategies they used to free themselves. The narratives highlight women's pluck and determination to survive and thrive. I continue looking at the contours of women's long-term survivorship in the next chapter.

4. Meaning Making and Post-traumatic Growth

This chapter continues exploring the ways that women make sense of their victimization and use their understandings of their experiences to move forward in their lives. I begin with a discussion about the lingering fears women experience after their relationship ends and how these circumstances help remind them of how far they have come and of what they should remain aware. Then the analysis turns to the critical role children play in relationship termination; for many mothers, children shape decision making, and women's hopes for their children's well-being facilitate their resilience despite the complications related to parenting. Finally, I look at the range of ways women react to their victimization and regain a stronger sense of self, restructuring their social world despite the cumulative (and continued) effects of their abusers' machinations to knock them off balance. Here I explore in detail the role of faith and religiosity (or the lack of such) and the call to activism in women's resilience and in the development of their individual and collective efficacy. In discussing all of these themes, I use the women's narratives to elaborate how they constructed meaning and what gave them the fortitude to move toward long-term liberation from violence and victimization.

LINGERING FEARS, DASHED HOPES, AND FLASHES OF POSSIBILITY

Assembling a life not controlled by an abuser is daunting. In what is never a linear process, women often move from relief to grief, such as a longing for what "could have been if only . . . ," and back to relief again. Although IPV/A survivors in general are not passive within their abusive relationships and even show dogged determination, forward momentum waxes and wanes. The past, at least in the initial separation, is never far away. As the post-traumatic stress literature has described, survivors encounter "triggers," experiences that cause them to recall a trauma and that contribute to an ongoing sense of threat, making them hypervigilant to familiar situations and behavior (J. Herman 1992; Van der Kolk 2015).

Given the entwining of past and present, the women I interviewed expressed concerns, after their relationship ended, about reading cues accurately and responding proportionately to them. They also worried about how the violent home had affected their children and how in the future this might shape the way they would treat their partners or expect to be treated. Though they described moving forward with hope and anticipation, they often felt as if they were being dragged back into a darker, more dangerous place where their fears re-emerged. This tension was heightened when there were continued ties with the abuser and his or her family because of prolonged court battles over divorce or decisions about child custody and visitation. As Megan aptly characterized this murky "in-between" period:

> I have such anger and resentment that I constantly have to work
> through. . . . I stay busy and I concentrate on the life I have now. That's
> the key. There's nothing I can do to change what happened before; I can
> only go forward. I have a relationship now where I love going home, and
> I never had that before, so I welcome that. . . . But at the holidays when I
> have to trade off the time with my son, I get that sick feeling again.

When women do not move to a different community, they face the stress of running into their ex or his or her family members and friends. Tina struggled with seeing her ex-husband and his family at "school events for the kids, weddings, and funerals," a complaint voiced by many of the women. Ellen explained, "Everywhere I go, I watch my back, because I don't trust any of his family; they were his enablers." Yet because of finances, schools, employment prospects, or family complications, relocation was not always feasible.

Sounds, scents, and situations reminded the women of the abuser or transported them back to when they had felt belittled and disrespected. Even years later, they often responded viscerally to these remnants from their past. Name-calling, for example, ignited bad memories for many of the women: as Megan explained, "When my ex got mad, he'd call me names, especially *stupid* or *dumb,* and those words will set me off to this day, anytime I perceive that someone is trying to bully me, especially when I'm dealing with men . . . and I work for men and with men, so . . . I'm always on the defense." Another common trigger was a man yelling at them, but the women were quick to add that now, rather than absorb the anger or accept rage emanating from strangers, they reacted. As Danielle described, "I couldn't just suck it up. I said to him, 'Don't you ever yell at me again. I don't appreciate your abusive tone. I already got rid of one man who abused me. Do you talk to your wife like that? You're scaring my kid.'" Some women channeled their earlier feelings of rage and helplessness to aid others in similar circumstances. Jazzy became livid and spoke up when she encountered a situation where someone was treating another person with disrespect. "It puts me back into that place where a man felt so entitled and didn't care about me or anyone else." Though she understood her reaction, she tried to take a step back and move from being "red hot angry" to being calm as she "call[ed] them out."

Even women who had been out of their abusive relationships for a decade or more experienced flashbacks when triggers appeared. Twenty-nine years after she left her abusive husband, Celeste vividly recalled: "I couldn't take a shower with the curtain drawn for about ten years after the divorce because that was one of the places he would attack me. I still have a very highly developed startle reaction. . . . Even if someone walks out of a doorway ten feet in front of me and I see them, I feel startled." Ellen talked about freaking out anytime she heard a loud muffler, since that was the sound she heard when her abuser drove into their driveway. These reminders made many of the women constantly on their guard, keeping their cell phones with them even in the bathroom, and being ever watchful in situations such as going to court. For court security reasons in many states, visitors were required to leave cell phones or pepper spray in their car in the parking garage; yet as Dale noted, "Anybody could hide anywhere. It's dark in there. Sometimes there's nobody around if you need help."

The longer the women were away from their abusers after the relationship ended, the less present the fear or the triggers—provided there was no protracted contact in court about visitation or custody issues, and provided that the abuser was not stalking them and did not attempt to murder them. But some women talked about being "stalked" in their nightmares even after the threat was no longer present: Florence, who had left her husband in 2005, still had nightmares where she woke up screaming (as did her daughter, whom he had sexually molested). Pepper, whose abusive boyfriend was dead (he had committed suicide after trying to murder her and her friend), said she still had "nightmares, visions of him, even though he is dead, I still feel like he is still out there. At the same time, I know that him dying is the only way I know I'm safe."

Women said these nightmares faded over time, but they stayed hypervigilant. They were innovative and proactive in documenting any continued abusive incidents they felt could be related to their exes. One woman, who felt her ex-husband kept track of her moves and occasionally stalked her neighborhood (someone spray-painted "Rest In Peace" on the side of her apartment building with her apartment number next to RIP), had a camera installed to try to film the graffiti artist. Another woman kept her same phone number for years because she wanted to record any threats and track calls with call logs to send to the police or to use in court if needed.

Dating was also complicated. With good reason, the women talked about the turmoil they faced when they were attracted to someone new or started dating and wondered if they could trust themselves to "pick" a better partner and not project their ex-partners' flaws onto their new partners. Most women internalized a list of warning signs and steered far away from potential dates who exhibited any of them. Not everyone in their social networks understood their concerns, and the women were often accused of being too picky or impolite. Haley's response was simply, "Men need to realize that women who are abused by other men—even though the men may be locked up . . . our lives will never be the same." Most of the women who ventured out into the dating world waited between one to five years, saying that they waited because of trust issues or because they needed to reestablish a family life for their kids that was stable and peaceful without the abuser. Jayde had learned not to get so enveloped by the giddiness of romance; now she "listen[ed] closely to things that people [were] saying" and watched more intently to determine if their words and behavior were in alignment.

Though women cherished their new freedom, a number had to work hard to conquer their fears when executing ordinary tasks that their abusers had forbidden them to do. For instance, after Amy's second abusive marriage (of ten years) ended, she had to relearn how to drive a car and also to venture into a grocery store to buy food: "I hadn't been anywhere by myself without him driving or taking me, like a grocery store. When I finally walked into one, I thought something terrible was going to happen." Katherine finally conquered her fear of leaving the house (and enduring panic attacks) by doing what scared her—driving a car—many, many times until she was desensitized to it and realized no harm would come to her: "I got my life back." Some women were inspired to tackle these obstacles because they wanted to be role models for their children and not live their lives governed by fear anymore. They also were acutely aware of what they had missed out on because their abusers had controlled so much of their lives. Jenny, for instance, was wistful when she saw groups of young women having fun at college: "I wonder what would my life be like if I hadn't had him with me for my four years at the university? . . . I never had the freedom to explore campus life on my own."

As Naomi described, "When I left him, I was pretty desperate and felt pretty powerless, even though I knew I was doing the right thing. I struggled, even though I had this whole network to help me out. . . . It took me a while to develop my own voice." Naomi was well educated with a high-status job, yet she shared the same concerns about regaining autonomy and becoming empowered for her own well-being as other women who were less privileged. For all the women, regaining their autonomy and self-confidence was a drawn-out and difficult process.

CHILDREN

Children represent a conundrum for women in abusive relationships; they are often what keeps women mired in the relationship because of a belief that it is better for the children to have a father or intact family, or because of the economic issues that hinder separation. But children are also often the motivating factor for a mother to leave in order to keep them safe or prevent further harm. Many women expressed deep remorse that the exposure to abuse might have affected their children who had witnessed it. At the same time, however, it was often not a choice. Surviving daily emotional attacks, threats, or actual violence while trying to keep their children safe drained the women's energy and contributed to their feelings of guilt. Often, what could be misinterpreted as inertia to outsiders would be more accurately understood as a reaction to being terrorized by the all-too-real possibility that the abuser would pursue the woman and the children if they left, a fear reinforced by taunts like Megan heard: "If you leave me, I'll take the kids and you'll never see them again." The women's terror about their exes' threats to kidnap children was not unfounded, as these kinds of tactics are well documented in research, and abusers employ them to continue to assert their control over their former partners after separation (Beeble, Bybee, and Sullivan 2007; Brownridge et al. 2008; Hayes 2012; Jaffe et al. 2003; Zeoli et al. 2013). Yet children could also be the impetus for leaving, often after a particularly dangerous threat or incident. Naomi, for example, explained that she had wanted to leave her abuser sooner, but it was his death threats against her son that had precipitated her departure.

IPV/A often begins or escalates when a woman is pregnant (see Charles and Perreira 2007; Hellmuth et al. 2013; Jasinski 2004; Saltzman et al. 2003; Taillieu and Brownridge 2014). Julia recalled:

> The violence and his drinking escalated after I became pregnant.
> Throwing things at me escalated. He often pushed me to the limit—
> like carrying many grocery bags up three flights of stairs in my ninth
> month. Leaving things for me to fall over. Not stopping to allow me to
> use a restroom when in the car, and of course rougher and rougher sex
> on demand. Anything that would degrade me. . . . When my daughter
> was born, she was sick and required a great deal of attention. This
> enraged him. He drank more and started smoking dope. Since I had a
> security clearance at work, he knew his dope smoking could hurt my
> career, but he did not care.

Several women believed that the abuser was responsible for their miscarriages or stillbirths and, for some, their children's disabilities. Reeva, for
example, felt that the stress of living with a violent and abusive man was
connected to her miscarriages, a stillbirth, and perhaps the birth of her profoundly disabled son. Although she and her husband were given the option
to terminate the pregnancy because he would have no brain functioning,
Reeva did not believe she could make that choice. This decision resulted in
more violent behavior from her husband, since he did not agree with her
about not terminating the pregnancy. Elizabeth also believed that her miscarriages were related to abuse.

Some of the women made a decision not to have children, or not to have
more children, with their abuser. Katherine had a child by a previous marriage but declared she was forever thankful that she never had a child with
her abuser. "I became pregnant in 1977 and I aborted the pregnancy because
I knew I'd be connected to him forever if I had his child." Robyn felt that
after having two children and enduring seventeen years in an abusive marriage, getting her tubes tied was wise. However, her doctor would not accept
just Robyn's decision about her own body: "The doctor wouldn't perform
the surgery unless I had my husband's signature. Thank God my husband
didn't care one way or the other. I had it done on my thirty-third birthday."
Though Robyn was fortunate in this example, reproductive coercion, as
practiced by abusive partners or husbands as a tactic of power and control,
and reinforced by physicians, is not uncommon (E. Miller, Decker, et al.
2010; E. Miller, Jordan, et al. 2010).

Many women stayed in the abusive situation for longer than they
desired because they felt they owed it to their children to keep the family
together and not to disrupt the children's relation to their father. Danielle,
for instance, explained:

> I didn't call the police because I didn't want him to have a record. As
> angry as I was, if he could get help and be a productive person, I didn't
> want to interfere with that, because he's still the father of my children.

When you involve law enforcement, that is a very serious thing, and I didn't like making decisions that affect somebody so drastically that it could cause their whole life to be a failure.

Of course, this benevolence changed after Danielle discovered he was sexually molesting her daughter. Once he was approved for overnight visits, the older daughter disclosed this information to her therapist because she was worried that he might shift his attention to her younger sister if they stayed unsupervised for an overnight visit.

> This was probably one of the worst days of my life. I hugged her, told her how much I loved her and how proud I was of her. But she was so scared for so long. . . . His name was in the newspaper, and my kids were stigmatized because we all have the same last name. I was afraid to change my last name because I was so afraid that the judge would assume I moved on with my life and didn't care. That is so crazy. You just can't pick up the pieces and move on with your life.

Danielle found out later from his sister that before she met her husband he had been institutionalized at a juvenile detention center out of state for sexually molesting other children. She remained bitter about learning of his past child sexual abuse history after the fact, given that they had four children together.

Casey similarly explained her persistence in the relationship as an attempt to preserve the family:

> I thought I needed to give him as many chances to get himself off drugs, since he was the father of my baby. . . . So I dealt with the verbal and emotional abuse longer than I should have because I was trying to be encouraging, even after he had been in and out of prison and jail for drugs. . . . But I needed to try so I could explain to our son that I did everything I could to help his father and I didn't just give up.

This theme—that the mothers could later tell their children they tried to keep the family together before finally leaving—was common.

The sense of an obligation not to harm the children's relationship to their father could extend even after the separation. Robyn, for instance, had two sons with a large age gap between them. The youngest one never really experienced the abusive situations that the older boy did.

> I never told him, and I'm technically sure that no one told him, of his father's abuse. I watch him have this untroubled, loving relationship with this man, and I played into that too. I treat my ex-husband like we're friends because they are our children and to ease tension during the times we have to be together, for family celebrations or funerals.

Finding some peace in this situation was hard, but she "wanted to be sensitive to my kids' relationship."

A number of women embraced a traditional belief that children needed to be raised with both a mother and a father. Danielle said that when she had been a very new wife, "I felt like having a mom and dad was important for certain parts of a child's life, it made them feel the most secure in life. I really believed . . . even if the dad had not been the best, that they would be better people with both parents." Later, however, she was able to see how her daughter had been harmed by her father's sexual abuse, and Danielle was relieved that he was locked up: "My daughter said to me, 'Mommy, I can go to the library and not worry Daddy is going to show up.' That's how scared she was. After he was arrested, she went from being this little closed-off flower into this free-form flower, like all the petals just came out." Joan's husband resented her children from a previous marriage, but for a long time she clung to a hope that he could become "like a father" to them, something she felt was important to have for her children, and she acquiesced to his demands, something she later regretted. Indeed, Joan's relationship with her children changed for the better once they left: "My parenting changed because before I was always trying to find someone to be a father for my children, whereas now I am definitely the father for my children."

Not only Danielle but several other women talked about their abuser targeting their children with physical or sexual violence. Abuse occurred whether the abuser was the children's biological father or their mother's partner unrelated to the children. In some cases with abusers who were the nonbiological fathers, children from a woman's earlier relationships became the target of struggles, and the abusers manipulated the children as tools to keep the women submissive. Joan talked about how her abusive husband treated her children from a prior relationship: "He kept saying that I am to hold him to a higher regard than my kids. He was jealous of my kids. I didn't agree with that—my kids were there longer and needed my support more."

Unfortunately, child abuse by IPV/A abusers is all too common. One of Florence's daughters from a prior marriage was sexually abused by her ex when she was around twelve. When they were safe in shelter, the daughter revealed the abuse, and child protective services interviewed her. Florence was crestfallen:

> I thought I was doing everything that a mom is supposed to do. . . .
> Everybody said I should have caught on when he bought me some
> fancy gifts. The thing that still bothers me to this day is not being able
> to protect her and knowing that she still has nightmares. But I took my

> kids to the doctor on a regular basis and nothing had been discovered. . . .
> I was told they couldn't prosecute him; it had been too long. That's a
> burden I have to live with the rest of my life.

Her daughter's disclosure was exacerbated by the public exposure to the family once his arrest was published in the local newspaper. She pulled her daughter out of school to begin home schooling to decrease her daughter's embarrassment once everyone at school saw the news story.

To keep their children safe, women tried many things to protect them, such as putting their bodies between the abuser and the children when he was violent. When Vanessa's baby was five and a half months old, her husband exploded in anger and lashed out:

> Blood is coming out of my face, and I'm gasping for air, and [my baby]
> comes over, and she is crying, "Mom, Mom, Mom," and at the point
> I looked up because I was turning around to pull her to me. He had
> picked up the hammer and was standing over me about to hit me in
> the head. So I flung her so my whole body was covering her, and I was
> crouched down, staying like that, waiting for the hammer to hit me.
> But instead he threw the hammer through the windshield of my van.
> At four in the morning, when the police finally came, they make me
> pack up my babies, even though he ripped open my C-section.

When Tina came home early from work and saw her husband beating— "disciplining"—their ten-year-old son, she began to scream. He pushed her out of the house and then refused to let her young kids say goodbye. Tina somehow got back into the house: "I had a paring knife in my hand. I saw the phone hanging on the wall. I called his brother and said, 'If you ever want to see your brother alive, you better come pick him up.' I think I had purpose in my mind that I was going to kill him since he touched my son." Megan was also concerned with protecting her children, even at her own expense: "I got to a point that I wished he would just beat the crap out of me and leave the kids alone. He was constantly at them with verbal tirades . . . but I was more afraid he would hurt the baby when he was throwing things at me."

Abusers often use children to manipulate the mothers, including threatening the children, mistreating the children to punish their mothers, and physically hurting them (Beeble, Bybee, and Sullivan 2007; Bemiller 2008; Hardesty 2002; Hardesty and Ganong 2006; Harrison 2008; Moe 2009; Slote et al. 2005). Celeste recounted:

> My ex-husband would threaten to do things, and he did things that
> wounded the children physically and hurt their feelings in the moment,
> but he would threaten even more horrible things, or actually start to

carry them out, and I would negotiate with him. He would say, "If you let me fuck you from behind, I won't pick our son up by the foot."[1]

National statistics reveal that in 30 to 60 percent of cases of IPV/A, the children are themselves abused—or neglected (Edelson 1999). Women described their desperate attempts just to feed and clothe their children when their abuser was taking all the resources for himself. Celeste, for example, made the decision to nurse her baby just so she could be sure the baby got enough food:

> His family thought it was crazy, that I was nursing. They're working-class people, so for them you get a formula, you put it in a bottle, you don't nurse—so they were really unsupportive. But I wasn't nursing because I was some sort of crunchy granola mommy. I was nursing because I didn't trust my ex-husband to provide [the money for] formula. He might withhold that to punish me, and I was afraid of him. And I was more convinced by the time I had my second child, I knew he would use that as a tool, so I wanted to never, ever be without a supply of milk, which meant nursing. He got mad at me because his family was criticizing me for the nursing and I defended it, and he felt like I was talking back to his mom and his stepfather. He is a hunter, and to punish me he put me in the trunk of the car with a deer carcass and left me there for I don't know how long. I didn't get out of the trunk on my own accord—by the time he got me out I think I had left my mind . . . a mental shutdown or something. I don't really remember much, except later when, post-divorce, I had reoccurring visions around that particular incident.

Just the witnessing of their mother's abuse harms children in many ways, as many of the women I interviewed painfully recalled. Victims/survivors often believe—or want to believe—that their children are oblivious to the abuse, claiming it mostly occurs when the children are asleep at night or when the children are playing elsewhere in the house. Yet more than three million children witness IPV/A in their homes each year (Carlson 1984; M. Straus 1992). Studies show that exposure to IPV/A drastically affects children's well-being. Their chronic stress is shown in a greater propensity to illness, frequent headaches or stomachaches, and tiredness and lethargy (Moylan et al. 2010; Graham-Bermann and J. Seng 2005). Florence was shocked when her son, who was in seventh grade, came home from school one day and told her that they had learned about domestic violence: "He said to me, 'If we don't get away from him, he's gonna kill us.' That really opened my eyes." Sometimes, the children are in the room witnessing the physical violence and try to intervene, putting them at a greater risk for injury or even death (Edelson 1999). Jazzy described one episode when her boyfriend was beating her: "My oldest boy retaliated and jumped on him, and said, 'Don't hit my mom, let my mother alone.' He was a kid, but he was feeling it." Jazzy felt relieved that neither of her sons had ever "put their hands on a woman," even though research evidence suggests that boys who witness IPV/A are more likely to grow up to be abusers (Carlson 1991; Smith-Marek et al. 2015).

Dale recalled the ways her children had been exposed to and affected by the abuse:

> One time he beat me terribly and the neighbor called the cops. My son was three years old and my daughter was one and a half. I had just put them into the car when the cop came and asked what was going on and my son told the cop the whole story. Every little detail—his daddy picked up Mommy by the neck and was ramming her into the wall.

Ultimately, her husband's violence extended to their son. He beat up their son when the son was a teenager and had just been diagnosed with cancer—not liking that he was afraid of getting blood drawn at a local lab site. On the day he tried to kill her, the children saw him pack the green "suicide bag," as they called it, and put it in his car that morning. They knew its contents: a Bible, a rosary, a hangman's noose, and suicide letters to the judge, the kids, his lawyer, Dale, and her boss. Today, the children (now young adults) still have a lot of guilt over not saying anything about their dad taking the bag—believing that maybe if they had spoken up, the attempted murder would not have happened.

At the time of the interview, Katherine was still distressed about what her daughter had witnessed, even though she herself had blocked out many of the details:

> I have to live with that forever. . . . She and I were just talking about that recently, and she hasn't forgotten or blocked out anything. . . . I'll say, "Well, I don't remember blah blah blah. Do you remember?" and she'll say, "Yes, Mom, he was chasing you through the house," or "He grabbed your hair and pulled your wig off, so I picked up the attachment to the vacuum cleaner and I was trying to hit him to get him to leave you alone," and "We had to crawl out of the bathroom window."

Though Katherine did her best to erase the experience, her daughter's memory was indelibly marked.

Winnie likewise reported that her children had seen too much violence:

> Once he came down and tackled me to the ground and starting hitting me with the hard sole of a shoe and with his fists from head to toe. The boys would be strapped in their high chairs and he would hurt me with

them sitting there watching. I could tell while looking at them they
were traumatized. I would just drop to the floor, behind the counter so
they couldn't see [since it got more violent if she tried to protect
herself]. I would just let him hurt me so the boys wouldn't see
everything.

Julia recalled that as time went on and her husband got more physically
violent,

I locked myself in the bathroom with the baby to try and get away. His
modus operandi was throwing things at me, kicking in walls and doors,
and pushing or chest butting me when I stood up to him. It happened in
front of my daughter all the time. Since I did not want her to see us
fight, I would back down.

Julia only later realized the full extent of the damage that the abusive relationship had inflicted on her daughter:

If you think you are protecting your children, you're not. I thought I
was keeping my daughter safe by staying, but the truth is my daughter
was deeply scarred by my staying. There were things going on that
I didn't find out about until years after we left. My fear was so strong
that it made my daughter afraid, despite the fact that she was only
four.

Robyn also expressed regrets on this subject: she had thought she protected
her son from seeing how violent his father was, but

when he was about two, I was sitting in a chair with my arm around my
husband's leg. I stood up and he started to kick me and his mother
walked into the room. She saw us and said, "Oh, stop it, you two." And
my two-year-old said, "Get back, Grandma, Daddy loves her." This
shows you a little about the family dynamics.

Later the women were adamant that they had felt impelled to interrupt the
cycle of violence so their children would not grow up and model this behavior in their own relationships.

The desire for children's well-being provided a strong motivation to
leave. Elizabeth described how she would not tolerate yelling and disrespect
in front of her son: "I don't mind having a disagreement, but I told him [a
new man she was dating] not to yell at me in front of my son, especially in
my home. He said, 'I'll yell when I want,' and that was the end of that."
Sara described an incident where her husband broke a heavy-duty broom
on his knee and brandished it: "I said, you are scaring me and you need to
leave. My kids are here and they can hear it." That was the last straw for
Sara, and he took her seriously and moved out.

Winnie "finally had the courage to draw the line . . . when the abuse was no longer limited to me, but it included my children":

> My son was in his little jammies, and said, "Daddy hurt me." I said, "Where?" He pointed and touched his leg and I saw these long red lines, raised. I laid my hand on it and they lined up. I kissed it and said, "Daddy's not gonna hurt you anymore." Once the boys were napping and my daughter was preoccupied, I told my husband that with me being a mandatory reporter, and being a mom—I pointed a finger in his face and said, "You can't touch my kids, we're done."

She called the police, and they arrested him. He never lived there again. A trooper did bring him back two days later to get some personal items: "He came in one car and left in the better one. At that time he also took a handgun." Winnie reflected later,

> I had rationalized that this was a marital problem and that as long as the children were not physically affected I should stick it out and try to encourage him to get counseling. When I started to lose hope in that, I started to grieve the end of my marriage and accept that I would be parenting alone with two kids still in diapers.

As noted in the previous chapter, for many women rationalizations no longer worked once, like Winnie, they could see clearly the harm endured by their children. When Katherine thought about leaving she did not know where to go, as there were no shelters or resources yet in her town in the 1970s. She felt her only option was to try to work on the marriage—until her nine-year-old daughter (from her first marriage) shocked her by taking a stand. Katherine and her daughter had been driving around after a fight and Katherine had been "trying to convince" her daughter that the two of them should return home: "I had been . . . talking about 'Oh, I can do some shelves in your room . . . paint it. . . .'" But her daughter was having none of it: "She was sitting on the little hump in my 1974 Corvette next to me, and she said, 'Mommy, you can go back and you can change the furniture and you can change the house but you'll never change him. So if you go back, I'm gonna have to go live with my daddy." Katherine left him.

But leaving also posed great risk for the children. Even when someone was offering the women help and sanctuary, the women had to weigh the very real possibility that taking up on the offer might only bring more danger. Julia's mother knew something was wrong and said that Julia and her daughter could come and live at her house. "But one of the things that I was afraid after my daughter was born—he would never let me go and take her. He always implied that I was mentally unstable and told me that he would cut my daughter in half before he would ever allow me to leave with her." Julia was afraid to leave for this reason, and also feared putting her mother in harm's way.

Women lived with the ever-present fear that if they left their abuser he would seek or obtain custody (see Saunders, Faller, and Tolman 2012). Julia spoke of having been "terrified about going to the courts for help. They scare you to death; it's all about taking your kids." This statement reveals the continuation of "coercive control" (Stark 2007) that women felt the courts exerted over them and their children. Very few of the women with children had positive things to say about their court experiences. This fear of turning to "authorities" for help increased their vulnerability, exacerbating their inability to be effective in court if their trauma re-ignited when they were faced with their abuser (see Pagelow 1993; Renner 2009). This secondary victimization—defined as "the victim-blaming attitudes, behaviors, and practices engaged in by community services providers which result in additional trauma" (J. Campbell 2005, 56)—erodes self-esteem, faith in the future, and trust in the legal system (E. Rivera, Sullivan, and Zeoli 2012, 237; see also R. Campbell et al. 1999; Orth 2002). When survivors of IPV/A experience post-traumatic stress due to negativity or unresponsiveness towards them in the courts, they are less likely to use the legal system in the future (E. Rivera, Sullivan, and Zeoli 2012), a response echoed by many of the women in my study. When women feel dismissed or disbelieved by a court system they hope will help them, their trust plummets further.

The women experienced their abusers' continued use of power and control tactics during legal proceedings, particularly during custody, visitation, and child support hearings. During the relationship, women had often felt guilty about not parenting their children adequately. They spoke of how hard it was to parent well when one was trying not to die. Celeste, for example, stated, "I was so fearful and so depressed and so utterly convinced that I was going to die that I was just going through the motions of life. I didn't nurture the children very well." Abusers capitalized on this, expertly manipulating the women into feeling worthless and inadequate as mothers. Julia reported, "He told me when I was crying during postpartum that if he had breasts he could be a better mother than me." Abusers continued to use this tactic during legal proceedings: indeed, such undermining of women's confidence as parents after separation is a documented method of continuing to exert control (Beeble, Bybee, and Sullivan 2007; Hayes 2012; Zeoli et al. 2013).

Some extensions of abuse into legal proceedings, well documented in the literature (American Psychological Association 1998, 2005; Neilson 2004;

Saunders, Faller, and Tolman 2012; D. Taylor, Stoilkov, and Greco 2008; Watson and Ancis 2013), may go undetected by judges because of its subtlety. For instance, Rivera, Sullivan, and Zeoli (2012, 236) discuss how "'a look' or a word that appears innocuous to an outsider can in reality be threats of future abuse" (see also Stark 2007).

Abusers also seize the opportunity of custody or visitation to sabotage the mothers' relationships with their children, since the abusers know that going after what mothers value the most, their children, is effective. Such sabotage often occurs during the relationship but becomes even more pronounced after separation (see Jaffe, Lemon, and Poisson 2003; Toews and Bermea 2017).

Five women did not have custody of their children, at least temporarily; their children lived with the abusive parent for at least a year. A few other women had to allow their husbands to have their children in order for them to be safe. In retrospect, Tina realized that her abuser had more power and legal clout than she could ever accrue, since he had been successful getting custody from a prior relationship:

> History repeats itself. He got custody of his daughter, even though he wasn't married to her mother. He proved her unfit. On record, he was the first father of an illegitimate child to gain sole custody in our state. He did the same thing to me. We had joint custody, but he controlled it. He determined when I saw my kids.

Things came to a head when one of her sons broke an elbow playing baseball and she rushed to the emergency room.

> When I took him back to his father's home from the hospital, my ex said, "You can come back. I really need help with the kids." I remember saying, "After what you did to me?" I wanted to be with my kids so bad, I could taste it. But I couldn't make the sacrifice to go back to be with him.

Rosa also felt she could not risk more abuse by coming back to her house. She had left him following a hospitalization where the doctor said she was at risk of heart attacks. He held out hope for her return, begging her to come back because it was too hard for him to cook for three kids and run the household. Rosa refused, prioritizing her own safety so she would be there long term for her children.[2] Research reveals that their experiences reflect the norm: noncustodial mothers are controlled further by their abusers when the fathers defy court orders and instead restrict mothers' access to their children, including communication and visitation (Bemiller 2008; Hardesty and Ganong 2006; Kernic et al. 2005).

After Reeva lost custody, she did not tell anyone. "I'm embarrassed. Who loses custody? Everyone thinks if you lost custody, what kind of mother are you?" When she finally confided in another woman, the woman shared her own story about losing custody. "My eyes cleared up because I thought I was the only one! I started researching it because I wanted to know how many women lose custody; nobody wants to talk about [it]." Reeva is indeed correct that many abused mothers lose custody; custody disputes in divorce cases are more likely to be adversarial when there is IPV/A (Haselschwerdt, Hardesty, and Hans 2011). Biases in the legal system work in the abuser's favor (Bryan 2005). As Watson and Ancis (2013, 167) state, "Although there is a common perception that a judicial bias exists in favor of women gaining custody of children, research has suggested that fathers obtain primary or joint physical custody a majority of the time when they actively seek it" (see also Arizona Coalition against Domestic Violence 2003; Heim et al. 2002). IPV/A is often not considered when judges make custody decisions (Bemiller 2008; Harrison 2008). Courts continue to demand higher standards of parenting for mothers than fathers, and punish mothers if they are not the "friendly parent" who tries to facilitate relationships between their children and the father (Jaffe, Lemon, and Poisson 2003; E. Rivera, Sullivan, and Zeoli 2012; Slote et al. 2005; Zorza 2007). Abusers are master manipulators and often convince the court that they desire joint custody; thus they are seen more favorably than survivors, who may be resisting joint custody and are perceived as unreasonable (Dalton, Carbon, and Oleson 2003; Hart 1990; E. Rivera, Sullivan, and Zeoli 2012). The women in Watson and Ancis's (2013, 175) research believed that many of the custody disputes were "driven by revenge or vindictiveness, as opposed to truly wanting to spend time with the children," especially since the fathers had previously been only minimally involved in their children's lives. Their finding is consistent with the reports of the women I interviewed.

Many women were dismayed about their abusers' complete lack of interest in the children unless they could be manipulated as a way of hurting their mothers. Courts often order supervised visitations so that the noncustodial parent can maintain some consistent contact with the children. Danielle talked about every-Sunday visitation being a joke:

> I bring my four kids for supervised visits. He can't handle it. The workers complain to me, every time I come to pick them up, that the kids aren't doing what they are told by him, they're this, they're that. I said, "I don't know why you are coming to me and telling me this when I take care of these kids every day; he has them for one and a half hours.

Don't tell me he can't handle these kids for one and a half hours, but yet he wants custody of them." He wanted custody because he wants the control. He just wants to say, "They're mine."

Terri also talked about how her husband would ignore their daughter until she left him the first time (but came back because she ran out of money and lost a place to live). Then he would pepper her with questions, such as "'Does Mommy love Daddy?' My daughter would actually say no. . . . It's not healthy for her. . . . So when I left the second time, I knew I had to cut the ties completely . . . My daughter and I didn't have a future. I wanted something better for us." Naomi obtained a restraining order. Although her husband had not been violent to her son, the order included the times when she was with her son: "He could still see him, like at day care, but there was no visitation at that time. A few months later, he received a court order for visitation, which he never used, because he was offended by the idea of supervised visitation."

Five of the women did not have children at the time of our interviews; these women noted that things seemed far worse for those survivors with children. Brenda put it this way: "I can't imagine when some people tell me their stories when they had kids. It took every ounce of me to get my life in order, so I give them special credit, because it doesn't just end the relationship because you have kids together." All of the women who did not have children with their abuser expressed relief as well as admiration for the stamina mothers needed to have since they never were able to truly "leave" their abuser.

MEANING MAKING

Victims often assert that there are ways they benefited from adverse life experiences. The secular explanation for this is that people need to find some meaning behind an undesirable experience or a traumatic victimization that shatters their perception of who they are or their belief in a benevolent world. The women I talked with tried to make sense of their situations after leaving their relationships. They did so in a variety of ways, drawing on personal faith, church connections, and activism, and seeking meaning within religious and secular realms, through private forms and in collective, public venues. Finding meaning in one's victimization is an adaptive strategy that is common, as psychologists report in research on incest survivors and other adults who have experienced different kinds of sexual abuse as children (Silver, Boon, and Stones 1983; McMillen, Zuravin, and Rideout 1995). In fact, there is a long tradition in psychological work to explore victims' meaning making and its relevance for post-traumatic growth. The theory of cognitive adaption (S. Taylor 1983) introduces three phases that help successful adjustment to traumatic life circumstances: finding meaning in the experience, regaining mastery over the experience, and restoring one's self-worth. The women in my study talked at length about how they would never be so naive, vulnerable, or dependent again. Kristen declared, "I vow never to be a victim and silent again," and Ellen exclaimed, "I'm the captain of my ship, and I can now steer it anywhere without fear." These quotes, and many more like them, exemplify the theme of renewed self-esteem and mastery. Meaning-making strategies involve reshaping one's view of the negative experience to fit into existing worldviews or changing one's worldviews "to accommodate the stressful event" (C. Park and Blumberg 2002, 600, quoted in Lim, Valdez, and Lilly 2015, 1066). The benefit is that it can move survivors forward because they will understand more about the event's impact and significance in their lives and what it means, so they can perhaps have more hope for their future and increased resilience. Without this kind of appraisal, their grief may be prolonged and may lead to more stressors and illness in the future (Lim, Valdez, and Lilly 2015). The damage is greater for personal traumas, such as betrayal by intimate family members or partners, than for nonpersonal traumas such as natural disasters (Janoff-Bulman 1992).

Although an in-depth exploration of the psychological issues related to meaning making and posttraumatic growth is beyond the scope of this book, it is worthwhile to look at some of the research that demonstrates a connection with my interest in resilience as a mechanism for the women moving forward and growing and learning from their victimizations. For instance, retrospective interviews conducted with many adult survivors of child sexual abuse indicate that they gained some value from their misfortune (see Himelein and McElrath 1996). One such study involved interviews with seventy-seven adult women survivors of father-daughter incest; the women who had at least one person they could talk to about the victimization and vent their feelings about it were more likely to find meaning in their experiences and to report less psychological distress and greater resolution of their experience (Silver, Boon, and Stones 1983, 92). Regardless of how successful they were in finding meaning, however, thoughts and mental pictures of their experiences were still sometimes present and could be triggered by other things happening that were reminiscent of their past (93). So although the effects of the trauma did not disappear, those who were able to make sense of their experiences achieved more psychological comfort than others who were still searching for meaning. A support system in which a survivor had a confidant was important but also could be challenging given the stigma that often surrounds cases of incest or rape (Silver, Boon, and Stones 1983). IPV/A is no less stigmatizing, so some of these same difficulties around finding support are present with survivors of abuse. Many women kept silent about their victimization while it was ongoing; not until they were in a safe place did they have the luxury of time to explore what happened and to derive some comfort from their retrospective assessments. The women believed that talking to a counselor who "got IPV/A" helped. Other women felt that leaving their abuser had reinforced their position as a role model to their children in that their kids would learn, in Vanessa's words, to "stand up for themselves and know they need to be treated with respect and equality."

McMillen, Zuravin, and Rideout's (1995) work explored victims' perceived benefits from child sexual abuse with a sample of 154 low-income women. Half of the women reported that their experiences with victimization made them feel stronger or more self-sufficient and thus increased their self-esteem, gave them more understanding about how to better protect themselves (in terms of being more aware and less naive), made them better parents because they could recognize signs and be proactive, and increased their knowledge of child sexual abuse, which also increased their empathy with victims of it. Here the authors are interested in how their findings could help clinicians influence adult survivors' reactions to the abuse. Thus they caution that raising the issue of potential benefits of a traumatic event "may be perceived as insensitive" and that "those who are encouraged to discover ways they have benefitted and find none, may feel that they are not doing a good job of adjusting to the abuse" (1043). Just as being unable to interrupt an abuser's coercive control should not be viewed as blameworthy, so too should survivors not be seen as "healthier" if they characterize their experiences as beneficial.

Lim, Valdez, and Lilly (2015) interviewed twenty-five (primarily unemployed, African American) survivors who had experienced IPV/A within the past six months to explore the strategies the women used to make sense of their victimization.[3] The most reported type of meaning making was self-blame. Some of this was situational self-blame, which attributed the abuse to something that could be modified, such as their own behavior. This was characterized as "better" than the characterological blame exhibited by some other participants, which attributed the abuse to some enduring trait they possessed as individuals. In order of prevalence, other strategies the participants used to devise meaning included making excuses for the perpetrator's actions, normalizing violence, attributing violence to karmic or divine intervention, minimizing violence and using social comparison, reappraising IPV/A as an opportunity for growth, and seeing IPV/A as the result of the absence of a protective figure or role model in their lives; a number of women did not report success with finding meaning. The women I interviewed reported many of these ways of finding meaning in their abusive past or in their present. For instance, the belief among women in Lim, Valdez, and Lilly's (2015) study that their suffering was related to God having a purpose for them resonated with a number of the women in my sample.

The literature on post-traumatic growth provides another way to understand how survivors can construct meaning. Tedeschi and Calhoun (2004, 1) describe post-traumatic growth as "the experience of positive change that occurs as a result of the struggle with highly challenging life crises. It is manifested in a variety of ways, including an increased appreciation for life in general, more meaningful interpersonal relationships, an increased sense of personal strength, changed priorities, and a richer existential life."

Much of the current psychological research on post-traumatic growth derives from social psychologist Ronnie Janoff-Bulman's work on rebuilding assumptions about the world and self following trauma. Her words capture the process that many victims follow as they cope with traumatic life events:

> In the aftermath of these extreme experiences, coping involves the arduous task of reconstructing an assumptive world, a task that requires a delicate balance between confronting and avoiding trauma-related thoughts, feelings, and images. Over time, with the help of personally meaningful cognitive reappraisals and genuine support from close, caring others, most trauma victims manage to rebuild their inner world. They can move on with their lives, which no longer seem to be wholly defined by their victimization. Victims become survivors. (1992, 169)

Coping and post-traumatic growth models in the psychological realm are helpful in identifying how individuals incorporate their traumatic experiences into who they are; when this micro-level work is linked with more macro-level sociological research, we get a richer picture of how victims' social location (race/ethnicity, social class, education level, sexual identity) and the social institutions with which they interact (service providers, family courts, police) influence coping, growth, and resilience. In other research, social and spiritual support has been shown to help victims make positive meaning out of their experiences (Anderson, Renner, and Danis 2012). This support can come from the collective spirit of support groups or activism or from one's spirituality or involvement in faith communities. With this in mind, I next explore some of the anchoring forces that facilitated women's understanding and growth after victimization.

Faith

In my project, ten women could be described as earnest believers—and I use the word *earnest* to indicate the depth of their devotion and joy they revealed when discussing God and religion. While other women talked infrequently about their spirituality or openly acknowledged their struggles and tensions with faith—often only when prompted by me—the ten "earnest believers" explicitly and emphatically infused their conversations with references to their faith. Six of the ten women were African American, one was Latina, and three were white; only one other African American woman in my sample was interviewed, and she was in the "less [overtly] religious" group. Some empirical research finds that African American women are generally more likely than white women to see religion and prayer as main sources of support (Short et al. 2000). The sociologist Hillary Potter (2007) has researched how spirituality and religion specifically help African American battered women to deal with hardship and heal. The women she studied felt that their ability to confront adversity rested on their use of "ecclesiastical resources," such as prayer, spirituality, and religion. In her work, Potter uses a definition of spirituality first crafted by Tracy West (1999, 4): "Apart from a relationship with God, spirituality includes a yearning and longing for connection with community, a need for meaning and purpose in life, a desire for the unconditional affirmation of one's personhood, and an appreciation for the intangible mystical wonder of being that exists in nature and humanity." Potter (2007, 264) believes that although spirituality should be distinguished from religiosity (see Mattis 2000) they are both important sources of healing for African American women. Even black women who said they had low levels of religiosity (i.e., church attendance and participation in formal religious activities) still maintained that religion and prayer (and social support networks, which would include their faith communities) helped them in their abusive relationships (Mattis, Taylor, and Chatters 2001). In fact, religion occupied a central role in their lives, and "direct and intercessory prayer" was key to their "effort to cope with a wide array of problems" (Mattis, Taylor, and Chatters 2001, 91; see also Chatters and Taylor 1989; Ellison and Taylor 1996; Giesbrecht and Sevcik 2000). Many of the women in my own study, particularly African American women, consistently identified prayer and religion as important and meaningful. The historical salience of the black church and its role in supporting resilience in the face of racial oppression and violence are discussed in the next chapter when I look more closely at social institutions.

Potter's (2007, 271) study revealed that most black battered women relied on a "Higher Power" (spirituality, rather than involvement in formal religious institutions) to endure and to end their abusive relationships. Though many of the women felt that their abusive relationships interrupted their connection to their religious practice in the formal sense (i.e., preventing them from attending church), they nonetheless maintained their spiritual connections, often believing that they would not have made it through alive without God there beside them; many also believed that a "blessing" that came out of the abuse was that their faith was reawakened and became stronger after the relationship ended (277). Senter and Caldwell (2002) found similar results for the nine women they interviewed who had left an IPV/A relationship and had been outside of it for at least three years, though they did not look at a specific race or any race effects (five of the women in their sample were white). The explicit religious theme that emerged from the interviews involved the women's affirmation of the important role of faith-based beliefs and practices as a strength and a resource during their relationship and after the relationship ended (see also Gillum, Sullivan, and Bybee 2006; Potter 2007).[4] Many attributed growth and healing, including new perspectives about self, life, and God, to leaving their abuser. In particular, the belief that faith in God who would provide guidance and would "get me through" resonated for many of the women. After the relationship ended, many women reported that their faith was strengthened; many also increased their church attendance and participation in church-related activities and described these as providing solace and support. All nine women affirmed their faith after leaving the relationship, though three of the women had to reconcile their religious beliefs with unsupportive clergy; ultimately, as time went on, all felt closer to God and more aware of his presence, though some had felt during the abusive relationship that their prayers were unanswered and that God had failed them as their protector (Senter and Caldwell 2002, 552). Even in the discussion of other themes besides religion and spirituality (Senter and Caldwell identified twelve themes altogether), some women brought up God or religion, whether in relation to acknowledging the reality of their relationship; being receptive to others' advocacy and acting on their encouragement; accepting others' support; making adjustments to a new way of living; acknowledging anger, loss, and fear; letting go; rediscovering themselves; focusing on themselves (looking within); reviving and strengthening supportive relationships that they had let go or been separated from; helping others and reaching out; or embracing a new perspective of self, others, and life (Senter and Caldwell 2002). Gillum, Sullivan, and Bybee (2006) similarly found that 97 percent of the 151 IPV/A survivors they interviewed considered their spirituality to be a source of strength or comfort. Anderson, Renner, and Danis (2012) found that thirty-one of thirty-seven IPV/A survivors believed that something beyond themselves helped them to rise above their suffering: they learned from their struggles, God gave them the strength to terminate their relationships, or they felt spirituality was a key to their healing.

The women I interviewed embraced a variety of spiritual and/or religious beliefs and experienced a range of responses when they sought help from their religious communities. Some found much support and comfort in their faith communities: Reeva, for example, described received much-needed assistance from her minister and his wife after her husband left. Once, the minister's wife had called to say,

> "You're just on my heart, so I wanted to know, what do you need?"
> At that moment, I didn't have enough diapers for my son. I ran out of
> formula. I just cried from humiliation. And she said, "We're on our
> way." They lived on the other side of our big city, but they picked me
> up and went to the store to get all that and food. It was just the grace
> of God. That's what I wanna do for women, to be used in that capacity.

Others reported that their troubles only increased when they turned to their faith communities for help. Some did not believe in God—whether because of the horror they experienced ("What kind of a God would make me go through this?")—or because they did not feel drawn to the formal aspects of religion but rather believed in more of a generic spirituality that was deeply personal and private (none identified as atheists). Some said they were spiritual but not overtly religious or members of any churches. Private prayer was a way some of the women used to keep their faith without belonging to a church. Ellen, for instance, said, "I don't go to church. I absolutely believe in God and did a lot of praying, and still do. I was raised Presbyterian, but church was not a source of support for me." Some also sought to make sense of their pain by becoming involved with secular activities.

My own study did find, consistent with other research, that religious connections, spirituality, and faith could contribute to abused women's coping and healing. It certainly was not the only factor: others, such as the role of children (just discussed) and the social support received from family and friendship networks and service providers, were also important. But many perceived their own resilience, as well as their actions, as being shaped by their faith. They talked about how their faith in God had helped them deal with problems that otherwise would have seemed unsurmountable. For instance, Joan was particularly moved by a church song about how even the weakest can accomplish big things with God's help:

> Part of the song says: If you have faith the size of a mustard seed, you can speak to the mountains in your life. . . . So God is telling me that if I have faith, this little or this big that I can speak to the mountains in my life. . . . I got to thinking about me, how I feel so little in my problems but I'm still useful and if I have that much faith, God can use me.

She bought a packet of mustard seeds and taped one to an index card and wrote, "God loves Joan" on it, then carried it around in her bra to remind her of God's love and how she could get through the day and ultimately move the mountains in her life.

Other women spoke about how, through their experiences, God had strengthened their capacity to endure. For Rosa, a devout Catholic, suffering was a coping skill that prepared people to carry on, regardless of the problems that they encountered, and "since God suffered for us, we suffer for others." Vanessa's childhood was characterized by poverty, abuse, and violence. She believed, "My faith is what got me through, nothing else. If it weren't for everything I went through as a child and teenager, then everything I went through with my ex-husband, I wouldn't have made it this far. . . . I would have lost my mind. I think God slowly prepared me and built me up to endure." When her daughters asked her how she was able to survive, or her counselor asked what stopped her from killing herself, Vanessa credited God:

> My girls would always say like, "Why don't you drink yourself to sleep, or why aren't you on drugs, or why aren't you going from guy to guy?" I believe my faith was what has gotten me through, that's the bottom line. I would be a basket case right now, but not for the grace of God. God prepared me every step of the way; God intervened every single time and met every need.

Many people turn to something that gives them strength when facing trouble or when in crisis; for some, this can be accomplished through prayer to God or reliance on some kind of a belief system, through private prayer, or through engagement with a congregation at an organized religious institution such as a church, mosque, or synagogue. Other people may find solace in nature or with being among supportive friends. Still others are alone and face their terror with whatever coping skills and strategies they have developed. Of course, these actions are not mutually exclusive—agnostics may still pray, fervently religious Evangelicals may still have highly developed coping skills beyond faith-based ones, and so forth. Often, however, looking for a way to make sense of something that defies reason is common when one is hurting or needing help.

As mentioned earlier in this chapter, Janoff-Bulman (1992) writes eloquently about the human need to restore balance after victimizations or other crises occur. One's equilibrium can be reestablished in many ways, but the crux of the process involves making sense out of a bad experience. Celeste astutely stated this: "Maybe when inexplicably bad things happen to people, we all find ways to rationalize their happening both as a means of coping and as a means of trying to avoid them happening again." Meaning making provides a sense of comfort to many victims so they do not feel as though the world is out of control. If they can identify what happened and what their part in it is, they may be better able to control things or manage trauma.

The attempt to make meaning can easily invoke victim blaming. But deeply religious battered women, in my sample, often were able to evade explicit victim blaming by believing that God had allowed bad things to happen in order to bring about a greater good for them and others. They claimed that God had some kind of plan that involved their triumph over the devastating cruelty at the hands of a partner they loved. Reeva, for example, insisted that "you go through things for a reason, even if it's difficult and unfair." Many women pointed to the fact that they had emerged from these horrific relationships with more strength and a greater sense of purpose, for example as activists, and that their suffering had been a necessary step along that path. Vanessa, for example, hoped to leave the business field and "be a voice for victims. I cannot believe that I've gone through everything for nothing; it has to serve a purpose." One woman claimed that her experiences of childhood sexual abuse, rape, and IPV/A had been part of God's plan to deepen her faith:

> I am who I am now because of all those things that happened to me. All of it led me to the Cross, led me to Christ. So, if I could go back and live my life over, would I have not done those things, yeah, I would have. It would have all went exactly the way it went. . . . and it has all drawn me closer to God. It all happened for a reason and all worked out for God's glory. . . . Like now I have this gift.

Another (Joan) very similarly stated that her hardships had made her who she was in the present; she was emphatic that she would not change anything that had happened to her, since it had all created who she now was:

> I would not do anything differently because then I wouldn't be who I am now. I really believe, what ten-year-old wishes to be raped, what thirteen-year-old wishes to go to foster care? I am who I am now

because of all those things that happened to me. I wouldn't take any of it back. I love my kids, I love the things I have experienced in my life, not everything, but it has all drawn me closer to God. It all equals Joan.

For Elizabeth, her abusive relationship had led her to recognize her own true worth. Before that point, she had had low self-esteem and was drawn to a spiral of bad relationships, drinking too much and getting high. But once she was able to engage more completely with God, "to really try to get to know that God called me to be who I am and to learn my identity through the Word," she was able to learn the "value of myself." By accepting that God wanted the best for her life, she was able to leave her abusive boyfriend and realize that she was worth so much more: "I'm really in tune now and have a good relationship with God, just knowing the Word, and knowing my value to him. It gets lonely sometimes. . . . But now I'd rather be alone than be unhappy . . . and settle for something less than what I know I deserve." Others believed that their trials were obstacles that God placed in front of them to test their strength and even prove their commitment to him; their endurance or triumph over obstacles built their character (as several claimed, "God doesn't give you anything that he thinks you can't handle").

For Jazzy, experiences of abuse had led her to a greater reliance on God in making decisions. She recounted that after she left her second abuser she needed another place to stay, and "God just stepped in, because things became so easy for me to get this other apartment. I went to work and talked to a coworker. I had no idea why I went to talk to her. I believe in divine intervention and being led, and so she helped me and I was able to leave him." When I asked Jazzy more about God's "choice" to lead her to the woman who found her an apartment but not away from a violent boyfriend, she said she had chosen the men freely herself and had not previously asked for God's guidance in selecting a partner; she now would let God lead the next man to her. "I believe in the Bible that a woman does not go out seeking; every time I was seeking, I found everything bad."

Yet for some women who had an unwavering faith in God and his plans, being in a violent or abusive relationship could challenge the idea of a loving God and create a lot of cognitive dissonance. Three of the nine women interviewed by Senter and Caldwell (2002, 552) were angry at God because they believed that their prayers were unanswered and that God was not hearing or helping them. This feeling of betrayal emerged in some of the women I talked with. Danielle's comment, echoed in several other women's interviews, that she had trusted that "God's gonna send the right person to you" was shaken to its core when the supposedly "right person" was anything but. She stated: "If you trust God to take care of you by introducing you to the right suitor, what does it mean when he shows his devotion by harming you?" Amy similarly spoke of initially believing "with every fiber of my being" that God would "rescue" her: "I just thought if I prayed enough, if I fasted, if I worked harder, if I honored my husband more, at some point I would have reached the faithful place and God would come and be faithful to me because I was faithful to him." She described crushing disappointment when the promises of her faith were not borne out:

> I don't pray anymore. I realized, "Nobody is coming." It got so bad that
> I realized I could die and my kids would be there and witness it; I was in
> real danger. . . . I thought if God wanted to do something, he had plenty
> of opportunities. I prayed every way—standing on my head. He didn't
> show up.

In the end, she said, "my faith broke." At this point she contemplated suicide. But she ultimately decided against it because "I didn't want to let God down." And she concluded, "I am not gonna kill myself if God doesn't love me anymore than this; I love me more than this."

The kind of distress felt by these religious women could be compounded when their religious communities added to the betrayal, questioning what they did to cause their abuse or siding with the abuser. Though religious communities could provide support, they could also reject women who sought a divorce if the dissolution of their marriage was against their spiritual teachings, or they could be judgmental and controlling. Florence stated,

> I think it helped to pray a lot each day. I still do that. . . . But no church
> that I reached out to for help came through for me. Even when I was
> out from underneath, I attended a Baptist church for a while. But then
> they started making comments because I didn't wear dressy clothes to
> church, so I stopped going.

Even women who described themselves as religious or spiritual did not necessarily accept the concept that their experience of abuse had been part of a divine plan. Jenny maintained, "I don't believe that bad things happen to good people to teach them something, like from a Higher Power. If God is so benevolent, why would this have happened to me?" Instead, she claimed, "Not all suffering is rewarded and not all cries for help are answered." Her spirituality was less oriented to doctrines than to a quest for experience of the divine: "I was raised Catholic, but I don't believe in organized religion. I do believe that there is a power or energy and I'm trying to connect with that through meditation and yoga, to experience a spiritual presence."

Six of the women had no strong religious leanings, either before their violent relationship or after, and were adamant that things did not happen for a reason or because of "God's will." As Abigayle described,

> I don't have any kind of religious background whatsoever. So that would not explain any of it. . . . I don't think things happen for a reason. I know other people do, but I struggle with that because there are so many bad things that happen to good people. I'm the kind of person that if I can't see it or touch it, it isn't here. . . . It would really be nice if there is something after death. I don't think there is. So for me it's okay, this is what you get and roll with it.

Celeste strongly agreed:

> I don't believe that things happen for a reason. I believe that things happen and then we assign reason to them to try to survive them, or to glorify them if they are good. Part of that belief comes from reading . . . informed by Engels and Marx and using faith to make sense of bad shit—I think that's just false consciousness. I think that's just a way of making sense of the world so that we can keep on truckin', but I never, I never bought into that things happen for a reason. I bought into shit happens, and if it's great then we glorify it, and if it's horrible then we try to rationalize it, and I'm not going to do that. I'm just going to . . . try to survive it, or . . . try to use it as a stepping-stone to something else. . . . Religion has never really been one of the things that helped me at all.

Several of the women, while not affiliated with any religious institution or organization, still credited God for helping them to protect themselves or to achieve something. For instance, Amy described receiving help from God in a mysterious way. She felt strongly that her husband was going to use his gun to hurt or kill her, so she hid it from him:

> I don't know how to even say this other than just to say it, and if I sound on tape like a nut job then that is okay. I was very religious at the time, and all I can say is that God told me. And I knew in my mind: "Hide the gun." I got the words "Hide the gun." So I wedged it between the sofa and the wall so even if he looked under the sofa he wouldn't see anything. Sure enough, in the middle of the fight that night he went looking for it. . . . All I can say is, it was right on.

Sandee believed that a Higher Power had led her to finally understand that her situation constituted dating violence after taking a college course that discussed it:

> It was like, oh my God, this is actually what happened to me; my boyfriend came with flowers to apologize, but then it re-escalated. . . . It

was almost like a blessing, like if there's somebody up there, sometimes you say, "Oh God, there's nobody up there watching over people because these awful things happen to people in the world," but yet, there must have been Somebody watching over me at that point.

Dale similarly said,

> I just take it one day at a time because of my kids. I guess faith and God might be there because how else did I get a job when I wasn't looking ?
> . . . But the biggest thing that got me through is people, friends I was working with. . . . I wouldn't have made it without their support. . . .
> Right after he tried to kill me, people called and sent checks and gift cards so I could go to the grocery store.

Many strangers sent her money because they were so moved—and horrified—after reading her story in the newspaper and wanted to help. Dale's description paints a picture of a hybrid response—having some faith but not letting it substitute for the tangible support and help given by individuals.

Faith can be a source of great comfort, yet it also can eclipse the very concrete things that women do to empower themselves that are examples of individual efficacy and free will. Sociologists like to talk about "agentic choice" that propels individuals forward in creating their own lives. With the women I interviewed, strength, courage, and resilience emerged in many ways, though some of them credited their action to a higher deity while others found the strength within themselves to persevere. Still others described a kind of hybrid combination of faith and guts. Vanessa, for example, though claiming, "My faith is what got me through, nothing else," also credited her own tenacity in achieving academically as playing a role in her survival: "Getting my second master's degree [one in human resources and one in public administration] helped." Megan spoke of the importance of religion in her life—"When I grew up, my mom took me to church, and I loved going to church and I always have. I've always held onto my faith. I still pray privately." But she also credited her own actions for her current stability: "Therapy wasn't helpful, so my therapy is going to school and staying focused on some goals."

Some women, though not religious, still followed certain rituals or superstitions that they said had emerged from their abusive relationships. For instance, Celeste explained,

> I never developed some kind of attachment to religion or a God or a Higher Power. I do have some beliefs that might be interpreted as spiritual in some ways, and one belief, in particular, might be connected to either how I coped or how I recovered or how I rationalized my life post-marriage. I came to believe that life required some kind of sacrifice

from me, that only so many good things can be in one life. That kind of thinking has tempered my ambitions some, and I've made deals with the cosmos (these deals are not unlike giving up something one loves for Lent, only in my case I give up something I love forever in order to make room for something I want even more). I made these kinds of deals during the marriage and frankly continue to make these kinds of deals. For example, while married, I would say things like, "I won't read that book I want to read because I want to have a good evening." My thinking was that I could only have one or the other, a good read or a good evening. Post-divorce, I came to see this kind of bargaining as a desperate attempt to control the uncontrollable, namely the abuser; but at the time it made perfect sense to me.

Women who were not religious sometimes relied on certain deeply held nonreligious beliefs as a source of strength in the face of abuse. Naomi, for instance, stated,

> I certainly don't believe that people are intended to abuse other people. That's not how we are supposed to be as human beings toward each other. It helped me to say, "I have a right to not be in this situation." But that's more about the self-confidence that my parents raised their children to have in our own abilities and voices.

Haley, not strongly tied to faith or spirituality or religion, quoted country music lyrics for inspiration rather than the Bible. In fact, many survivors drew on country music rather than church hymns, mentioning songs by Travis Tritt, Rodney Atkins, and Carrie Underwood.

For women who did not turn to a religious analysis of their situation, meaning making was initially framed by some internalization of self-blame such as Lim et al. (2015) reported for women who had experienced IPV/A in the last six months. But after a couple of years, attempts to make meaning through self-blame gave place to women's more charitable understanding of the pressures and terror under which they had lived. It was at that point—as they recognized their lack of role models if they grew up in an abusive household, or if they acknowledged their low self-esteem and naïveté while in the abusive relationships—that the women spoke of their younger selves with greater empathy. The women's stories reveal multiple and intersecting paths to meaning making and resilience.

Religion and Activism

There is a long tradition of social justice advocacy by people of faith (Faver 2004; Gutierrez [1973] 1988; Lee 2004; Lee and Barrett 2007; Ovrelid 2008; Singletary 2005), among women in particular,[5] and this connection is particularly ingrained in black churches, both Protestant and Catholic (Cavendish 2000). For instance, the abolitionist movement in the 1830s (and later the civil rights movement of the 1950s and '60s) connected black and white women who were active in religious and benevolent organizations prior to joining the abolitionist movement. This intersection of antislavery groups and feminism highlighted the belief that both slaves and women needed emancipation. For instance, the Grimké sisters, Sarah and Angelina, were white Quakers who believed that they had a special calling to do God's work in combating slavery (Grimké [1836] 2016). More contemporary congregations continue to forge connections between social justice movements and their religious beliefs (Caputo 2005; Harris 1994; Sleeper 2007; Verba et al. 1993; Verba, Schlozman, and Brady 1995). This commitment to social justice issues was very present among the women I interviewed;[6] they believed they could use their abusive experiences as a springboard to activism, sometimes beginning with educating fellow church members.

Danielle tried to educate her church elders on the laws concerning domestic violence.

> When they were arguing with me about how I should give my husband a chance, I sent them a photocopy of a newspaper article that said, "If you allow your children to witness domestic violence, then you are responsible for committing a crime"; there was a bill signed by the governor saying that even if you weren't the one perpetrating domestic violence, you are guilty of exposing children to DV and not taking action. . . . Whoa—I'm not going to go to prison when he's the offender.

At the time of the interview she no longer attended that church and missed the social events and camaraderie that her children had enjoyed. But Danielle did not miss the church's responses when members disagreed with their policies. She was proud that she was the only person who did not get a letter from them criticizing her for not following the church policies.

Anita similarly challenged beliefs supporting IPV/A in the context of her church but found more support from church leadership:

> In African American culture, it's all about religion, and black women are so subservient. A person on TV said it best: "Why do women of color feel like their paycheck belongs to everybody else?" . . . God doesn't want me to stay in a bad relationship. He doesn't. He wants us to be treated well. That's why my pastor asked me to speak to other women. I see so many women, older black women, who put up, put up, put up with it and keep their mouths shut. We can't depend on the criminal justice system because they are already pretty racist. The women don't want their men to go to jail.

Some women were more eager to join a group like WIND because of their involvement in social justice in their churches and their positive experiences of working together to challenge oppression. Several of the African American women described the historical connection between black churches and political resistance and saw fighting IPV/A as a continuation of their efforts in this vein. The majority of WIND members had previously been or were currently engaged with organized religion and had been, or still were, regular attendees. Activism was an extension of their already familiar activities with their congregations. The other WIND members who did not share these kinds of religious affiliations and activism were equally motivated to be part of a group that expressed condemnation of violence in all relationships. This shared purpose manifested in powerful collective efficacy. Chapter 5 will continue to look at the role that churches, as social institutions, play in women's lives.

Other Kinds of Activism

Activism that was wholly secular was another avenue through which survivors made sense out of their experience by trying to help other women in similar situations. I am loosely defining activism here because some of the women's acts were more private and personal than others. For instance, Megan, Jayde, and Katherine mentioned that although they did not want to share their stories publicly, they told coworkers and new friends what had happened to them whenever the chance arose, just in case their experience of IPV/A and their hard-won knowledge of the labyrinth of the criminal justice system could help another person. This sense of altruism has been defined as activism by other researchers, since it indicates a purpose undergirding the acts of helping others, similar to participants' willingness to be interviewed for this kind of research (see Senter and Caldwell 2002). Casey, who left her abusive partner when their son was ten months old, stated, "It's not a taboo subject for me. My son very much knows that his dad was abusive to me and was abusive to himself [drug addiction], . . . but I wouldn't broadcast my family business." She used her own situation to talk with other nurses and patients about the signs of abuse and addiction, though she was unwilling to speak in more public venues. Another woman, now a social worker in the secondary education system, was not publicly or formally involved in the fight against IPV/A, but she was vigilant in looking at signs of troubled families; she often used her own story of abuse to break the ice with any of the parents who indicated there were problems at home, and they invariably ended up confiding in her.

Thus all of the women, regardless of membership in WIND, engaged in some kind of activism. At the time of interview, many of them worked in the victim advocacy field or actively reached out to survivors of IPV/A through volunteer work. Women in the community-at-large sample of survivors recalled various ways that IPV/A influenced their volunteer work or other activities. Sandee, who had ended her abusive relationship in her first year of college, did an internship two years later in family court where she helped battered women obtain civil protection orders. Later, when she was a candidate for a master's degree in social work, her final project entailed writing a children's book about children who had witnessed domestic violence. She said, "Who better to do this than someone who went through it, as a child and later as a young adult victim?"

Five women in the community-at-large sample had volunteered at some point in their lives with organizations created to help IPV/A victims; three of the women (Sara, Celeste, Jazzy) volunteered after their relationships ended, but two of them (Abigayle, Jenny) volunteered while still in their abusive relationships, an irony they had not acknowledged until our interview. Their ruminations made clear that they had been searching for help or for a way to put a name to their experience but that they were not ready to admit at the time that their lives were similar to the victims they were helping. Jenny explained,

> I was trying to detach myself. I went through the whole training, learning about power and control, cycle of abuse, thinking it was very similar to my situation. I volunteered at the shelter to take care of the children and in their self-help library . . . behind-the-scene kinds of things. I was trying to do something, and maybe trying to reach out.

All of the women could trace how their own experiences with IPV/A filtered into their work. Joan said of IPV/A's influence on her career: "Because of what I've been through, I have greater empathy and am less judgmental about women's situations." Casey, a nurse, was more acutely aware of addiction issues and abuse with her patients because of her ex-husband's addiction. Sandee decided to pursue social work in a school setting so she could try to identify adolescents' problems and risks related to family or intimate partner violence or abuse. Abigayle's job involved educating women about financial issues, and she was most concerned about women going through a divorce and their precarious economic well-being. She enjoyed helping empower women who were making transitions: "helping them from a financial perspective certainly, but also helping them find their confidence and moorings." Celeste volunteered at an anti–domestic violence organization that also was antiracist and antipoverty, which "helped me to develop critical thinking and new knowledge streams around those subjects, and I had support from the people who worked there." Megan was training to be a police officer and wanted to work in the child abuse division because she knew firsthand about the harm children experienced witnessing their parents' volatility. Sara felt drawn to her current career working in the social services sector because she could give back. She felt that there were not enough resources for victims and that since she understood their plight she was in a position to assist them. For her master's of social work practicum, she hand-picked assignments in alternative schools (where kids who were unruly and kicked out of public schools ended up) and conducted presentations about teen dating violence. Jazzy, in her midsixties and finishing her baccalaureate degree, had wanted to work with prison re-entry issues until she participated in a summer internship in family court, helping victims obtain restraining orders.

The motivations of women from the community-at-large group struck familiar chords: they wanted to work in their own way, and on their own timetable, to prevent IPV/A or to intervene because they understood the arduous task victims faced when disentangling from abusive relationships when they felt trapped. Some of these women used their educational and career opportunities to find ways to reach others, or they volunteered in organizations devoted to helping IPV/A victims and their children. While they did not engage in the public speaking or political activism that many of the WIND members were involved with, they spoke up when opportunities presented, and they worked to raise awareness in their social and work spheres. Even when their considerable efforts were acknowledged by me, not one considered herself as an activist.

In contrast, the members of WIND worked against IPV/A publicly as a group. They felt connected with others who understood their ups and downs, and they often remarked how working together for the same cause was energizing and exhilarating. They felt that their lives—the bad parts—*mattered*. At least half of the WIND members mentioned that they liked that "WIND isn't a victims' group. It is a survivors' group, and that's where I am mentally." Several of the WIND members were labeled as "high-risk" victims by the criminal justice system because their abusers had tried to kill them or harm their children, but they found that WIND's support increased their confidence to speak in public, promoting strategies to establish escort services for high-risk victims in and out of family court and weighing in on other policy issues in the state. Terri aptly summarized the motivating force behind their desire to join WIND: "There's more power in numbers. I had reached the point where I can help people; it's nice to be on this side now." Haley similarly commented that "all of us want to help make a difference. Women are really supporting other women. Some of us are more public with our stands and that's been really inspirational for the others."

Members of the WIND group described a variety of avenues for making a difference. Several WIND members (and one non-WIND member) spoke at churches. Other projects included reaching out to teens about the warning signs of dating violence, talking with inmates in prison through a victim sensitivity program (designed to facilitate victim empathy), and speaking to community groups or in college classrooms. What also gave WIND members great pride was the opportunity to speak to elected officials and in legislative sessions; their personal stories and experiences informed and educated officials and the lay public about the tribulations they faced when encountering the police or court or social services. As Joan describes,

> I am very proud to be a part of WIND. Helping in the community, like speaking out about domestic violence, has been very helpful long-term. Being able to go to a legislative session and they acknowledge our existence, and then talk to individual senators and representatives and say, "This is what I support, are you on board?" Being able to go to senators' offices and say, "Thank you." That helps me, and then when something is pending in legislation, being on that e-mail alert list and being able to call our congressional representatives and say I am [gives full name], and supportive of this, or, I am against this—that makes me feel awesome. . . . Someone stood up for me, before I even knew it, and helped get legislation passed that helped me, so now I can return the support.

A number of women gravitated to participating in public art projects like the Suitcase Project previously described in chapter 2. The member who orchestrated the project, Terri, also had an art business on the Web dedicated "to empower females who are going through abusive relationships, and the money is donated to the organizations that have helped me the most." Three WIND members (though I did not interview one of them) had self-published books about their experiences.

Telling one's story in a variety of public venues is not easy. Joan stated, "It's not like I get pleasure in telling it, but it makes me feel good to think that I'm going to speak to fifty people, and one person out of that fifty is totally going to relate to me and know that she has another option." In fact, that was why Brenda joined WIND: she had attended one of Amy's public talks and felt a strong connection with her because they both had endured emotional abuse and it validated her experience. Two white, upper-middle-class women, one from each group, talked about the "shock value" of their public speaking; both said that their appearance, demeanor, and profession made them credible spokespeople because, as one put it, "I am not crying; I'm not 'woe is me.' I don't fit the stereotype, so they probably think if it can happen to me, it can happen to anyone."

Two WIND members had once served on their state's coalition board and felt that their presence helped the board members better understand some issues. One mentioned that serving on the board "was an awesome opportunity for somebody like me. All the other board members are well educated, work at these high-powered jobs, and I am just a receptionist. But I bring a different opinion to the table." Other WIND members were already deeply involved in independent, but public, activism prior to joining WIND. Elizabeth worked with youth groups at her church and as a full-time empowerment speaker for church groups: "I'm the biggest mouth about God, domestic violence and sexual abuse. There's a lot of women hurting in church who hide behind God and the Word. I write plays to perform at churches. . . . You never know what story is going to resonate. . . . We all have a common thread." Anita also did some public speaking on IPV/A to many congregations in two states, as arranged by her pastor. Ellen created a private Facebook page for women to talk about abuse, custody, and related issues, where she moderated confidential chat rooms so women could support each other and share resources worldwide on the Internet.

The collective efficacy of WIND members highlights how group support empowers women to move beyond their comfort zone to accomplish important goals. Despite individual differences in temperament, faith, race, education, and social class, the women prioritized the same goals and supported each other in efforts to reach them. Whenever outside agencies or the coalition asked them for help, they volunteered quickly and freely. Their efforts were very successful—as evidenced by their influence in the legislative hall and the times their opinions and experiences helped influence policy issues. This reinforced the power of the group, empowering them to think about tackling larger projects. Being able to attribute significance to such a horrible (and for some women embarrassing or shameful) part of their lives was very rewarding. The group identity and cohesion of WIND members were foremost in their descriptions of who they were and what they did, indicative of a Goffman-esque "master status." In contrast, the community-at-large group, unaffiliated with any official survivors' group, made independent choices about when to reveal their past and what activism to undertake. They were no less effective but drew their strength through situations of individual efficacy. These women, too, found a deep satisfaction in using their private horrors to inspire other women who felt entrapped. All of the women's stories reveal the paths they took to find courage to reach out to others in need, draw meaning from their hurtful experiences, and discover the power of both individual and collective efficacy.

This chapter used the women's narratives to reveal common themes that emerged surrounding the many obstacles survivors faced long after they exited their abusive relationships. All of the women experienced lingering fears, which were stoked by the abusers' continuing threats, intimidation, violence, and intrusion into their lives. Women's actions were greatly shaped by the presence of children, and the women were fiercely protective in seeking to prevent the children from being hurt. For mothers, children played a central role in maintaining forward movement, though parenting often placed women on shaky ground as they still had to negotiate issues around visitation, child support, and custody that continued to put them in proximity to their former partners. Reclaiming even small tasks that had been "forbidden," such as driving a car or writing checks, reinforced their independence and gave the women a deeper appreciation for all the things now under their control. These small victories reminded the women that the dissolution of their family was worth it, despite their earlier worries that their departure from the abusive relationship would hurt their children and their concerns about being alone. Women, with or without children, embraced their hard-won freedoms and believed their lives were far better than they had been with their abusers.

In this chapter, I also explored the women's experience with post-traumatic growth. Victims/survivors strategized to make meaning out of unfathomable circumstances and propel themselves forward, often turning to their faith or to other people who helped ground them. Resilience reflected how the women incorporated the traumatic events into their worldview or altered their worldview to fit the events in attempts to better understand the impact and significance of their experiences and how these could help shape a more satisfying future. Though no one would choose to endure an abusive and violent relationship, positive adaptation and understanding helped shore up the women's courage to face the unknown. Their coping strategies, in addition to some women's religious faith, included pursuing education and job training and reconnecting with estranged family members and friends. Their enhanced sense of self-worth and personal strength is seen as the hallmark of posttraumatic growth (Tedeschi and Calhoun 2004). Activism also emerged as a way to help others learn from their experiences, and these activities reinforced the women's sense of fulfillment and their post-traumatic growth. For instance, WIND members exercised collective activism when they testified about survivor issues to legislators or spoke to residents at battered women's shelter, while women who were not part of WIND used more one-on-one connections to support victims, or reached out to them in other ways, such as through social media. Both individual and collective activism worked well to educate the public and to provide validation and support for women still in abusive situations. Achieving a sense of purpose that emerged from utter hell was one outcome noted by many of the women and indicated that growth could occur following trauma alongside the vicissitudes of fear and sadness. Many women talked about how their faith was tested during their journeys, while others talked about how their spirituality was awakened and gave them strength to persevere. Religious communities could provide solace and support, but some were judgmental and offered support to the perpetrator because of adherence to traditional patriarchal gender-based social roles. Faith was complicated, though many of the women attributed their coping and healing to their belief systems. However, many women encountered resistance and obstacles as they entered and interacted with the systems (social services, criminal justice) they had hoped would help them. The next chapter explores the help and hindrance the women experienced in these systems and other institutions from which they sought help.

5. Support Networks and Structural Challenges

The IPV/A literature is unequivocal in reinforcing the importance of social support and institutional help for women in abusive relationships and for those explicitly seeking to end such relationships (see Belknap 2015), despite the recognition that not all people or institutions are helpful (Rose and Campbell 2000; Barnett 2001). Given the enormous obstacles and the strength needed to overcome them, the journey to a life without violence and abuse is long and arduous. This chapter continues exploring individual and collective efficacy in women's lives and the ways women gained support from their networks. Also discussed are the obstacles they encountered when trying to achieve support, such as isolation, learning to trust outsiders with their private problems, dealing with other people's judgments, and responding in ways that resulted in the women's own arrests. Finally, three institutions that play a significant role in resilience and long-term survivorship are explored: the church, social services (such as shelters, victim advocacy, and legal representation), and the criminal and civil justice systems.

INFORMAL SUPPORT NETWORKS

Although all the women I interviewed expressed relief that the abusers were no longer in the house, their resilience had peaks and valleys. It was a challenge to move from being controlled to being in full control without feeling some bewilderment—and even grief—at times. As Megan said, "There were days when it was hard to get out of bed when that was finally over. Everybody thinks you should be happy it's over and click your heels, but it's not that easy." Amy and her husband had talked together with five different marriage counselors, but her husband had dismissed them all as "devils" because they suggested his behavior was cruel. So she decided to try talking privately to a friend who was a therapist: "I tell her, 'I am so stuck and feel so trapped and paralyzed.' She says, 'You are not paralyzed or else you wouldn't be here. You have already taken the first step—you just haven't realized it yet.'" This observation gave Amy clarity, yet she was fearful of the future:

> I will lose my entire identity. I am a minister's wife, and when I leave my husband I am not a minister's wife anymore. We own our own company, and when I leave my husband, I won't own a company anymore. I will be unemployed. I will be homeless. I was forty-nine years old. When I started over at thirty, I was not afraid; when I was young I was invincible. You get older, and you realize you are no longer invincible, and your retirement is near. When you are thirty, retirement is not on the radar yet, but at my age it terrifies me because I had not planned on starting over. But it was life and death for me and I was dying.

She summoned internal strength and left him.

It was common to many abusive relationships that women had become isolated from their friends and families (Stark 2007; Walker 1979). Some of this isolation was due to the abuser's efforts to separate them from others and to keep them from telling others what was going on. But the women also isolated themselves. Sometimes they did so to avoid their abuser's anger. As Dale explained, "It was a pain in the neck at social occasions to pretend all was well but also to placate him, and later isolation was easier than getting into battles with him." Also they could be too embarrassed to have others see their abusive relationship up close. Women maintained that it just became simpler to lie to outsiders. Often the abuser as well as the women themselves made sure that family and friends were exposed only to the "good side" of the abuser, so they would not believe things were that bad in private.

As noted in chapter 3, the women whose parents had not approved of their marriage felt a lack of support from their parents as well as embarrassment in having to tell them they were right. Megan's mother told her, "We don't want you to get hurt, but you should try to stick it out." Several other women said their parents had cautioned them not to break up their marriage because their abusers were "good providers." There was a lot of judgment: Megan recalled that her mother also admonished her: "You ran off and got married when you were sixteen. You let all that stuff happen in front of your kids." Haley's mother said similarly told her, "You weren't raised this way; I don't understand why you're with him," and Katherine heard the shame in her parents' voices when they told her, "You have already failed in your first marriage." Families of origin where the women had experienced IPV/A were even less supportive, as noted by three women. Katherine described an incident when her husband's father saw him hit her and said, "Well, you must have done something to get him that mad." Robyn's mother-in-law warned her, when she was hospitalized after a particularly violent incident, not to tell anyone and not to press charges ("Nobody needs to know about this," she said pointedly).

Not all women were cut off from familial support. For instance, Sara said that since her mother had experienced abuse, she wanted Sara to leave him and provided the money for Sara to file for a divorce and retain an attorney. Other women talked about their family stepping up to the plate once they were told what was really going on or saw their daughter or sister terrified or badly injured. After Terri confided to her parents that she planned to leave her abuser for good (the second time), she called them daily from her car on the way to work or while she was driving alone: "Every day, I would run my plan by them. They would tell me things that he might catch on to or that didn't make sense. . . . That helped a lot because there were things I wouldn't have even thought of; they were very supportive, I was very lucky to have them." Florence received some emotional support from an aunt, who lived about an hour away, but her aunt was visually impaired (she had been shot by her own ex-husband) and was limited in what she could do. Yet the aunt's personal experience with an abusive husband facilitated rapport and trust between them.

Sometimes parents meant well but helped the abuser, in the misguided belief that they were supporting their daughter's marriage. Danielle, who had four children (one with a serious illness), explained,

> My parents thought he was going off the deep end because of the pressure of this sick child, and my dad invited him to stay at their house where he could get straightened out with his medications. I was persuaded because the kids love their dad, so I'm living in the house and he's living in my parents' house and going to church with them every week.

This arrangement soon ended badly, with Danielle's husband wrecking her father's car and swinging at him. Jenny recalled that although her parents did not like her husband they felt sorry for him:

> When we were going through the divorce, he even called my mother and talked for a couple of hours. For several years prior to this, she took his calls and he spoke badly about me; I couldn't believe my mother accepted his collect, international calls. Finally, I explained the whole thing to her and she stopped accepting his calls. But that was one way of stalking.

Though Jenny told her mother the reason for the divorce, she told her father only that things had not worked out; since her father had never liked her husband, he paid for her attorney and accompanied Jenny to all proceedings.

Many of the women with brothers felt some pride in telling me that their brothers wanted to beat up their abusers once the women shared what was really going on; they hastened to say that the brothers were not aggressive but wanted to protect their sister. Although fortunately none of the brothers carried out their threats, the sisters admired their loyalty, though they wondered retrospectively in the interviews whether, if their brothers *had* done something, the abuse would have stopped.

Celeste talked about the pivotal role played by her sister, a social worker:

> My sister said, "Maybe you're fooling everybody else, but you're not fooling me. I know, and I don't want you to pretend I don't, in part because it's insulting to be assumed that stupid and in part because I don't think it's good for you." And I remember being really rattled by my sister saying this, but it made me braver to tell other people that I'm a survivor of domestic violence.

Later, when everything fell apart, this sister helped Celeste negotiate the legal system. Celeste was afraid that her children might be taken into foster care. Her sister forced her to be more forthcoming about the abuse so that other people who had power over her and her kids would understand what was really going on and would provide assistance rather than respond punitively. Ellen and Abigayle also said their sisters had offered them shelter but they were too proud to take it. In the end, however, these women relied on their sisters for tangible help with finances and child care and lived with them for a while.

Many women emphasized the need or desire for a strong support network. Some were wistful about not having had one or about the ways the people who had been in their lives had failed to support them. Robyn, for instance, wished she had had a close friend to confide in: "I had no girlfriends that were mine. . . . I associated with the wives of his friends. . . . I think if I had a girlfriend, outside of the lives of the men who were his friends, I might have been able to talk to her and get some kind of a reality check." But she did eventually get in contact with one distant friend: "She said, 'You need to go to college.' And I said, 'I'll be forty-five, that's too old,' and she said, 'You'll be forty-five anyway.'" Her friend's comment proved the catalyst for Robyn to start community college and then to leave her abusive husband.

Other women similarly highlighted how valuable it had been to them to confide in at least one person who refrained from judging them. Megan's coworker stressed that her husband "didn't deserve what he has" rather than saying judgmental things such as "Why do you stay? Why do you keep going back?" The coworker came from a "normal family" that gave her an alternative picture about how people lived, leading her to question her own home life. Casey had two really close friends who did not know what was going on during the relationship but were there afterwards for her once she confided in them. Dale met a member of WIND who quickly became her confidante and friend; she accompanied Dale to court and helped her write statements for the judge in various proceedings. Joan's godparents proved very supportive, though they had introduced her to the abusive husband. They severed their loyalty to him, offering Joan and her kids transportation, baby sitting, and emotional support. Such accounts support the finding in victimization research that it is the quality and not the quantity of friends that helps survivors the most (for instance, see Rose and Campbell 2000). And even strangers could be valuable sources of support. When Dale's husband ran her down with his car and put her in the hospital, her situation was well covered in the news media and strangers sent cards and money. "It felt really good, and like, I gotta be strong for these people that are supporting me."

Going to school or having a job outside the home gave the women an opportunity to meet new friends and gain new sources of support, unless their efforts were compromised by their abuser's insecurity. Some of the women sought jobs or interacted with people or received accolades from supervisors at work, which threatened their abuser. As the women gained confidence, their abuser felt more like he was losing control. As Dale tells it:

> My boss was complimenting me at my job, building up my confidence, and other coworkers agreed I was doing a great job, and for the first time in my life, I had this group of people telling me I did something good. My mom never did tell me that—she said I was ugly and stupid— so it was the first time I was really popular, at my job, in church. . . . He didn't like that, he kept trying to get us to change churches, to get me out of the spotlight. My boss said I should go back to school and that I put myself down too much; I was starting to get really confident, and then my husband got worse.

Telling a supervisor—though embarrassing—often resulted in support and validation. Terri also spoke about how wonderful her boss had been; he had assured her that her job was secure and had let her take time off with pay to go to court. "I was very lucky. It would be very hard if I had lost my job going through all of that—I would lose my economic ability to take care of my daughter. . . . I wish there was something they could do for single moms who are going through all of this where we don't have to go to court every time the abuser files something bogus." Ellen's boss loaned her several thousand dollars to catch up on the bills that her husband had run out on. Brenda's boss went above and beyond anything expected, letting her nap at work and giving her paid time off to handle things: "He was amazing. I had to tell him because there were days that I came in without sleep when my husband would keep me up arguing. I'd show up at work, looking a mess. I was trying not to lose my home; that's why I think I stayed strong enough to work despite my husband's threats." At her former job, Pepper worked for a bank and told everyone what was going on "because I came to work with black eyes and bruises, and I brought them my restraining order. I let everybody know. They gave me parking preference in the employee lot; they didn't want me walking out of sight." When she began a new job, she decided to hide her private life from her colleagues and boss but later realized that in doing so she had probably missed out on valuable help:

> I was starting my career. I worried more about what people would think about me, even though all the girls knew because they could hear the phone calls and threats. But as far as the higher-ups, they didn't know he had held a knife to me or he held the gun to me for four hours. So I didn't tell them I had a restraining order. When he shot me and it hit the newspapers, they were shocked. . . . If I had let them know something, they probably would have been supportive.

When Naomi left her husband, she began graduate studies, moving with her son into university-owned housing. She talked at length about the challenge of being a single mother and starting back to school. "But there were other single parents in graduate housing. . . . We exchanged child care . . . and the time period was very politically charged about the danger of single mothers, so there was this political context of you being told that your family is wrong." Exacerbating this was that her son was biracial, but given that graduate students came to study from all over the globe, he fit right in. She also was able to join a women's therapy group and developed strong friendships with several women in her department.

Some women turned to a therapist for support and understanding. Their experiences were not always positive. Winnie, for instance, went to one of the few therapists available to her (her options were limited because of insurance) after the abuse started, when her baby was about a year old:

> I told her what was going on, and I said, "I think I am going to get a divorce. I need somebody I can confide in along the way because I have this baby." She talked to me about this and said, "I think I can save your marriage," which is not what I was asking her to do. I said, "Do you

think it is salvageable?" She said, "Yes, a lot of times babies are stressful and you are both working. Why don't you bring him in?" I said, "What for?" She said, "We'll just talk through some things and see." So he agreed to come, and then the focus ended up being on his parents and how they were meddling, and how they were coming to our house all the time, stirring up trouble. That was not the real issue. She coerced him into talking to his parents and setting some healthier boundaries, which did need to happen, but that was not the cause of our problem.

They stopped seeing her, and the abuse began again, worsening. Winnie went back to her alone and asked what she should do when he hit her, and the therapist said, "Just don't hit back."[1] Naomi also had a negative experience with therapy when she and her husband went together. The therapist asked Naomi what she did to evoke his anger. Naomi was disgusted by this, but later, after she had left him, she went to a different therapist for individual counseling and found it immensely helpful.

Therapists could play a crucial role in providing external validation to the women when they doubted their own assessments of the danger and abusiveness of their situations. Ellen found strength and support from a therapist "who actually was originally treating my ex, because I made him go to counseling":

> I went and met her a couple times—even she was scared to death for me. So when all shit broke loose at the end, and I told her what happened, she told me, "I'm done seeing him . . . he's not accepting my help, he's coming in here bullshitting me." So I started seeing her, and she broke the ties with him, and we started off fresh, because I was comfortable with her.

Unfortunately, one day the counselor left the practice without telling clients in advance. Ellen never knew why, and she never sought counseling with someone else because she did not want to start explaining everything to someone new.

Dale and her husband sought marriage counseling after the first time he beat her up. After several sessions together, the counselor suggested that she see them individually. One of the first things the therapist said to Dale was

> I should go to a domestic violence victims' support group. She told me that she doesn't suggest to people to get divorced, but she suggested that I get out of my relationship right away. But I was married; he watched every move I made, tracked every dime I spent. I didn't know how to find a DV group, and I couldn't tell him, "Oh, I'm gonna go out tonight to a victims' group for DV." I'm not a good liar so I wouldn't have been able to say I was going to a friend's house.

However, the therapist had planted an important seed: "For years in my marriage, I always thought of that counselor who said that I should get out." Later, after Dale's husband tried to kill her, she saw a therapist again. The therapist understood her fragility—and her financial situation—and never charged her for five years of sessions.

Meaningful social support is crucial, especially when women are geographically isolated and also socially isolated on account of the abuser's control. When women desperately reach out for help, trying to gain support from a therapist or friend, but are thwarted because of that person's victim blaming or zeal to keep a marriage intact, the results are devastating, both emotionally and practically. Women may never have another chance to connect when their intricate plans fail, increasing their isolation: "I kept it a secret after my effort with the therapist failed. I lied to my doctor, my boss, my coworkers, family and friends. It was safer that way."

Tina summed up the importance of a supportive and nonjudgmental network for its impact on resilience:

> Anyone coming out of an abusive relationship needs a strong support system. Being around positive people and almost adopting a selfish attitude, like, I gotta do what I gotta do for me, and . . . cutting all the ties with that person, who's treating you like a dog, and everything related to him. . . . I had a really strong network of females and church friends who were always there for me, even the board I was on, with mostly white people [Tina is African American].

Though some negative encounters were setbacks to postrelationship independence and growth, the women met friends, employers, and other confidants who reinforced their resolve and emerging self-esteem. And for some women, when friendship networks were unreliable or absent, trained, compassionate professionals could fill the void.

CHURCHES

Potter's (2007) research summarizes the reactions of various religious communities, including Muslim (Hassouneh-Phillips 2001), Jewish (Graetz 1998; Kaufman 2003), and South Asian (Abraham 2000), when IPV/A is revealed and their sometimes unhelpful responses to abused women in their congregations, such as avoidance, victim blaming, and lack of investigation. Often these religions are grounded in beliefs about traditional gender roles for women that include childbearing and obeying husbands; such precepts leave women vulnerable to abuse (Knickmeyer et al. 2003). Some research demonstrates that women stay in abusive relationships longer if they are more connected to their religious group (Horton, Wilkins, and Wright 1988), and religious teachers sometimes use scripture to excuse batterers' behavior (see Potter 2007, 266). The women I interviewed had mixed experiences, finding that sometimes their faith and their religious community were helpful and provided solace, while other times—though their own faith endured—their religious communities trivialized the abuse, failed to hold batterers accountable, and even blamed the women. For these women who felt that God or their churches had abandoned them, a growing recognition that they had survived so far, and an inchoate belief that they could make it if they persevered with their goals of leaving the abuse and being safe, shored up their strength. Other support materialized—or was embraced by the women as potential sources of strength—such as a vigilant victim services advocate or a family member or friend. Though this varied across individuals, some of the women continued to have a deep faith, hoping that as they helped themselves their spiritual journey would also evolve and they would reconnect with God. Indeed, a few of the "earnest" believers' retrospective accounts of this "falling out" with God revealed that, to their welcome surprise, God had not really abandoned them at all but was helping them find their own strength. Other women severed their connections to their faith communities or jettisoned their belief in a just God and opened up new relationships with others in their lives.

Women were quick to differentiate between having faith in God and belonging to a church, as detailed in chapter 4. Many of the women had been very involved with their church—Sunday school and summer Bible camp for their children, Sunday worship, and participation in many groups (choir, Bible study) during the week. After giving so much time and so much of themselves to the church community, they felt betrayed by their fellow worshippers and the minister or priest who had failed to support them in their time of need because of views that they were breaking religious doctrine by leaving their husband or filing for divorce (i.e., actively resisting the Christian doctrine of submission; see chapter 3). Other women reported not only that their church had not supported them for doctrinal reasons but also that clergy and congregation had felt sorry for the husband who was "losing his wife and family" and had turned against her—even when they knew he beat her. The hypocrisy and the betrayal were devastating, and many women left their church.

Julia thought she had married a fellow Christian; he said that he loved God and did not drink, smoke, or gamble, and he identified as Christian—all before the marriage. Although she taught Sunday school and was very involved with various church groups, such as women's Bible study and the flower committee, he attended church only about once a month.

But then as soon as we split up he went running back to the church and boo-hooing, "I let Satan into my life. I lost my wife. I need forgiveness." All of a sudden, people from the church starting calling, not to see how my daughter and I were, but to tell me to forgive him. So, I'm not too big on church now. I'm still religious, and I still have a very strong faith, but I've got a real hard time with organized religion.

Tina similarly felt betrayed by her church once her husband's abuse was exposed:

Faith was a part of giving me strength, except that I was in a church where his family members were the key players, and so I didn't get much support there. When I left him I was labeled by the church community, with people saying I left him so that I could fool around. When I came out about the victimization, a lot of people said I was lying and that he was a good dad and husband—even though the woman that he ran to be with was right in the church.

Winnie also lost trust in the church. She tried to stay with her husband at first, having taken her marriage vows of "for better or worse" very seriously, and supported his taking medications for stress and going to counseling. Their lives were very entwined with the church—her daughter sang in the choir, and all the kids were in Sunday school. But

When we split, I found out that they embraced him and there was no place for me. They put him on the softball team. They reached out to the dad, the husband; they never called me. And, it wasn't just me— there were other women in this prominent church that this happened to [IPV/A leading to a separation]. . . . In the days following the separation, I drew on my faith very, very much because I had two kids in diapers and another kid, I was teaching, working sixty to eighty hours a week, and my daughter involved in advanced studies, sports, band. . . . I was just trying to keep it together. . . . I had a criminal no-contact order plus a civil restraining order, and he refused to pay any child support or help with the mortgage and bills for three months. . . . It was really hard to lose the emotional support from my church friends.

Amy was afraid to ask for any help from her church because she occupied a position of respect there and feared that her good reputation would be tarnished:

I kept it hidden until towards the end because my husband was a drug dealer and I was a Sunday school teacher. I thought, "Who would listen to me?" They are all lily white and I am covered in mud. Finally I did start talking a bit; gossip went through the church like wildfire because my life was like a cheap paperback novel. Ladies came over just to hear the latest story about me because it was so wild between his other women and his drug use. . . . Visits were more for entertainment than support.

Even when acknowledging the risk of her own murder, Amy did not feel she could leave her husband. Her church and her family had taught her that you could not leave your husband unless he was committing adultery.

It is till death do us part. My parents always taught me, you make your bed, you lie in it. The way it is, is the way it is, not everybody's happy. . . . You have to stay because of the kids; it is your religious duty. So if the men were running around on you, that's one thing. I never felt bad a day for leaving husband number one because of all the women. But with this second one, there weren't any women. And no matter how hard I looked in the Bible, I couldn't find where it said if he is crazy, then you can go.

Amy's struggle and pain when she felt that God was ignoring her pleas for help are described in chapter 4. Talking with a therapist was the catalyst she needed, and it helped her to put her feelings about God into perspective. At the time of the interview, she believed she could still have faith and feel close to God without joining a church; at the same time, however, she saw the church as potentially a place where she could connect with women who are experiencing similar crises:

I still want to get into the churches to talk with people about domestic violence. That is where my heart is. . . . I still can't get into church for myself. . . . I can't do the religious thing at all. I pray all the time; I have no problem with God. I would like to be able to talk in churches. I don't know if I can reconcile those pieces, because it is not exactly a harmonious fit. . . . Or I could do a small Bible study, I could do a women's retreat.

Despite all of her disheartening experiences with her church, Amy did recall one time when a visiting minister had come over for dinner, and after having a couple of hours of observing their relationship had pulled her aside: "'You have got to get out of here, you have got to leave this marriage,' he said. 'Life is way too short.' Wow, especially from a Pentecostal minister. But he could see, this is a crazy guy." His intervention encouraged her to call a toll-free religious hotline for advice on how to leave. But "The lady hung up on me. This is a prayer line major ministry on TV, and she hung up on me. I was beyond her ability to help, and I understand her naïveté, but I was very typical of the way a victim is, and if it was that simple to me I would have just done something years ago."

Although Joan was very happy with the church she belonged to at the time of the interview, the church she and her husband had gone to during their marriage was problematic. When she spoke to her pastor about the abuse and asked for counseling,

> The first thing he said . . . was "Are your tithes paid up-to-date?" I was one payment behind, and I had to go on to the computer and find the cancelled check and print it out to get counseling and fax it over to him. I told my pastor this was just for me and I explained what was going on, but when I got to the appointment, guess who was there? Him! My abusive husband! The pastor wanted to keep us together—even though I told him about the abuse.

This effort made her question the church and her time commitment to the music ministry in contrast to the Bible study side.

This was a difficult time for Joan because it challenged all the good she thought the church symbolized. "I started seeing that the church hurt me. I started seeing that pastor different. I had held him in such high regard but in church, all he asked was for money, money, money, and I felt this is not about the money, this is about the people; I stopped going to church."

Her bad experience did not stop her from looking into other congregations where she might be happier. "I just couldn't be without the connection because God had saved me from so much." She ended up loving the first church she visited, but then her past came back to haunt her when she applied to work with the baby room on Sundays. There was a record of her arrest when she had fought back against her husband's abuse; she had to spend a lot of time and money to get it expunged so the church could hire her to work with children.

After Danielle filed for a restraining order and her husband began attending court-ordered anger management classes, he moved in with her parents because the family believed "You don't just get rid of people if they have problems; you try to help people through those problems." But then he started acting out with my dad, coming back from anger management class and assaulting my father, after everything he's done for him? That's crazy. But we just didn't want to put him out in the street." So her brother called the church, but the church did not have a place for him to go.

> They wanted me to stay married to him because they said that he hadn't had an affair, he hadn't sexually cheated on me or something, and that's the only cause for a divorce. They wanted me to come in to a board of elders and have a trial in front of the church elders with him there. I have a restraining order. I'm not going in there with him.

As a compromise, he started going to counseling with the people at the church. "They wanted me to reconcile. They were sending the elder wives to my house to do emotional, spiritual, and maturity counseling."

Meanwhile, Danielle was completing her BA in psychology, raising four children on her own with one of them very sick, and "trying to figure out what he's gonna do next, while the church folks told her that I'm some sort of heathen." She was a pariah and felt disassociated from every person from the church except one friend who also decided to leave the church because, she said, "she can't be in a church that does this to you and where all the women walked around on eggshells all the time. . . . I don't want my daughters growing up thinking that's okay."

Florence especially needed support from her church because of her disability that limited her mobility. "It helped getting through by praying a lot each day. I still do that . . . but no church that I reached out to helped." Florence was steadfast in her faith, yet lost respect for formal organized religion after she felt mistreated. Robyn also lost faith in the church. When she sought help from the minister,

> He told me that I should be worried about my marriage and challenged my faith. He asked, "Were you behaving in a Christian manner when this happened to you?" and I couldn't figure if I was or not because I had been a good wife. That started my questioning and withdrawal. . . . Religion was never helpful to me. I am not a believer in organized religion or that any asshole can say he is a harbinger of God's will. . . . Or that there's this big guy in the sky that loves us and we have to turn our pain over to him.

Not all churches betrayed the women. Some women received invaluable emotional support and tangible assistance. Reeva, whose parents were both ministers (and who at the time of interview had become an ordained minister herself, but was not when she was still married to her abusive husband), felt that her religion had taught her how to forgive; in fact, in 2012, she talked with her ex-husband about forgiving him (never forgetting) after he made an overture of apology to her: "We have made amends. I choose to forgive because I have to move forward . . . and when you choose to forgive, it's not about you freeing the other person. You're not absolving them in any way, but you're really freeing yourself. Lifting a burden." Reeva believed that prayer was the most important but also felt grounded by her church. She trusted her pastors—who knew her story—when they sent women from the congregation to her for advocacy. She wanted to give back, especially since she believed she had gotten away from her abuser by the grace of God, who had helped her and given her the strength to fight back.

Anita also talked about forgiveness: "God gave me the strength to forgive him . . . . I wrote him a letter in 2006 and said, 'If I have done anything to you, I apologize; that's what God wants me to do. And if you don't, that's between you and God.' It was like a weight was lifted off me." She also had been asked by her pastor to speak about domestic violence to other women; at the time of the interview, she was speaking in ten different churches in two states.

> People see me, and say, what? That's a battered wife? I like my jewelry, I like nice things. This is the day I will wear makeup (when I speak). I'm not letting myself go. When they see me, they say, this happened to someone like you? I talk about how it's a terrible feeling to think that you can kill somebody fighting back against DV. When he put that burning hot iron up to my face, something just went off in me and I knew I had to get out of there because I was gonna kill him. I thank God for stopping me because I could be in jail for the rest of my life. So I promised God that if I ever got out of this situation, I would give back.

Although Naomi never officially joined the church they attended, she felt the congregation was warm and welcoming (she was white, with an African American husband and a biracial child). She played the organ in her church, and her son was in vacation Bible school.

> They were very, very kind to me and my son. I think that they felt a responsibility to me and to my child, and not to him [her ex-husband], because he really didn't have a relationship with them. What they knew about him was that he periodically flaked out on taking care of my son so that I had to bring him to rehearsals. I don't know how much it was their religious belief, I think it was also that it was a social network and they were protecting us. . . . One of the ways that he taunted me was he called me Christian. He would say like, live up to your Christian values, and he told my parents that if they were Christians they should tell their daughter to uphold the sanctity of marriage.

Thus some of the women's stories are encouraging: help was provided from clergy or members of congregations. Such positive responses have increased as state and national coalitions have begun to recognize the enormous positive role that religious institutions can play in IPV/A prevention and support for victims and their families.

SHELTERS, VICTIM ADVOCACY, AND LEGAL REPRESENTATION

From the earliest days of the battered women's movement, shelters have dominated as necessary options to address women's safety (Schechter 1982). Only five of the women I interviewed had fled to a shelter for battered women, and they felt very supported and safe there. Vanessa's middle-of-the-night call to a hotline directed her to a secret safe house where she and her children could stay for thirty days. When the staff discovered that Vanessa had been awarded a four-year, fully paid scholarship to any college in the state but had dropped out when she became pregnant, they arranged for her to stay at a second safe residential facility for six to twelve months and helped her re-enroll in college, where she went full time while her children were in school (at the time of interview she had two master's degrees). Joan had tried to leave her abusive husband several times before by going to a shelter but always went back to him because she could not get to her workplace and could not pay rent. Once she was connected to a shelter located on a bus line with a route near her job, Joan was able to take public transportation and live at the shelter with her children until she had enough money saved to rent an apartment. A police officer transported Celeste and her two children to a shelter in another state; everyone feared that her husband—a police officer—could find Celeste if she stayed in their home state. This was her first time being exposed to other battered women. The shelter was run with a feminist philosophy and had a collaborative, supportive environment. The experience was eye-opening and reassuring to Celeste, reinforcing that she had done the right thing by leaving. Terri also had a great experience with a shelter. She made connections with people there the first time she fled her abuser but remained in touch with them even after she reunited with him: "They'd ask me how I was doing, and I kept them always as a contact. They gave me some money this second time toward the new apartment and child care expenses. When we went to court, they matched me up with a lawyer at my civil hearing who really helped me too." She said that the resources they told her about were so valuable that sometimes she would drop in just to check out what materials were available for victims: "It made me feel less alone and more determined to leave."

Women had a variety of reasons for not going to shelters. Many did not know about shelters, or there were none where they lived, or they considered them too disruptive for their situation with children in school. Relocating to a shelter, even temporarily, entails inconvenient ramifications, such as arranging for pet care and changing children's schools or securing transportation to get children to and fro. Amy did not even consider seeking refuge at a shelter: "I never called a shelter since I wasn't being beaten, I didn't think that I qualified. Where's my marks? I didn't have any. I didn't have violent stories or hospital bills. I never went to the hospital, so I didn't think I qualified. I always figured that's for someone who is in more danger than I was." Amy was chased around the house with a gun and isolated and stalked, but in her mind that was not enough to justify her seeking safety.

Domestic violence advocates, victim services, and hotlines were a lifeline for some women who were unable to leave yet. For instance, Tina would call a domestic violence hotline on the weekends and just hang up. "It was enough to hear them answer the phone with 'domestic violence hotline'— then I could endure another day, and then on Monday I would go back to work and have a reprieve because I wouldn't be under his thumb all day long."

Women's experiences with the criminal justice system were less positive. More details on these are provided in the next section. But victim service professionals, whether working with the state coalition or hotline or with police and prosecutor's offices, were often helpful in connecting survivors to financial and legal resources and acting as liaisons to the criminal justice system. Women frequently needed legal representation to equalize them with their exes when their exes hired counsel; having a lawyer was often the key to achieving custody or financial goals. As Amy said on this point:

> You can't negotiate again with the devil. . . . He told me countless times, "I will destroy you." He is brilliant . . . but my mind doesn't work like his. . . . With all these twists and turns of manipulation, lying and cheating . . . I needed a lawyer. I owe this lady lawyer some two thousand dollars. . . . But I needed her there because I needed to be able to trust what was being decided. Even at the final settlement, I just kept turning to her, asking, "Is that fair," and she would say yes or no. If it's fair okay, it is what it is.

Those who could not afford a lawyer could sometimes qualify for pro bono assistance: many women who sought help were directed to their state's Coalition against Domestic Violence or to advocates in the courts or the prosecutor's office.

Other kinds of legal help were also valuable. Many survivors of IPV/A find themselves in a position where they have joint assets but the abuser absconds from the lease or car payment, ruining their credit. Joan recounted how her state senator had intervened in her case and introduced a bill changing the landlord-tenant code that would allow her to be released from her lease.

Women also mentioned many other kinds of assistance from professionals and agencies. Ellen talked about how a victim services worker at the probation office had provided extra assistance by informing her about a state program that paid the security deposit for the first and last month's rent, electricity, and heat. Since her ex-husband was on probation for a year for assaulting her, that department knew her case well, and the probation officer called the victim advocate to warn Ellen of his anger. Florence connected with a terrific social service worker who helped her figure out disability and medication issues, and her kids' SSI money, in addition to relocating her to a different county. Julia overall despaired about the criminal justice system, but she could still recognize that individual people at family court helped get the capital police to escort her to the car from the courthouse, could identify individual police who validated what was happening, and could recall certain lawyers in the attorney general's office who seemed to care. Several women praised the child protective services counselors who had helped their children, and the supportive role the state coalition and the WIND group had played in buoying their spirits and providing practice and tangible assistance when most needed.

THE (IN)JUSTICE SYSTEM

For many victims/survivors, the justice system is unfamiliar and mysterious. Most people have a general understanding about how the system operates for offenders, starting with *Miranda* rights and the right to have an attorney, and they know about how the opposing sides of prosecution and defense battle before a judge and jury. But victims/survivors often believe that once they can tell their stories and expose the abuse, fair decisions will follow, not realizing that a system primarily concerned with the rights of the accused is not designed to be victim centered (Goodmark 2013; Tobolowsky et al. 2016). Then, when victims/survivors feel that their stories and wishes are disregarded or minimized, they feel betrayed by a system they thought was in place to help them. Despite some positive experiences with truly caring justice professionals, for many victims/survivors the system becomes another domain in which they are overpowered and voiceless—a situation that mirrors their experiences with their abuser—and they lose faith in their pursuit of justice.

Victims/survivors question the fairness of both the process and the outcome of their cases. Procedural justice scholarship demonstrates that individuals who feel the process was fair are more likely to accept an outcome that is negative (Tyler 1984, 1988). If individuals believe the process was unfair, they are less likely to turn to the formal criminal justice system for assistance in the future (S. Herman 2011). For the women in my project, experiences with the justice system ranged from excellent to truly horrendous. But although sometimes a survivor could point to a police officer who went above and beyond the call of duty, or a compassionate judge or prosecutor, the women expressed an overall dissatisfaction with law enforcement responses and bewilderment over the system's handling of their situations.

Police

Neighbors, not victims, are more often the ones who call the police when situations escalate to violence. Although sometimes abusers keep the victim from calling the police (women I interviewed spoke of how their abuser grabbed the phone out of their hand or ripped it out of the wall), it is also the case that many women are reluctant to call police. Women expressed several reasons for this reluctance. Danielle, as discussed in chapter 4, was apprehensive about giving her husband a criminal record and potentially ruining his life. Experience and knowledge of racial injustice could make women even more apprehensive on this point: Anita, an African American woman, described how "the black community, they don't want to give the police any more power because they are already pretty racist.... When I first called the police on my boyfriend, his own brother had pulled a gun on his wife and son when he was drunk three weeks earlier. But both his wife and I didn't want the men to go to jail." Vanessa, though white, was mistrustful of police because she had grown up in a racist rural community where they were intertwined with the Ku Klux Klan: "I was terrified of the KKK. We used to pass the police barracks and there was a huge gigantic cross near it, and the police used to stop us coming home from church service and hand out KKK applications in their full KKK garb with their uniforms underneath it.... I never wanted to get the police involved because they are useless."

Some women did not want to bring police in because of an impulse to be generous and forgiving toward their abuser and to give him more chances; as Danielle put it (chapter 4), "If he could get help and be a productive person, I didn't want to interfere with that." Elizabeth aligned herself with the abuser even when he showed extreme brutality toward her. In an early incident police were called by neighbors, busted through her front door, and found Elizabeth so badly beaten that her face was gushing blood. They arrested her fiancé and took her to the hospital, as she thought, "I'm gonna die or I'm gonna be alone" and his pleas for forgiveness echoed in her ears. After the ER stitched her up and sent her home, all Elizabeth could think about was defending him, going to see him where he was jailed, and feeling sad about their shared good times and her several miscarriages. She called in sick to work because her face was bandaged and she did not want anyone to know what had happened, particularly since she was determined to make their relationship work.

> I would wash my face and not even look in the mirror. . . . Then the police came to my door one day with a court subpoena. I didn't press charges, but they did, and said if I don't show up they will arrest me. . . . . I needed to be there so they could prove their case. . . . Looking back, they seemed to care more about my life than I did at that time. I just wanted everything to go away. I wanted us to go back to where we were. . . . I went to court. . . . I forced myself to be unemotional, giving facts and telling them what I did . . . and that he didn't charge at me. I'm trying not to implicate him. He's there in the room. They have me tell my story twice. The third time they bring out this mirror and they put it in front of me and they asked me to remove my bandages. I take my bandages off and the whole court room just like gasped.

Elizabeth told herself this was not happening; she was still reeling from her fourth miscarriage and saw her abuser as her (potential) child's father and her fiancé. "For me, my life was not in danger. It was an accident. Maybe if I would have never put my hand up and just let him talk, it would have never happened. When I looked in the mirror, I finally saw my face. I still tried to tell my story without crying or being emotional. It didn't work." He was convicted and sentenced, and they let her leave the courtroom. There was no follow-up with her, such as connecting her to victims' services or a counselor. When her fiancé's release date came up, a little under six months later, she was the one who picked him up. When the police were called again during a fight, Elizabeth used her rent money to post his bail. The night before the next court date, he left her a note that he was going to take her out to the movies that night, but he never came home. He skipped out on bail, leaving Elizabeth to contend with the bounty hunters who hounded her at her apartment—banging on her door in the middle of the night, at family members' residences and her job because they thought she was hiding him. When her fiancé finally contacted her, Elizabeth discovered he was staying with another woman, whom he had been seeing, and the other woman was pregnant. Even at this point, her reaction was to blame herself:

> So here I am, having paid two bounty hunters, and I'm left with my face cut up. . . . Everything I believed in and fought for at my own expense, just up and left without a second thought. . . . I was at my lowest low . . . and I thought that something was definitely wrong with me, because nobody loves me, I don't even love myself. I'm not lovable. I went into the deepest depression. I would think about the molestations, the rape, the miscarriages, and feel neglected and

lonely ... and just sit there and just scratch my arms until I bled. I
would go to work, hide in the bathroom and cry my heart out.

Pepper showed even more ambivalence: she called the police, obtained
restraining orders, and testified in court, but afterwards she still would reconcile with her boyfriend, even when he was spending weekends in jail and
she found out she was the third woman with a restraining order against
him.

Some women spoke of not calling the cops out of embarrassment or
worries about exposing their private hell to public scrutiny. Katherine
recounted how she had threatened to call the police but her husband had
just laughed at her, saying the police would not do anything so she should
go ahead and call. This was in the 1970s, and Katherine never had heard of
the police getting involved in marital quarrels. She said that back then it
would have been considered "mortifying" to have a police car come to your
house; it would indicate that there was something wrong with you, and
neighbors would gossip. So she quickly discounted the police as a resource.
Winnie said, "I didn't call the police at first because then it would be in the
paper. I didn't want him arrested. I work with professional people. I don't
want lights in the driveway or cops in the house scaring my kids." Racial
considerations could influence this concern as well. Tina wanted to avoid
the police coming to the house because "we lived in a primarily white
development and we were one of the first black families to move there.
Both sides of the next-door neighbors were white." She did not want to
draw negative attention to her family or reinforce racial stereotypes.

Many women didn't call police because they were too terrified of retaliatory abuse after the police left. And indeed seven women reported experiencing retaliatory violence after police were called. One time, Joan called
the police when her abuser beat her face so badly that she could not open
one of her eyes or go to work. She knew her husband would retaliate for the
arrest, and he did, beating her even worse after the police left and threatening her not to call the police again or she would truly regret it, even though
her choice to proceed had been taken away from her when the state pressed
charges against him. Later, the specter of worse beatings if she further
involved the criminal justice system loomed large, and she hesitated to call
police again.

Sometimes the call to the police did not even present the opportunity to
press charges. Reeva told how her abuser would flee the scene before the
police arrived. Other times the abuser lied to the police and managed to
convince them that there was no problem. Florence described multiple
times when the police were called to her house and her husband finessed

the situation by talking to the police before they questioned her. He would warn the police that Florence had a mental problem that affected her memory and resulted in her fabricating incidents when she could not remember what was going on. Florence felt the police never doubted him; they never questioned her separately, and they ignored her pleas for help.

Police could be jaded about IPV/A in ways that discouraged the women from pursuing legal recourse. Joan's reluctance to call police a second time was reinforced by what she had overheard them saying out on the porch when they had arrived at her house ("You know how these women are, you know what they do, they change their minds as soon as we take their men in"). Brenda talked about how once police had seen her abuser attack her in public and had stopped to question them. At the time she felt respected, since they asked her if she wanted to press charges and they informed her about the protection order process, but Brenda just wanted the police to leave so they could go home. And the police left. Looking back, she wishes they had been more insistent, since their nonchalance conveyed the message to her husband that the abuse was private and the law would not intervene.

When abusers had some kind of connection to local law enforcement, victims' safety was further compromised. For six women, their abuser either was a police officer (Jayde, Megan, Celeste) or was close friends with police officers (Amy, Vanessa, Robyn). Amy explained how this entrapped her further:

> I only called the cops once and will never do it again. . . . I was dealing with a person with no fear of the law whatsoever. . . . I called the cops because he broke in the door and I was terrified. I called 911 and they came, but I wasn't bleeding so nothing happened. They told him, "Go cool off, just, cool off." So he goes to the bar. Guess who shows up at the bar—the arresting officer. . . . I find out later that the arresting office beats his wife, and here they are, having beers together. Apparently the arresting officer tells him, "Best thing you ever did was that you didn't punch her. I would have had to arrest you." . . . So he validates him. He comes back home. What happens? He walks in the door and rips the phone out of that wall and says to me, "All right, bitch, who you gonna call now?" . . . I never called the police again.

When Vanessa's neighbors called the police after overhearing a particularly loud and vicious beating,

> The police showed up. But his first wife was a police dispatcher, so he partied with all the police, so any of the times the police would actually show up, they'd take him around the corner, do drugs with him, and bring him back more jacked up than what he was, and they would be like, "Yo, this is his house, you don't have nothing, you're [meaning

Vanessa] from the street, you should go back to the street." So I never had anyone to back me.

In another instance, Robyn reached out to the police after her husband threatened to "blow my fucking head off." Several of the officers had gone to high school with her husband, and one warned him, "If something happens to your wife, I have to come and take you to jail." Robyn reported, "My husband was furious." Though the officer may just have been trying to prevent further violence, he compromised her safety by letting her husband know she had called them without getting her consent.

Jayde was between a rock and a hard place: her (female) partner was a police officer, and there had been no physical abuse until the day her partner and two (female) police officer friends beat her up. Earlier that evening, their yelling alerted a neighbor who called the cops, and Jayde was asked by an officer, whom she didn't know, whether there was any domestic violence going on.

> I said, "There's no DV here." He said, "Are you sure, because you look a little shaken up." I said, "No, we're having some problems, but we're okay." I remember these next fateful words—he said to me, "Do you have any fear of her? She is a law enforcement officer and she carries a gun." I looked at him, saying, ". . . No, I'm not afraid of her; she has never hurt me." He said, okay, and they left.

Soon after, the doorbell rang and it was her partner and two female officer friends. Jayde was puzzled, especially when they said they were there to help her, so she locked herself in the master bedroom that she and her partner shared. The officers started pounding on the door, demanding that she open a shared room; Jayde became afraid. They broke down the door, tearing it off the hinges. At that point, Jayde threw a phone at them and one of the officers started screaming that she had assaulted an officer and they were going to arrest her. One of them pepper-sprayed her and she could not see or breathe and started to have an asthma attack. Jayde went limp and the three officers dragged her across the room, making her lie down, and put handcuffs on her. Other officers arrived, separated Jayde from the women, and took her statement. Their line of questioning revealed what Jayde's partner had already told the newly arriving officers: she was afraid Jayde was going to hurt herself, she and her two friends had been forced to break down the door to rescue Jayde, and Jayde had then become combative. As Jayde gave her very different account to a male officer, realization dawned upon him:

> He said, "Wait a minute, you were in your room and they demanded that you open the door and they broke down the door when you didn't?"

Did you throw a phone at them?" "Yes I did, in self-defense. I had three armed police officers coming after me in my own home." He said, "Does somebody have a handcuff key? Take these handcuffs off her," and he got real scared. I told him, "I'm being held hostage with these handcuffs on." As I was saying this stuff to him, the look on his face was "Oh, shit, we did something wrong." That was it and then they tore out of there and my house was completely empty.

Jayde was in shock and all alone. She called a friend, who came over with a blank temporary restraining order to fill out (her friend was a lawyer) and brought Jayde to the ER. Jayde resisted at first because she was afraid that her partner would lose her job, but when she called her father, across the country, and he agreed she needed to go to the hospital, she went. She had black and blue bruises springing up all over and a broken wrist, in addition to her eyes being red and smarting from the pepper spray. The intake nurse was very supportive and told Jayde they had seen many DV cases involving police abusers; Jayde gave her all three officers' names. The ER physician's assistant, who had to count all the bruises, from head to toe, was also sympathetic. After finding out that Jayde had been with her partner for eight years and it was the first time, he warned her, "Don't go back. He said, 'She did it once, she'll do it again. I say it to everybody I deal with in domestic violence. Don't go back.' He asked me, 'What does she do for a living?' Again, I said, police officer, and he said, 'Say no more, say no more.'"

Jayde did not see her partner again, although her ex threatened her with a restraining order and forged Jayde's name to break the lease. The hospital sent a report to the police department, but Jayde never found out if her ex had experienced any punitive action. Jayde followed up by calling the watch commander and demanding to press charges.

> He was very sweet to me on the phone, and assured me that we could handle all this right now on the phone. He said to me that he knew the two of us were going through a rough time now. Then he advised me to just leave her alone and she'll leave me alone and we'd both be done. I refused, because I have twenty-eight-plus bruises on my body and a broken wrist, and he said, "They will heal; do you realize if you press charges, she will probably lose her job and then that will be devastating to her." I said, "Well, she should have thought about it before she put her hands on me." He said, "I see your point, but now you have to go to court, and prove that all of this had happened."

Jayde assured him that she has photos of the unhinged broken door, her injuries and hospital records, and the police reports. He urged her to think about it and call him back if she decided to move forward with formal charges. Jayde then called her father again, and he advised her not to "mess with anybody's career; just let it go." Jayde thought her father trivialized the abuse because it involved two women: "If this had been with a man, my dad would have been on a plane and would beat the hell out of the guy. But I think because it was two women, my father didn't take it seriously."[2]

Yet sometimes the police were helpful. Haley received a resource card from a police officer when the neighbors called the cops to report loud fighting. She called a victim services number on that list: "I credit an advocate I called for saving my life, and everything she did to help me."

Some women noted that their racial or class status probably helped get them respectfully treated by police. Naomi believed the police were more protective toward her and more antagonistic against her husband because she was white and he was black. He raped her the day before she left, but she was told upon calling the local battered women's shelter that marital rape was exempt from the law.[3] The police still took a report, which she used to get a restraining order. About ten days after she left him, he asked to meet in a public place to talk things out, and Naomi agreed to meet him. He was very calm and charming and offered to go with her to their apartment to get some more clothing for their son. When they arrived, he blocked the door and prevented her from leaving, then called the caregiver who was watching their son, telling her to bring him to the apartment. The caregiver heard Naomi screaming in the background and called the police. Six police barreled up the stairs and surrounded him. They were all white, Naomi said, "and I'm sure the racial context of the relationship also made a difference in how they behaved." Abigayle stated that when the police arrested her for assault against her long-term boyfriend on the basis of his account of the incident and were about to take her to the station to book her, "the police officer said, 'We can do this one of two ways; you can either ride with me or follow me. That way, you will have a car—but I'll still be watching you so don't do anything stupid.'" She thought they were so considerate of her because it was clear, from her neighborhood, race, and speech articulation, that she was not "riffraff."

Fighting Back: Arrests and Self-Defense

Sometimes pushing back against abusers' coercive control results in a victim's arrest, a dual arrest, or a police threat to arrest, as was the case for six women in the project. The women's experiences mirror recent work on the conundrum faced by the police when operating under an ostensibly gender-neutral mandatory or proarrest policy for "domestic violence": anyone who uses force in a relationship is arrested (S. Miller 2005). Following the emergence of such policies, women with IPV/A victimization/survivorship histories have been increasingly swept up in arrests (Haviland et al. 2001; Henning and Feder 2004; Rajan and McCloskey 2007) because these policies ignore the motivation, consequences, and injury involved in IPV/A, thus decontextualizing the use of force and ignoring the different reasons victims/survivors and abusers use force (Goodmark 2008; S. Miller 2001). Primary aggressor training, which is becoming more common, distinguishes between aggressive and defensive use of force and guides police to investigate the context of the incident, specifically addressing the question "Who will have the most fear when I leave the scene?" (Larance and Miller 2016). Unfortunately, however, not all police officers consider motivation, consequences, and context in IPV/A situations, leading to incorrect identification of the true victim and offender, and often resulting in arrests of victims who fought back or a dual arrest of both parties (Dichter 2013; Osthoff 2002).

One instance of dual arrest occurred when Megan's husband cleaned out their bank accounts and had his wild trip to Florida (mentioned in chapter 3). She decided that was it, turned to a friend to find a place for them to move, and started packing.

> When my husband came home and saw all of the boxes, I got a horrible beating. The police were involved and we were both arrested; that just sealed the deal for me. I had been having second thoughts right before that incident, wavering because the kids love their dad and same old crap. When he said, "You can go, but you're not getting the kids. You're never going to see them again," my youngest starts screaming and there is a tug of war, and it just turned into a physical fight. Then I said, "All right, all right, just put the baby down. And let's end it." As soon as he did, I grabbed my son and took off to the bathroom, and my ex-husband's trying to knock down the door. My niece walks in and called the cops. They showed up and I had the fat lip and he had a bite mark on the inside of his arm, and we both went to jail. When I was sitting there in that cell, booked and printed, I was like, "What, am I nuts? Don't think about giving him a second chance or a third chance," and that was it.

Tina offered an account of an incident in which she was the aggressor:

> One time, he had me arrested because he said that I assaulted him. He had called me a bitch and I smacked him in the face. . . . When he went to strike me back, he slipped. The warrant said his face was scratched, his shirt was torn, and his glasses were broken. . . . He also had me arrested for telephone harassment, or at least his girlfriend did. It was a mess.

Ultimately, however, she was released when the larger context of his abuse of her was recognized. "The police kept me in a holding cell. They sentenced me to jail and suspended it for probation. The probation officer visited the home twice and then wrote a letter to the judge saying that she didn't think that I needed to be on probation, given my years of victimization by him."

Sara got in trouble with the police for threatening one of her husband's girlfriends. Her husband had been violent to her, and the first time he tried to strangle her she called his commanding officer at the base.

> I lost it—how dare he? Then he said he was sorry. . . . We tried again. The army had a discussion with him, so it stopped for a couple of months, but then he had another affair . . . and he kept abusing me, I had a black eye and bruises. . . . I went to the military base hospital and the police came. They arrested him and were going to press charges and make him take an anger management course.

But he sweet-talked Sara into trying again, and they got back together. When his cheating continued, it was a girlfriend who became the direct target of Sara's anger: "One of his girlfriends said she was pregnant. I saw his car at her house and I went there, yelling, 'If you don't open this door, consider your career over; I'll report you for fraternizing, you are a lowlife, how dare you break up my family.' . . . She never answered the door." The police arrested Sara the next day on terroristic threat charges. Ultimately the case was *nolle prosequi*,[4] but Sara endured a good deal of stress and expense to fight the charges. Here Sara displaced the humiliation she felt because of her husband's cheating onto a "safer" target who did not have the violent history that her husband did, in an illustration of what Larance and Miller (2016) call "horizontal hostility": a woman uses force against a third party in a situation typically orchestrated by her abusive partner/former partner; although the third party is also female, she is not in an intimate relationship with the woman. Instead, the third party is usually a past or current girlfriend of the abusive partner, whom the partner may flaunt openly. Sara also responded more conventionally in self-defense later, when her husband tried to kill her: "I also got arrested for DV when I threw a magazine when he was threatening (again) to strangle me. It didn't even hit or cut him." If police had been following primary aggressor training, they would have understood more about the context in which Sara felt she had no choice but to defend herself.

Joan was arrested for fighting back when she knew from past experience that her abuser could severely hurt her. She was put on probation and sent to an anger management class.

Jayde also was threatened with arrest when she fought back against her police officer girlfriend and two other officers accompanying her girlfriend; different police officers, who arrived on the scene, without knowing what had occurred, warned her that striking at a police officer was a serious offense. Without an understanding of the context, police officers assumed that "a hit is a hit is a hit," wholly discounting any gendered understanding of IPV/A victims' self-defensive behavior (see Osthoff 2002).

Abigayle was arrested for assault on the basis of her boyfriend's account of the incident: she threw something at him. However, Abigayle felt she had to do something since he had her cornered and she needed to escape further injury. Later, when Abigayle appeared in court to respond to the charge, the prosecutor invited her to

> step into the stairwell and let's make a deal. He told me, "This is what I'm prepared to offer you." I said, "I'll tell you what I'm prepared to offer *you*. You have no witness. He's not going to show up because if he does, he has to perjure himself on the stand. So you have no alleged victim, you have no witness, you have no evidence whatsoever. I also have subpoenaed the worker who had taken my statement and his. I am absolutely not taking a plea. I'm looking forward to going in that courtroom, so let's go."

The prosecutor dismissed the charges. Abigayle recognized that

> someone with a personality that wasn't as strong as mine definitely would not have handled it that way. I was absolutely forthcoming and said, you have nothing. But there's so many people that don't have the confidence to self-advocate, and for a long time I had lost my voice. I have always been a very confident person, very independent, and he sucked that life out of me. But I knew at that point in court that I wasn't going to get pushed around. I was done.

Although their actions did not end in arrest, an additional 20 percent of the sample described times when they resisted their abuser's violence by self-defensive behavior. The women did not passively take their partner's or husband's physical abuse. At the same time, their defensive actions did not curtail his violence. For instance, Pepper recounted: "I fought back as much as I could. Every single time. If he hit me, I hit him. It was just like that— that's my personality. I'll never let anybody walk all over me." Pepper was very petite, however, and her attempts to hit back did nothing to stop him; in fact, they merely increased her boyfriend's anger. At one point, Ellen brandished a switchblade to defend herself but later hid it so her husband would not find it and use it against her. Julia and Vanessa fought back verbally and also physically when they could, but, as Vanessa explained, "He overpowered me, and my lame attempts to fight back never threatened him or deterred him." Julia added, "I tried to cover myself to avoid the more direct hits, and I pushed him when I could. But he used it against me to taunt me later, saying I was a bad mother because I was violent."

Other women talked about fighting back by using the system. Haley described how, after her husband had persuaded her not to show up at court, she had decided to go anyway as a way to regain some self-respect.

> We would have court dates and he would convince me not to go. The first time, I went anyway because the night before he was going to court, he didn't call me and I thought to myself . . . he needs to show me respect. I'm cutting him a break by not going tomorrow and he's not gonna call me tonight? So . . . my mind-set was: You're not getting away with this, buddy. So I showed up [at court] and he lost it. He saw my car out front, came in, he's screaming, I'm gonna pay the consequences, I have to leave.

The security staff even asked the judge if they could escort her to the parking garage, fearful of what he might do since he was so visibly angry. "Long story short, I had him arrested pretty much every time. . . . I fought back any way I could. . . . With my self-esteem smashed to bits by him and my family not supporting me, trying to keep a new job, I just trying to juggle all the balls in the air so I could survive."

Research unequivocally reveals that when victims/survivors use protective and self-defensive actions against their abusers, their use of force in their intimate relationships is not that of a batterer who tries to assert power and control over a partner (Dasgupta 2002; Larance and Miller 2015; S. Miller 2005; Swan and Snow 2002). The stories of the women I interviewed illustrate how the criminalization of victimization reveals the fallacies of an incident-driven criminal justice system that fails to take the complexities of IPV/A context into consideration, creating a host of collateral consequences for victims.

Restraining Orders

Interactions with the civil courts did not offer much more satisfaction. The women spoke of bewildering and seemingly arbitrary norms and practices of the civil court process that determined whether protection orders (also called PFAs, or "Protection from Abuse" orders, in some states) were granted. Yet there is another side to it: judges are trying their best to decipher "the story" within a battle of high emotions and contested versions. Judges are all too familiar with game playing and drama that may go on with both parties—or at least that is often the characterization of the process. Stakes are high and both sides are invested in winning.

Casey experienced this kind of game playing when her ex-boyfriend and father of her first child used the legal system to target her new fiancé. After almost five years of being single and not really dating, Casey had met her soulmate. Eight weeks before the wedding, when she was addressing wedding invitations,

> My ex's mother called me and she accused my fiancé of sexually molesting my son. . . . It was their last-ditch effort to keep me as "his"—like it was another emotional blackmail from his family. The police came and my fiancé was taken away. We ended up working with social workers and really quickly going to court, where it was proven that my fiancé had done nothing to my son.

Judges' cynicism, however, does not necessarily help them to reach an objective decision and may cause the victims/survivors feel degraded or disrespected. The women I talked with who went to court to get a restraining order and were able to document their abuse were confused and dejected when they seem disbelieved. As Dale said, after demonstrating to the judge all the records of her husband's abuse,

> I wanted to tell the judge, "I hope you learned from this so the next woman that comes into your courthouse, you won't think she is exaggerating." Yet I can understand because there are so many people that do exaggerate and lie; I mean, nowadays, if you want a divorce, the first things you're supposed to do is get a PFA, that's what everybody does, so judges don't believe us when we are the people who really did need it, and that's what happens.

Sometimes there were special legal obstacles to getting a restraining order. Haley couldn't get one against her abusive boyfriend because they were not married, although the law in her state has changed since the time Haley was in court.

Ellen was frustrated with the protection order process because she could not extend it past one year:

> My biggest fear is him showing up at work—I've been at the same place ten years—or my daughter's day care. The day care won't let him leave with my daughter, and she won't leave with him. . . . I know he was calling but I blocked him, texting me from other people's phone numbers, still driving by, and I couldn't prove any of it with him, and they told me that they are only allowed to extend it one time. . . . The judge's words to me were, "Let's hope he doesn't do anything." . . . I have cop friends now, weapons in the house, but still scared of this guy. Really? You can't extend it? So I now have weapons to protect us that I didn't want to get when he was there because he could have easily used them against me.

Restraining orders did not necessarily provide the women adequate protection. Casey's boyfriend routinely violated the restraining order against him, leaving Casey to believe, "A restraining order is a joke; if someone wants to cause some harm, they're going to. You learn quickly that the system isn't going to take care of you and the system is not just or fair." A number of women felt they had no choice but to let their restraining orders expire because their former partners were "having more fun violating the PFA," forcing the women to keep taking off work to respond, as well as finding child care and transportation and paying the exorbitant parking fees at many courthouses.

Women could be embarrassed when getting a protection order came with requirements of workplace notification. Joan worked for the state, and policy dictated that you had to inform your direct supervisor about a protection order.

> We had security cameras; my director made me e-mail him a picture of my ex, which he enlarged in color and printed out, and every person working there had a picture of him, including me, and it also had to be at the front desk. So if anybody saw him, they could call the police. . . . So, while I had just escaped, now I have a picture of him on my desk, and as I walked around the office, everybody had pictures of him on their desks.

Those four months were difficult, but she was relieved the photos did not remain on display for the entire length of her protection order (one year). "I wasn't talkative, and now everyone knew my business . . . I immediately started applying for other jobs. I couldn't take it. But I was stuck, since I couldn't find another job."

Custody Evaluations

In some states, when parties do not agree on custody, a custody evaluation is required before the parties appear in court. For four of the women, there was only one court-approved psychologist in their area able to conduct the evaluation, and many of the women in WIND (in addition to social workers in the county) believed he was biased toward fathers. What emerged from four in-depth interviews I conducted, reinforced by two service providers and two additional women from WIND, was the injustice stemming from his evaluations, which cost approximately $6,000. The psychologist framed the issue in terms that advantaged the (male) abusers over the women by maintaining in the written evaluation and at the oral presentation to the judge that deep conflict existed between the mother and father and that the mother was not "motivated" to work with the father or include him. Moreover, her failure to resolve their conflict demonstrated that she was alienating the children against their father. But the psychologist's reasoning did not offer any understanding of the power dynamics of IPV/A in which fathers hold the power; in fact, the psychologist referred to the offenders as "Dad" in court, essentially erasing their abusive behavior. The psychologist tended to argue that the two parents would provide a safe environment for the children. He was able to minimize the abuse because most IPV/A charges in the women's state were misdemeanors, not felonies, and because over 80 percent of the time, according to the service providers who routinely reviewed these cases in the state where WIND met, consent protection orders were granted without any finding of abuse, leaving women with no evidence to present to the court. Offenders were portrayed as fathers who were willing to make the custody work, while the victims were presented as stubborn, vindictive, and untruthful. Other studies similarly reveal that custody evaluators are not guided by a rich understanding of the complexities of IPV/A, such as understanding risk factors or the dynamics of power and control, but make their assessments based on "safe parenting" plans regardless of severity of abuse (G. Davis 2011; M. Davis et al. 2011; Saunders, Faller, and Tolman 2012).

Courts

Women found many aspects of courtroom procedures intimidating and mystifying. Many said they had not been "vocal" enough during court proceedings because of worries about antagonizing the judge and other legal authorities. For example, one of the women feared for the safety of her children because of her ex's collection of hunting equipment at his residence. She believed that if her ex-husband "thinks it's okay to shoot a bow and arrow in the middle of daylight with people walking their dogs, there's no way he's going to make a safe decision when he's got the kids." But she was afraid of being seen as argumentative if she raised the issue in court. When women stopped in the middle of their reading of the Victim Impact Statement (that they were invited to provide to the court), or when they got nervous and flustered when answering judges' questions, the judges' impatience would remind the women of how their batterers had demeaned them or questioned their reality. Further, they were discomfited to see the familiar terms on which court professionals interacted before court proceedings started. Professionals who work together day in/day out develop a kind of familiar pattern and rhythm of interaction that often becomes invisible once a session is called to order (Eisenstein and Jacob 1977; Hucmann 1977). Since victims/survivors are frequently in the courtroom before the offender is brought in, particularly if he is coming from jail or prison, they are likely to witness this familiarity. If the case does not go well for the survivors, it is no small stretch for them to think that it was not taken seriously enough or that there would have been a different outcome if the "players weren't obviously friends."

Women were particularly taken aback to discover that the system was more concerned with safeguarding the defendant's rights than theirs. It seemed wrong to them that defendants could get free copies of the court transcripts, whereas survivors, who needed the transcripts as well, had to pay (very high) prices for them. Women also were amazed that only defendants had the right to appeal, and that their abusers were appointed a "free lawyer" while the women could not afford one or were not represented by a lawyer other than the prosecutor. Many women talked about the difficulty of getting legal help. When the household income had been high, the women did not qualify for free legal assistance that considers factors such as home ownership and family income, even though economic control by the abuser meant that the women themselves had no access to the money. Further, pro bono assistance was not necessarily very good. Danielle received a copy of an invoice that her pro bono lawyer had sent to the judge showing what he was being paid on her behalf (he met with her only once for several minutes before heading into a court hearing). She commented,

> It is disheartening that he wasn't getting paid enough to represent me better. So you get what you pay for, which is nothing. . . . I'm not saying I wasn't grateful, but I did think that if I had gone in there myself without the lawyer, I could have made the judge more aware of the problems because the lawyer did not take the time to make the judge aware of things like my husband brought a knife to supervised visitation. . . . But because my lawyer didn't take the time to talk to me . . . he couldn't make any good recommendation to the court on my behalf. So I was very frustrated.

As one woman concluded, "It's sad the system is so fucked up. There is no fair system and I was very naive going into it. I thought the system was there to help victims and I had truth on my side. Then he was able to manipulate the system and lie on the stand."

The women I interviewed felt blindsided by what they experienced as gross injustices in the courts. Dale felt like "Alice in Wonderland going down the rabbit hole" after being in the courtroom for two days, hearing her former husband of seventeen years cry fake tears and tell

> lies about how horrible a person I was, with no opportunity for me to defend myself. Nobody heard that I was written up for my volunteer work, coached sports, and was active with my kids' schools. . . . Instead, they heard that I dragged him to a Mexican restaurant while he was on a diet—and he's six foot four and almost three hundred pounds—that

I did devil worship with my children, and that I charged him twenty dollars every time he wanted to have sex with me.

Dale sat with the victim's advocate connected to the prosecutor's office, but she felt that there was no one representing her position. Also bewildering was that a juror kept falling asleep but no one seemed to care. At sentencing, the judge said he believed everything her husband said and that "I deserved what I got." Dale mentioned that her husband was well educated and she did not have much education compared to him, so "I don't speak well. So when I got on the stand, I was a nervous wreck just being in the same room as him. . . . Here I am facing this man who I am seeing for the first time since he tried to kill me, and I was asked to remember exact dates and times about this and that event." Her experience led her to declare, "I am more scared of our court system than I am of him."

For Tina, court processes were similarly disappointing and humiliating:

Court was awful. Every time he tried to change an order for visitation or custody or money, I would find myself against a lawyer who made me look like a slut. Losing my children made me a bad mother, and so on. . . . The judge didn't even try to understand things. . . . Women don't leave their husbands. Back then, it was a big deal. . . . I also wasn't as vocal as I am now. I needed to speak up and say, "That's not true." But I just said okay and cried and felt guilty. They couldn't have cared less. . . . You left your husband *and* your kids, moved on and have a boyfriend. They don't say anything about him cheating and beating on me all those years.

When Winnie went to court, her abuser was represented by an expensive lawyer, while she had an attorney with no domestic violence experience. Her ex-husband had beaten her as well as the children (the latter being the final straw that made her leave after thirteen years of marriage). But her husband got custody of the children based on "the best interests of the children." "I will never forget the judge saying there is no evidence of domestic violence. I had pictures, there was an arrest record, there was a criminal no-contact order. There was a civil order of protection. He was in a diversion program. He was in a treatment program, twenty-six-week domestic violence class. Nothing was presented."

The judge failed to ask the necessary questions in a custody case, and her lawyer was "clueless." Winnie was afraid to challenge the court because she would be seen as angry and unreasonable and not a "good mother." She then retained a different lawyer, who filed for a custody modification, using evidence from her children's school reports (one child was depressed and expressing suicidal thoughts, and the other had bruises from being hit by her father); it still took seven months to get a court date to have the modification petition heard. In the end, Winnie was granted joint custody, but for years she continued to worry about her children's safety when they were under his care.

Often women were shocked by how minor legal penalties for the abuser turned out to be. Amy said of her court hearings.

> Talk about disappointment. Every time you turn around, there were legal problems with my children or legal problems with a man, I kept thinking that at some point there will be justice. . . . We get to court, and the public defender tells him, "Just sign here and sign that and you are guilty and get out of here." Okay, so that was a farce—Sign here, sign here—what was that? Then my husband goes to anger management classes, and each night when he got home, he would tell me, "These classes are a bunch of bullshit." So he finishes his anger management classes and he does the whole deal, so there is an arrest record, and there is a court agreement, so this arrest is expunged and done away with.

Joan similarly noted that legal proceedings against her husband accomplished very little, even though during those proceedings the state looked up his record and discovered that he had had past domestic violence incidents with his first wife. He ended up on probation and was ordered to attend a batterer intervention program. He was also ordered to surrender his gun, but since it was not registered in his name he was able to keep it. (Winnie had similarly thought that her abuser's guns would be seized if he were arrested and convicted of IPV/A, but her abuser scoffed at this, knowing that he would hide the guns with his brothers and that he would still retain many sharp and big hunting knives.) When Sara reported her husband's violence to the military police on base, they took him out of the residence and said they were going to press charges, "but then his direct supervisor said that he would be placed in an anger management class and urged me to forgive him and start anew." (Ironically, Sara herself would be arrested later for making threats when she confronted the military woman her husband was having an affair with, as described subsequently in this chapter.)

In many instances the women were not even notified when their abuser was released from jail or prison.[5] And Dale recounted that when her ex-husband was taken off the ankle bracelet he wore after being released from prison, "the court forgot to tell me about it so he is free to come [try to] kill me again."[6]

It is common practice in many jurisdictions to use mediators to iron out the details of agreements about children prior to an appearance before a judge. But many women recounted meetings with mediators in family court during which they were silenced out of fear, or their abuser lied, or their abuser charmed the mediator into doubting their words. Consistent with these stories, research by Rivera, Sullivan, and Zeoli (2012) has found that mediators do not always believe that physical IPV/A has occurred, even with documentation, and that they often ignore women's allegations of abusers' emotional abuse and controlling behavior when the abusers do not act belligerent or threatening in their presence. In Rivera et al.'s study, the women said they would avoid returning to family court because of their negative experiences.

Batterers often continue or increase their violence and/or abuse after a breakup (Fleury, Sullivan, and Bybee 2000), and as discussed in chapter 4 these abuse dynamics may continue for years under the guise of proper legal proceedings. Direct abuse occurring within the ongoing relationship can transition to more indirect abuse after a relationship ends, particularly through the courts. "Paper abuse" is a control tactic utilized by offenders to harass the victims/survivors of IPV/A through the court system after the relationship ends. It involves frivolously filing paperwork, making false reports of child abuse, and taking other legal actions as a means of exerting power, forcing contact, and financially burdening their ex-partners (S. Miller and Smolter 2011). Victims are often legally required to attend multiple meetings and hearings and may not have the resources to protect themselves legally or financially. The lengthy process can involve multiple judges who may be unaware of the history of abuse (see Logan et al. 2006). Paper abuse is similar to stalking because of the forced contact between the victim/survivor and the abuser (S. Miller and Smolter 2011) and the intent to harass (Mechanic, Weaver, and Resick 2008). Custody and visitation battles become means for ex-partners and ex-spouses to harass or intimidate their former partner because the abusers know how much the children mean to their mothers (see Goodman and Epstein 2011; Watson and Ancis 2013). A recent study interviewing twenty-two divorced mothers who reported IPV/A during or after their marriages reinforces the contention that abusers use the courts as an arena to exhaust women's financial assets after separation (Toews and Bermea 2017). Of the twenty-five women in my own study who had children when they were in their relationship with the abuser, twenty-four recounted the use of such tactics. (The twenty-fifth, Naomi, stated, "I'm kind of grateful that my ex-husband wasn't involved with my son and that I didn't have to deal with the courts; it made things simpler," but was adamant that her ex-husband would have made use of that venue if he had had more resources.)

The continuation of power and control exhibited by their abusers meant that women faced even greater challenges to their healing and resilience until their children were no longer young enough to be the pawns of custody, child support, and visitation hearings. Many of the women who participated in my project spoke at length about the ways in which their abusers manipulated the courts with claims centering on their shared children. This is a powerful and devious means of harassment: everyone presumably wants the best for their children, including the court, which is supposed to act in the "best interests of the children," so one would think that abusers' counterclaims of child abuse and their use of children as pawns to continue coercive control over their ex-partners would be closely examined for disingenuous assertions. Time after time, however, the women described a failure of the court system to do this. As Amy said of her own court experience, "The courts think they are fair by listening to him, but all of his lies obscure the truth, and the judges just don't seem to ask the right questions." Exacerbating their frustration was the judges' stance of gender neutrality. Though courts strive for fairness, such neutrality in IPV/A situations dealing with child custody and visitation is often misguided: it can mean ignoring the father's abusive behavior and dismissing the women's protestations that his "interest" is feigned and a way to perpetuate abuse within the legal arena (see Dragiewicz 2011).

Many women spoke of court-imposed visitation arrangements that put their children in danger from the abuser. In Celeste's case, the father was awarded unsupervised visitation even though he had withheld formula and food for the children as a way to punish Celeste and even though the children had had to witness his emotional and physical abuse of her. Fearing that he would kidnap the kids—since he took drugs and was a reckless driver, in addition to being vindictive after she left—Celeste moved out of state because she did not want to run the risk of losing her children if she did not follow through with the unsupervised visitation.

Danielle described a time when her ex-husband brought a pocketknife with him to the visitation center where he had supervised interactions with their children. He was using the knife to fix a toy, but he knew that he was on camera at the center and also that weapons, which included knives of any sort, were not allowed on the premises. The incident reinforced Danielle's concerns about his poor judgment: "What was he going to do when he is given unsupervised visitation, if he couldn't handle supervised visitation for an hour?" Indeed, her concerns were realized. Even when her ex-husband was accompanied by a court-ordered parent aide, he used every opportunity to scare the children and reassert that he was in control of them. Often the parent aide had to call Danielle to come to the rescue because one of the kids had run off to find a safe place away from the father. So when Danielle's attorney, assigned *ad litem* to her children, insisted that Danielle contact her husband to work out custody and drop-off plans because she was legally responsible for doing so, Danielle balked: "I'm thinking, do you know anything about domestic violence? No, she didn't, because she's just a regular divorce attorney; meanwhile, my kids are in danger." Danielle was indignant yet impotent when the court did nothing to rectify the situation. The judge told her that he wanted more time to see if her ex-husband improved under supervision.

During their separation phase, Amy and her husband had shared custody of their daughter, although he was able to convince the judge that he should have primary custody. She was forced to pick up their daughter at his house and bring her back there. "He insisted I come into the house; at every visit he would get me into the house and then the verbal abuse would just be constant and vicious, in front of her." Amy realized this was incredibly harmful to her daughter, so she had the court order changed to state that the drop-off and pickup would be at the curb, hoping to curtail her daughter's exposure to the verbal vitriol. Amy started to prepare her daughter for the change, "because I knew if I tried to just drop her at the curb, as the custody order says, if I did that he's going to say to her, 'Your mother doesn't love you, she dumps you off like a sack of garbage,' because I heard him say these words in front of me." Amy also had the foresight to begin carrying a tape recorder so she could document his ongoing verbal abuse each week. "I have a whole stack of tapes in my bedroom because I thought if I ever had to fight for custody, it would be a contrast to him showing up in court in a three-piece suit, looking perfectly normal. It doesn't feel very powerful being on this side of the fence, when he is accorded such respect in the courtroom and I am painted as the crazy one."

Consistent with such stories, research has found that judges often make crucial decisions regarding child custody and visitation that display little training or understanding of the issues related to IPV/A (see Kernic et al. 2005). Their guidance by "best interest of the child" factors allows them enormous discretion in contested cases. Custody decisions show not only a gender bias in favor of men but also a professional bias in that judges prefer psychologists (a group more likely to be male) to social workers (a group more likely to be female) as custody evaluators and take them more seriously (Saunders, Faller, and Tolman 2012); this has major repercussions given that "psychologists were more likely than social workers to believe that DV is not important in custody-visitation decisions and that alleged victims make false DV allegations, alienate the children, and hurt the children when they resist co-parenting" (88). Judges perpetuate this bias by ignoring IPV/A and its effects on the children and imposing joint custody arrangements (Hannah and Goldstein 2010); one study found that 40 percent of fathers who had committed violence against the mothers were granted joint custody (Morrill et al. 2005).

Many women feared that their sexual histories or their relationships after leaving the abuser would prejudice custody decisions against them. For instance, after Celeste left her abusive husband, she was terrified about any information he might raise in court to gain custody and was particularly anxious that he not find out she was dating a woman. "I kept everything separate from my children—they never knew about my personal intimate life because I feared their father would use it against me in court and I would lose custody." Such worries could be justified: Reeva described how her husband went to great lengths to hurt her by exposing past private and painful events in her life and using them to portray her as a bad mother so he would be awarded custody. She discovered he was keeping a journal on his computer where he documented

> all of the secrets I told him as my spouse—that I was molested as a little girl, that I was raped later on in life, miscarriages . . . and used my words later to show that I'm not a fit parent. And he didn't even want the custody! He just wanted to mess with me because he knew my kids were my world. I lost custody. When he put all of those little things together, they equaled "She's mentally unstable and she cannot handle taking care of our kids" to the judge.

Some women told how their abuser had threatened or manipulated one of their children to say damaging things against them in court. For instance, Tina described the devastating experience when her ten-year-old son testified against her. When her son grew up, he admitted that "his dad convinced him that I had abused him, and that I had allowed someone else [uncle] to beat him." At the time of being interviewed, Tina said her son now totally backed her but still felt the sting of having to be in the middle of their custody battle. He told Tina he wished that when she wrote articles or got in the news about IPV/A as an advocate, she would do it anonymously so his grandchildren would not find out about their violent past.

Vanessa similarly reported that after their separation, her husband had begun to shower her youngest of three daughters with attention. (This daughter had some mental health issues and was easily confused and manipulated.) Their father had never been involved in the daughters' lives before the divorce, and his brand-new attention was a way to taunt his wife.

After he and Vanessa had been separated for almost a year, one of the older daughters had a party at Vanessa's house at which a young man who attended slipped a drug into Vanessa's drink and raped her after she passed out. Vanessa took the case to court, despite her fears that her husband could use it against her, because there was physical proof (forensic evidence in the drink cup), she had eyewitness accounts of the evening by two of the rapist's friends, and her youngest daughter had seen it happen. But she discovered that

> there is no slam dunk in court. I had a rock-solid case. . . . I had my daughter as an eyewitness, the guy who did this has a past record, we have the senior nurse's report and that one thing about this tear in my vagina showing forced entry . . . but my youngest daughter talked to the judge alone and the case was dismissed. [Why?] Because the state troopers took a statement from her and asked, "How do you know your mother was unconscious at that time?" And my daughter said, "Because her eyes were closed." . . . My attorney said, "But that's the reason, that wasn't the right answer." I said, "What do you mean that wasn't the right answer? What was she supposed to say?" So my attorney told me that my daughter said that my eyes could have been closed because I was enjoying it. It was only months later, after a huge falling out occurred between this daughter and my ex-husband, that I found out he was coaching her about what to say in court.

Some women I interviewed spoke of unjust laws that hampered them from getting divorced even under conditions of abuse. Megan lived in a state where couples were required to wait a year before a divorce could be finalized—even if one of the parties was in a dangerous situation and children were involved—in case the parties reconciled. Her lawyer advised her not to date, not to be seen with any men or have men in her home, and to live a pristine life. Megan worked with all men in the police department and they were her friends and protectors, so she agonized over this because too many women she knew had lost their children for not following similar advice. So she moved to an adjoining state, which meant giving up the job she loved and disrupting her children's schools, because the waiting period was only six months. A similar situation occurred with Celeste when she sought a divorce; she had finally mustered up the courage to leave her husband, and the lawyer said he could take her case. The welfare department offered help, but only if she got a divorce. When she met with the lawyer, with her six-month-old baby in tow, he said at the end of the meeting, almost as an afterthought,

> "The only thing that could put a hitch in the get-a-long is if you were pregnant. You're not because I see you have the baby," and I said, "Uhh,

yeah, I am pregnant." He said, "No, no, no, no." I said, "Yes, I am pregnant." And he said "You can't get divorced in this state if you're pregnant." And I remember thinking, "This is terrible and I'm in a bad spot, and I'm gonna have to go back to him."

Celeste tried to understand why it was impossible to get a divorce, wondering,

> Why would lawmakers do this? They must think they are doing something good. They must think they are saving a family, that pregnant women shouldn't get divorced. Or lawmakers must think they're helping pregnant women be supported. I remember thinking that they have no idea—they don't know what it's like for pregnant women like me. They're operating from . . . the lawyer's office, from fancy desks with a lot of books, and not as one knocked-up, badly beaten pregnant woman in front of them.

This was the beginning of things making sense to Celeste on a social structural level, and not resting on meaning making that had to with pathologizing him or pathologizing her. It characterizes the path that many women journeyed in the years following the end of their abusive relationships: they moved away from self-blame to a broader understanding of how our patriarchal culture trivializes and tolerates IPV/A. The women's revised understanding can be attributed to positive experiences with therapists who understood the power-control dynamics of IPV/A, feminist pastoral counseling, access to information about IPV/A, and support from IPV/A-related victim services that helped women shift from internalized blame toward a greater awareness of the gender inequalities that shape the dynamics of and responses to IPV/A.

What is striking in the women's accounts is how often their abusers succeeded in getting the courts to see their side and negating the atrocities they had committed against their intimate partners. The women, who had initially believed that their voices and victimization would count for something, were often blindsided by these maneuverings. But it became increasingly clear to them that they were often powerless against their abuser's legal machinations and the court's assessment of their situations, leading to a deepening mistrust of the criminal justice system. Their abuser was using that system as a way to prolong ties with them, inflicting pain and fear and exerting control over them even after they had ended the relationship. Though the women I interviewed wished to be free of mediators' and courts' revictimization, they were forced to continue their struggles around child support, custody, and visitation. Yet they persevered, attempting whatever they could to protect their children. As Amy declared about her daughter, "She will not be a casualty of my war."

Social institutions such as religious organizations, social services, and the criminal justice system often have goals of bringing justice and comfort to those they serve. But for many of the victims/survivors I interviewed, these institutions, rather than recognizing the abusive tactics of coercive control, reinforced the vulnerability of the women and contributed to their continued abuse, though it might take more indirect forms. A number of the women described not only how their religious institutions had failed to condemn IPV/A but how some congregations had supported the abusers. The justice system in particular, in both its civil and criminal components, needs more informed IPV/A policies around gender inequality so that the concern to preserve the rights of the accused does not eclipse the needs of victims/survivors and their children. Women often felt silenced in judicial proceedings because they were intimidated and bewildered by many aspects of the court process. They worried that any challenge to court authority could result in their being penalized for "acting out" or accused of making false allegations, so they felt pressured to acquiesce. Lack of legal assistance exacerbated these concerns, especially when their abuser had an attorney in court. The court's paternalism and control often mirrored the very abusive patterns the women were trying to escape; nowhere was this more pronounced than in child support and custody battles. Women also often recounted difficulties in obtaining or extending civil protection orders. The criminal process was no less troublesome; for the six women arrested or threatened with arrest for their use of force in the context of the abusive relationship, the sense of betrayal and injustice was profound. Police, as the gatekeepers to the criminal justice system, can bear the brunt of people's anger and frustration, and many of the women I interviewed recalled instances in which they believed their trauma was compounded by the way police had treated them when they sought help. This sense of injustice was exacerbated when the women's partners were police officers themselves or were friendly with police, who then looked the other way when the women needed them. Although only a few women stayed at battered women's shelters, the victim advocates and service providers gave the women a lifeline as they contextualized the abuse in a way that led to a deeper understanding of the women's situation and a connection to resources the women drew upon for many years after their relationships ended.

Strength, courage, and tenacity are needed to combat IPV/A, both in the home and later in the various institutions with which women engage. The women were frustrated, stressed, and fearful, but although they wavered at times they were determined to secure safety and justice for themselves and their children. Many had encountered victim blaming and judgmental attitudes from people they turned to for help. Fortunately, however, the women also were embraced with compassion, understanding, and resources by people in their own family and friendship networks, landlords, employers, and coworkers, as well as by a number of dedicated professionals working within social services, the justice system, and religious communities. Both emotional and tangible support greatly assisted the women not only in the early months when they left their abusers but over the long haul. The final chapter continues this discussion of postabuse strategies that contributed to maximizing women's growth and resilience, explores the women's multiple pathways to long-term resilience, and develops policy recommendations derived from the women's experiences.

6. Paths to Survivorship and Suggestions for Policy

This final chapter addresses the broader significance and implications of this work. In particular, it explores the meaning of long-term recovery and resilience by recognizing the multiple pathways to survivorship and well-being. Though exploring battered women's narratives is not new, the in-depth analysis of their experiences in their many years living violence-free may assist programs in developing long-term support for survivors as well as provide inspiration to abused women still enmeshed in violent relationships. Not only does the analysis add to our thinking on identity integration, but the gendered perspective adds to our understanding of the ways in which patriarchal power and privilege frame abusers' sense of entitlement and the power wielded by the criminal justice and legal systems over the lives of IPV/A survivors. In this chapter, drawing on the experiences of long-term survivors of IPV/A raised in both the in-depth interview data and the ethnographic fieldwork, I summarize the context of the women's lives after abuse, where resilience is best characterized as a roller-coaster ride, and the ways they have found meaning and experienced personal growth in the aftermath of abusive relationships. I then use my analysis of the women's tumultuous journeys to formulate policy recommendations that could anticipate the needs of long-term survivors of abuse, while augmenting measures that are already in place and creating new ways to support victims/survivors.

LIFE AFTER ABUSE: "AN UNEASY PEACE"

For years following the end of their abusive relationships, the women in my project lived in a liminal space. Social anthropologists have conceptualized this state as one of being "betwixt and between" (Turner 1967) as it relates to identity reconstruction, and the field of human relations within organizations speaks of "before" and "after" identities, such as those of a temporary worker who succeeds in becoming permanent (see Beech 2011; Fiol 2002). Identity comprises both an internal self-identity and an external identity that is contingent on interaction with others (see Blumer 1969); individuals "constitute and [are] constituted by their social situations," so identity is "the intersection where structure and agency meet" (Beech 2011, 286; Ybema et al. 2009). Fluidity is also a feature of identity, as people move between identities that coexist (Whittle, Mueller, and Mangan 2009): for example, the identities of being a target of bullying and being an ex-victim (see Lutgen-Sandvik 2008), or here, being a victim and being a survivor living without abuse. In liminal space, multiple meanings coexist and are temporary, though they can extend over a long period; identities can be reconstructed, and transformation can occur depending on changes in the individual's meaning construction and in the relationship between the individual and society (Shotter 2008; see also Goffman 1974 on "rekeying," or shifting something on the periphery of one's life to make it more central).

While Dale's words in the title of this section capture the relief many women felt that grew over time as they realized they were no longer exposed to daily, relentless belittlement and abuse, the fear of their former partner lingered. Several women in my project expressed fears of being "found" and hurt by their ex-partners. These fears were exacerbated by the women's knowledge of their ex's anger and weapon possession, and their ex's oft-repeated threats to kill them if they left. Their experience with threats of harm from weapons (including knives and guns) led many of the women to consider safety precautions that had not been at their disposal when their abuser lived in the same house, such as purchasing Mace, getting a dog, installing an alarm system if there was enough money, and putting extra bars on the doors. However, these precautions did little to assure them of their safety if they shared children with their abuser. Indeed, a recurring nightmare for one-third of the women was that their ex would kidnap their child(ren) from day care or school, regardless of whether there was a court order to prohibit this possibility. Women with children had to deal long term with the abuser's coercive control, often facilitated by civil and criminal courts, and the power and control exercised over them by state officials. Though over time their fear of imminent violence and abusive attacks diminished, the consequences of their victimization lingered: financial problems, health problems, mental stress, trauma, damaged self-esteem, fears about falling into poverty (or deeper poverty) as their former partners continued to hide money or assets, and concerns that their children might have suffered lasting harm from their years in an abusive home. The women unanimously reflected that there was no real stability after abuse; indeed, abuse was so woven into the fabric of their lives that it actually helped to constitute stability since they knew its contours. These beliefs echo Blankenship's (1998) earlier sociological work on thriving, which underscores the importance of social context: some violence that outsiders see as horrific may seem routine or ordinary for someone used to experiencing life that way.

It is often argued that trauma shatters people's basic assumptions about self and others (Janoff-Bulman 1992) and disrupts their belief in a just world (Lerner 1980) that is meaningful, predictable, and controllable (Epstein 1967, cited in Janoff-Bulman 1992, 99). Such beliefs help people feel safe. Yet Gilfus (1999), in a psychological study of how survivors rebuild their identities and lives in the aftermath of trauma, maintains that many individuals—including racial and ethnic minorities, poor people, and abused children or battered women—may *never* have felt the world was kind or fair or predictable. Indeed, their experience has been one of vast unpredictability and well-founded fears of being hurt intentionally by other people who are more powerful and upon whom they may be economically dependent. In this context, a loss of belief in the just world hypothesis could be viewed as a healthy response to trauma when survivors do not feel safe in their own homes. This may be particularly salient for women who experience violence in their families of origin, as did one-fifth of the women I interviewed. When these women reflected on their worldviews in the years following their departure from their violent relationships, they described the need for caution but also the slow development of a sense of themselves as worthy and a sense that the world could be safe and people trusted; at the very least, the women were emphatic that they wanted these different worldviews for their children.

Over time the women's self-esteem and sense of efficacy crept back steadily but with great fragility. Eventually, however, the women felt less diminished and more firmly established at the helm of their lives. They described how although they kept moving forward they maintained a "healthy skepticism" regarding their future. One woman said, "It was months, maybe years, before I imagined a life free of violence because the fear permeated the way I lived long after I left. Until you are living without that constant suffocating fear, you are not surviving," and another said, "I didn't think leaving would mean some kind of sea change, some kind of liberation; I expected it to be terrible, just less terrible and less lethal than staying." For the majority of the women, this liminal state extended over many years. As they moved forward in the five or more years after their abusive relationships ended, their resilience had highs and lows; the women talked about being empowered in some areas yet still struggling to cope in others, much as Luthar, Cichetti, and Becker (2000) have described for recovery from other painful situations in women's lives. Overall, however, they shifted from blaming themselves and seeing themselves as victims to seeing themselves as survivors and questioning the limitations of the criminal justice and social service systems.

HARDINESS AND SOCIAL SUPPORT: INTEGRATING PSYCHOLOGICAL AND SOCIOLOGICAL PERSPECTIVES

The women in my project talked at length about dealing with the trauma of an abusive relationship, reconstructing their lives and their identities, and finding meaning in their horrific experiences. Their stories exhibited the personality trait of hardiness (see Kobasa, Maddi, and Kahn 1982)—a trait psychologists believe can act as a buffer when a person is exposed to extreme stress. Hardiness has three dimensions, all of which arise or are brought to the foreground in the aftermath of trauma: "being committed to finding meaningful purpose in life, the belief that one can influence one's surroundings and the outcome of events, and the belief that one can learn and grow from both positive and negative life experiences." With the help of these beliefs, "hardy individuals have been found to appraise potentially stressful situations as less threatening, thus minimizing the experience of distress. Hardy individuals are also more confident and better able to use active coping and social support, thus helping them deal with the distress they do experience" (Bonanno 2004, 25; also Florian, Mikulincer, and Taubman 1995).

Although my project did not measure hardiness, the women's narratives clearly illustrate the three dimensions of hardiness at the micro level. These dimensions interact with social support and social structures at the macro level, but it is important to look at the internal compasses that guide these women. With regard to the first dimension, finding a meaningful purpose in life, many women with children found strength to leave their abuser for their kids' well-being and future. Many also found meaning in their faith, or in helping other abused women to believe in themselves and find the courage to live violence-free. Over time, the women also believed they could influence their surroundings and the outcome of events, exhibiting the second dimension of hardiness. Although they had often been able to redirect violence or "clean up" in their abusers' wake during their relationships, now that they had left their abusers it was sheer joy to achieve more positive outcomes. This was especially evident in WIND members' statements about how proud they were to be making a difference politically, but similar feelings of efficacy were also expressed by women who engaged in more private efforts to help other women through their work, their volunteering, or their personal conversations. Further, the women expressed delight in a newfound ability to shape their lives in the ways they wanted. Although during their abusive relationships they had made many daily decisions that kept them and/or their children safer during their relationship, often these choices were circumscribed by their abusers, limiting the women's ability to self-care. All of the women talked exuberantly about the freedom in their lives after the relationship—the ability to make all big and small decisions. Tina, for instance, stated: "Twenty-five years after leaving him—I'm more independent, better educated. . . . What thrills me the most about being free from that violence is that I can think and make decisions for myself." The women were able to think about their future without the threat of their partner's abuse hanging over them, curtailing their dreams. Robyn, for instance, was able to step back from her life and think about what she wanted to do long term: "When I turned thirty-two, I thought, 'Oh my God. I am not who I wanted to be. If my life is going to be good, I'm going to have to change it.' . . . So I started community college." Indeed, fourteen of the thirty-one women pursued further education after the abuse.

The third component of hardiness—the belief that one can learn and grow from both positive and negative experiences—was revealed in the ways the women made sense of what they had been through (chapter 4), as in Joan's affirmation that "I wouldn't take any of it back. . . . It all equals Joan." For many, it was closely aligned to their recognition that they could draw on all their experiences to assist other women in similar situations.

Many of the women talked about their "core" self and the inner strength they had to summon to finally terminate the relationship for good. But they also spoke of their serendipitous discovery of or deliberate search for others in their social world who supported their determination to live violence-free lives by offering emotional and practical assistance. Formerly estranged family members and old friends, new friends—often other female survivors of IPV/A, employers and coworkers, and helpful service providers, victim advocates, and some criminal justice system professionals—played key roles in allaying the women's uncertainties and paving the way for them to progress toward their goals. As Bonanno describes above, the women's beliefs that together constituted hardiness made them more able to draw on such support, but the reverse causation was also true: the assistance that they found or sought facilitated their understanding of their own strength and resilience by validating their growing confidence and rejection of self-blame, challenging the abusers' construction of their faults, and reinforcing their new understandings of their situations and potential for well-being.

All of these findings reflect the psychological view that resilience is composed of traits, processes, and outcomes. But the integration of a sociological view suggests that women can have strong protective factors composing their individual personalities (agency) that interact with social networks and institutional support (structure) (see Dutton and Greene 2010) in ways that move them forward in the transition from victim to survivor.

ROADS TO SURVIVORSHIP

There was no single template for women's journeys to survivorship. Early studies conducted by psychologists found that most people responded to trauma by struggling with anxiety and depression, while others rebounded eventually to reach an emotional state similar to what they had experienced before their trauma (for a review, see Tedeschi and Calhoun 2004). Yet newer work on post-traumatic growth demonstrates that more than 50 percent of people undergo positive changes following trauma (Tedeschi and Calhoun 1996).

A key ingredient for recovery is the recognition that one is not to blame. As Harvey et al. (1991, 518) note with respect to sexual assault, "Long-term successful adjustment likely involves the development of an account that provides more in-depth understanding of the event and an interpretation that takes the onus off of self as the responsible agent." Feiring, Taska, and Chen (2002) found in their study of victims of sexual abuse that self-blaming was often associated with higher risk for PTSD and depression. However, it takes time to change one's beliefs about who is responsible for one's victimization. Over time, the women I interviewed moved from feeling blameworthy to questioning a society that tolerated men's violence against women. By realizing that the abuse was not their fault, and that they were not doomed to their situation, they discovered hope for the future for themselves and, if they had children, the family. The recognition that even in the face of abuse and humiliation they had finally asserted some control re-ignited long-extinguished pride in their resourcefulness. Acting on their new self-realizations was not easy for most of the women, especially those additionally held back by poverty, low levels of education, limited housing options, and lack of social support from friends and family. Yet they persevered.

Sometimes a particularly horrendous abusive episode catalyzed the decision to end an abusive relationship; other times a more usual episode simply proved to be "the last straw." Leaving was more difficult for women whose families of origin were characterized by IPV/A, parental alcoholism, or past experiences of child sexual or physical abuse. Dysfunction in the childhood home "normalized" the women's own experiences of abuse and left them with no one to turn to in their family of origin who could understand the abuse or support them in leaving the relationship. The women were most reinforced in leaving by validation from external sources. Many recalled how other people in their lives had suggested that they did not have to live with abuse. Some women discounted these messages, thinking that they did not really apply to their situations, but options for a different life remained beacons of hope in the back of their minds. As time moved on, many women made choices to try to talk with a therapist again, or their pastor, or to reach out to an estranged relative or long-lost friend. Often they found the most encouragement, not from relatives or old friends, especially if the abuser had further isolated the women from these people, but from new friends they might have met in a shelter or church, a victim advocate, an understanding employer, a coworker, a teacher, a landlord, a probation officer, a police officer, or a lawyer. These supportive people reinforced women's growing ability to cast off internalized blame, shame, and guilt.

The women's journeys were not easy; sometimes many felt that it would be easier to "deal with the devil you know" in contrast to an unknown future. They struggled at first with isolation in the years following the relationship's end, as they felt ashamed about what had happened or wary about disclosing their painful past to people in order to explain their absence from relationships that had lapsed. Nevertheless, many found new or revived connections to other people that took on deeper meanings and helped sustain them as time progressed. These connections gave women the energy to reassert their autonomy despite cynical lawyers, unhelpful judges, and other people who challenged their increasing independence, though this road was not always smooth and women sometimes faltered in their optimism. Such informal support has always been recognized as benefiting victims/survivors (Barrett and St. Pierre 2011; DuMont et al. 2005; Gover, Tomsich, and Richards 2015; Sabina, Cuevas, and Schally 2012). Vital to women's resilience was continuing acknowledgment by important people, such as friends, family members, or professionals, that what they had experienced was indeed horrible and not their fault. Validation of their experiences from significant people in the women's lives never ceased to be welcome.

Both spirituality and religiosity have been found to be sources of healing (Potter 2007), even for individuals not affiliated with a formal religious institution. The women had a complicated relationship with both their faith and any religious affiliations. While one-third of the sample described themselves as deeply religious, both during and after their abusive relationships, they were not necessarily churchgoing. Some women, after leaving their abuser, found solace in a new church, particularly if they had not received emotional support from their former congregation. Some said their faith had been rekindled and they no longer felt abandoned by God or the church as they had during their abusive relationship. Others turned to spiritual practices such as prayer, meditation, or being in nature. Many felt they would not have made it through their horrific experiences if not for the "grace of God." Thus faith of one kind or another was a strength and a resource for many. For some women, faith did not offer any solace. Even they, however, found ways to understand and draw meaning from their abuse.

Over one-third of the women credited journaling or writing as something that saved their sanity and helped them find meaning in their lives once their relationship ended. In her recent book describing her resilience after her husband died suddenly while they were vacationing, Facebook's chief operating officer Sheryl Sandberg (Sandberg and Grant 2017) credits the therapeutic nature of journaling as a way to handle emotional pain. Writing about one's traumatic experiences has been found to be healing since it uses both the emotional and the analytic parts of the brain (see Frattaroli 2006; Pennebaker and Smyth 2016); like meditation, it is an exercise often encouraged by therapists to help their clients process experiences (Rosenthal 2013).[1]

Many women went back to school, some of them completing a college education that had been interrupted by their abuser. Others started college for the first time, since they had believed their abusers' comments that they were too dumb for college or that a "good wife and mother" did not work outside the home. Pursuing an education or a career was a cherished freedom, along with finding a quality therapist who could support their budding confidence and transformation. Women also sought education for specific, problem-solving reasons: they wanted to know everything about the legal and criminal justice process so that they could curtail their abusers' attempts to stalk them or to manipulate them by sabotaging civil protective orders, or they sought knowledge about any kind of local, state, or federal programs that would help or educate them financially.

As time went on, the women's feelings of personal competence expanded, helping them confront new challenges. This newly gained independence to make their own decisions and gain confidence in asserting their preferences is reminiscent of what Sharp-Jeffs, Kelly, and Klein (2017) call "space for action" in describing survivors' restoration of agency and freedom in their study of one hundred women who left abusive relationships and were followed for three years after accessing IPV/A services in England (see also Kelly, Sharp, and Klein 2014).

Women also moved past feeling weak on account of their victimization and instead highlighted more valued traits that reflected survivorship, such as tenacity, empowerment, and courage (see Dunn 2005; Leisenring 2006). This process was bolstered by their interactions with other women who had experienced victimization but had been transformed from victims to survivors (see Naples 2003). Although they acknowledged their victimization, they shifted their perspective to one in which the abuse no longer defined them. Abigayle's admonition to women trying to leave their relationship was "Don't let it become who you are." Gaining mastery over their past meant that their first story was no longer about their abusive past. The women saw themselves as multifaceted in that their past contributed to who they were now and who they no longer wished to be. Thus, in Goffmanesque terms, "victim" was no longer the women's master status, even when women spoke in public about their abusive former relationships.

For many of the women, it was not until they began to help others, whether through the kinds of legislative and speaking activities conducted by WIND members or through the one-to-one advocacy that others practiced, that they realized they could contribute to the movement to eradicate IPV/A. All of the women experienced a desire to change other women's lives for the better. Their efforts raised their self-esteem, and most of the women talked with pride about how they had tackled and accomplished things they had never expected to attempt. Three women completed master's degrees and three completed PhDs. Half of these degrees were in areas that had something to do with victim services, social justice, or global violence issues. Survivors becoming advocates is not uncommon, and many of the women discussed how their own experiences gave them greater empathy and understanding of other abused women's plight. The women's paths here are consistent with Wood's (2017) finding that over 80 percent of her sample of women working in IPV/A-focused agencies were survivors themselves who believed they had a greater awareness of victims' situations and a strong calling to their jobs. In my project, women not working directly with IPV/A agencies were still engaged in the cause. One woman, with her new husband, regularly hosted a fundraiser at their house that was connected to state efforts to end IPV/A. Another woman helped get a bill passed in her state that allows financial compensation for innocent victims of crime. Activism, a commitment to social justice, or a willingness to talk about one's personal struggles and triumphs either in front of a group or in a private conversation with one other person gave the women hope for a more fulfilling future. As committed individuals using their individual strengths or their combined assets to work toward a common goal, they showed both collective and individual efficacy.

Women repeatedly described how constrained they were by gender ideals in terms of the police or the court judging them as "unfeminine" or as undeserving victims if they challenged their abusers or demanded certain protections or assurances in court. Since gendered assumptions about women align with their victimization, more empathy accrues to victims who conform to a portrayal of the battered woman as quiet and passive. These traits were ones that abusers expected as well, so women who did not acquiesce to their ex-partners' demands risked retaliation. The court, with all of its power, mirrors the power imbalance and lack of control that women experience in abusive relationships, particularly with regard to proceedings around custody, support, and visitation. Yet as women moved away from the control of their abusers, they challenged the courts' paternalism in trivializing their sufferings and fears and the courts' outright bias in treating abusers with more respect than victims. One of the more striking ways in which the women changed once they were five or more years away from their abusive relationship was that they moved from being passive in their interactions with system professionals to feeling validated and legitimate in voicing their concerns. No longer under the eye of their abuser, they felt empowered to ask for what they wanted or needed. At the same time, they recognized that their situation could become more difficult and that their plans could backfire if they were too assertive and were considered difficult to deal with. Despite this frustrating situation, they were buoyed by something they had not had or allowed themselves to think about while still in the relationships: hope. Hope fortified them in their determination to protect their children and to break the cycle of abuse in their children's generation, and allowed them to see opportunities for personal growth as their courage grew. The women's renewed self-worth, which developed over time following relationship termination, facilitated their assertiveness with the criminal justice system when things mattered. They shared their experiences of navigating the labyrinth of the civil and criminal justice systems and opposing gendered assumptions about their appearance and comportment with other abused women who were still early in the process of separating.

For all the women in my project, resources from people or institutions were crucial in their recovery from IPV/A, whether these consisted of money for first and last months' rent for a new apartment, the loan of a car or the cosigning of a loan, child care assistance, help navigating the baffling process of filing civil protection orders or dealing with the criminal justice system, or information about student loans or scholarships or job training programs. This vital help went beyond the immediate crisis, extending for years after the relationship ended and profoundly affecting women's survivorship.

GROWTH

Despite the positive outcomes addressed so far, as mentioned in chapter 1, many women continued to struggle to incorporate their past experiences into their present identities. They believed they had overcome adversity and faced down the sheer terror of their abuser, yet about half were reluctant to say they were thriving as O'Leary and Ickovics (1995) define it: going beyond functioning to growing vigorously and flourishing. Like the rest of the population, some who have experienced severe trauma and some who have not, the women did not see their lives as particularly remarkable. Joan emphatically declared, "I'm not broken into a ton of pieces, but I'm also not a superhero." At the same time, however, all of the women told me about risks they had taken that surprised them and successes they had had, such as negotiating their employment or a raise or having another child with a new husband. Two of the women had written books for a general audience about their own experiences with IPV/A, and, as mentioned previously, one woman had written a song and donated a portion of her CD profits to help survivors; another woman donated a percentage of her earnings from selling artwork to help battered women. The majority of women said that watching their children grow up in a healthier environment gave them strength to persevere after their relationships ended.

Learning to trust a new partner was a challenge. Three women asked me if I knew about any research that determined when it was safe to start dating seriously again. However, fourteen of the women either had remarried or were engaged, and five others were in serious relationships; only two of the women said they were not dating at all. Only one woman had married another abuser, and this ended in a second divorce, but her third marriage— much to her surprise—was to a wonderfully respectful and gentle man.

One woman determined that she would never be able to trust a man again and at the time of interview was involved only with other women:

> I think I was becoming aware—unconsciously—of the structural and social forces that facilitate violence against women and their children. Although I blamed my abuser for his acts of violence and terrorism against me and the kids, I equally blamed a world that enabled his violence and denied me liberty. And I know . . . that my liberty was denied not only because I was a woman but because I was poor, and that those things were inexorably intertwined with motherhood.

Three women's abusers died in the years after their relationships ended, and these women felt enormous relief. As Pepper put it, "That's the only way this man would have ever left me alone. I have never mourned about him being dead. It's not because I'm mad at him anymore for what he did to me. It's just such a relief."

One emotion that figured prominently in some of the women's discussions of growth and resilience was anger. For Dale, expressing her anger was important because "I was never allowed to be angry. Only he was allowed, and all of his anger was directed at me." Julia stated, "It took time for me to get that strength back. I had to get angry. . . . I knew I had to hold on to my anger, because I knew my anger was my strength."

And although IPV/A is no laughing matter, humor often surfaced as a strategy of resilience. Sociologists have long recognized the functional role of humor in dealing with aspects of social life (Zijderveld 1968), enabling people in similar situations to collectively bear their anxiety; humor is used in this way by patients in hospitals (Coser 1959) and police officers (Pogrebin and Poole 1988). Strategic use of humor can reinforce solidarity in a group that understands the meaning behind the humor in their shared concerns and experiences. "Joking relations among peers generate feelings of implicit understanding and camaraderie, thus strengthening group norms and bonds" (Pogrebin and Poole 1988, 184). Humor can also be used as a coping strategy when individuals need to manage situations that are outside their direct control. Studies support the psychological and health benefits of humor: patients recuperating from surgery who watch comedies ask for 25 percent less pain medication (Rotton and Shats 1996), heart rates are lowered by laughter (Newman and Stone 1996), and soldiers who can use humor with their situations cope better with stress (Bizi, Keinan, and Beit-Hallahmi, 1988, cited in Sandberg and Grant 2017, 214–15).

The interviews with the women and the survivors' task force meetings of WIND often featured irreverent humor, showing how the use of humor in groups can transform tragedy into something less threatening (see

Orbdlik 1942). During one of the WIND meetings, one woman said she felt stigmatized about currently living in a trailer park (she had lived with her abuser in an upper-middle class neighborhood) but believed it was safer to live closer to her neighbors; one neighbor had said that he could look into her bedroom from his living room and that he had a gun in case her ex showed up and caused trouble, at which point she said to the group, "Note to self: wear a robe!" Although humor about situations that appear potentially fatal to an outsider might seem callous or trivializing, for "in-group" members it has both a bonding and cathartic effect and serves to diminish feelings of vulnerability and being alone in the battle. Throughout my fieldwork with the WIND group, stories shared during the meetings used humor to normalize threatening situations, inspiring a sense of mastery over problems (see Holdaway 1984). In my interviews, women sometimes poked fun at themselves when telling stories of their abusers' bizarre behavior and their own former acceptance of it as "normal" or "okay."

Rich, thick narratives emblematic of qualitative research add to quantitative studies about post-traumatic growth of IPV/A survivors. Psychological studies consistently report that 75 to 90 percent of survivors find benefits after trauma (Calhoun and Tedschi 2006). Post-traumatic growth literature is guided by social psychologist Janoff-Bulman's work (1992, 2006) that explores how trauma survivors incorporate their experiences into a worldview that gives them a greater appreciation for life and a sense of purpose; survivors are moved to create a more meaningful existence through goals, interpersonal commitments to friends, family and community, and self-determination. For instance, using quantitative measures to investigate post-traumatic growth in survivors, Valdez and Lilly (2015) found that a positive assumptive worldview change (a more positive sense of meaning and value in their lives) occurred only for women who did not experience revictimization in the one year between assessments. Revictimization included a range of experiences, not just IPV/A.[2] The survivors I studied had been out of their abusive relationships for at least five years, often many more than five, providing a much longer time frame to assess post-traumatic growth and resilience. They were successful in integrating their abusive experiences and envisioned the world as a less threatening place. Overall, they were optimistic about their journeys and their futures. This optimism was somewhat tempered for survivors still enmeshed in the court system on account of custody and visitation issues, but these women kept struggling and drew upon their honed skills and psychological resources, not succumbing to former patterns of self-blame and doubt. Though they expressed their frustration with social institutions such as the courts or the church, they became more astute navigators of these institutions and systems over time.

In what was not a linear process, resilience waxed and waned, but post-traumatic growth manifested more and more as time passed. The women created deeper connections with people in their lives and talked about their increased appreciation of their lives and their greater satisfaction with their own well-being. These outcomes are consistent with recent research on military veterans who endured great emotional difficulties and struggled with PTSD but ultimately experienced a greater awareness of possibilities, enhanced inner strength, and other benefits of personal growth (Morgan and Desmaris 2017). Despite inevitable twists and turns on the path to survivorship, the stories of these women reveal their achievement of resilience.

POLICY IMPLICATIONS

Social and Economic Services

Narratives of women's lives offer many insights on policies that can be helpful for women who have left their abuser and are beyond the immediate crisis. Not surprisingly, many women I interviewed raised financial concerns as obstacles to their full autonomy for many years after their relationships ended. Recent research finds that the economic consequences of IPV/A can persist for three to six years after the relationship ends (Adams et. al. 2013; Crowne et al. 2011; Schrag 2015). In addition, the frequent tendency to lose informal social ties during an abusive relationship hinders women's development of a social network that can help with further employment and career opportunities (Kelly, Sharp, and Klein 2014; Sylaska and Edwards 2014). Without money of their own, women have few resources to help them hire attorneys, obtain divorces, fight custody and/or visitation battles, challenge frivolous court proceedings initiated by their abusers, find a safe alternative place to live, get job training, or cover educational costs. When abusers block their partners' access to family finances, as Joan noted, "the simple act of leaving is daunting, much less having no prospects for money for the future."

Neoliberal policies to privatize social services, cut back state funding of programs, reduce public services, and promote citizens' personal responsibility to achieve economic independence rather than rely on government assistance are particularly onerous for women trying to leave abusive relationships (see Peled and Krigel 2016). Brush's (2011) work excoriates these policies for trivializing the experiences and real needs of low-income women who are hemmed in by intersecting class, gender, and ethnic/race barriers and often are victims of IPV/A. Danielle, who had several children, one with a disability that entailed many hospitalizations out of state, and another who needed a lot of therapy once it was revealed that the father had been sexually abusing her, depended on the $400 a month she received in child support. But she fell under the "welfare to work" restrictions, which prevented her from finishing her education and getting a job that would pay enough to support her children. "Welfare to work is a joke," she concluded.

Other women I interviewed similarly described how governmental agencies such as child and family services and disability, health, and social security offices not only failed to aid them but, in Reeva's words, put "salt in the wounds." Dale experienced a catch-22 situation involving government red tape: her ex-husband got his sentence reduced from six to three years (after attempting to murder her) by claiming a disability. Dale fought it because she knew he was not disabled and wanted him to serve his full sentence. But since the court ultimately ruled in his favor, she received an extra $500 a month from social security, which allowed her to buy laptop computers and extracurricular lessons for her children. Then the court reversed the ruling and Dale owed them $12,000 in back social security. Earlier, when she was still fighting for her life in the hospital after her husband attempted to murder her, the state came after her over his gambling debt.

Health insurance—its availability and affordability—is a big issue for victims of IPV/A. The women in my study often brought up long-term health issues stemming from their exes' abuse, such as problems with kidneys, noticeable burn marks, vision problems, and stress-related concerns. Dale had to have her own insurance company sue her abuser's health care provider to pay her medical bills for hospitalization when her abuser hit her with his car because his action—attempted murder—was premeditated and not covered. If survivors' insurance policies do not cover injuries caused by the abusers, it would be helpful for all states to enact policies that allow them to apply for health-related financial help from victim compensation funds. Several provisions of the Obama administration's Affordable Care Act (ACA) help victims of IPV/A, including domestic violence screening and counseling with no copays, protections against insurance discrimination, and outreach programs for women experiencing IPV/A during pregnancy and after the birth of a child. As the new Republican administration gets under way in 2017 with its promise to reform or repeal the ACA, new worries abound for the continued protections in place now for IPV/A victims.

Abusers' refusal to "permit" women to work outside the home or get further education, because of the family's real or imagined need for a parent to stay home with the children or because of concerns of jealousy, put some of the women at a disadvantage both before and after the relationship ended. Jazzy strongly believed in women's abilities to parlay skills they already had into a real job: "If you can cook, if you can bake, you can make money. I made money by selling my spring rolls. You take your everyday skills and you learn to use them." Her entrepreneurial spirit under the bleakest of conditions is emblematic of the motivation with which women sought out employment opportunities. During a relationship with an abuser, women are subjected to increased IPV/A when they work outside the home (Brush 2011), but for the women I interviewed, their work gave them temporary relief from their stressful situations and seemed well worth the risks (see also Sauber and O'Brien 2017). And once the relationship was over, many eagerly pursued more job training and education that would increase their employability.

Although shelters can provide short-term aid for women in immediate crisis, more long-term interventions are needed. Peled and Krigel (2016, 133) urge that programs to help IPV/A survivors gain financial independence "go beyond the personal" to encompass a wide-ranging structural response: training social services workers to become more aware of the problem and better able to address it; crafting responses to the unique cultural challenges of marginalized populations; lobbying politicians to sponsor legislation that removes barriers to economic advancement; strengthening protection orders; and partnering social services with higher education and job training. Long-term financial security needs to be the goal. It would be helpful to consider reentry programs, like those for former inmates or for war veterans, that would target IPV/A survivors and provide them the resources to reintegrate successfully into community life—for instance, through victim compensation funds for housing or job training assistance, or through Pell grants to subsidize college for students with financial need. Peer mentoring could also aid with establishing a continuum of care for the extended period of time that long-term survivors of abuse may need. Clearly there is a vital need for transitional housing while survivors work toward establishing and maintaining employment and long-term housing solutions, with respite from the abuse and stress they endured, since shelters provide only short-term refuge for immediate crises. Difficulties in securing social services are exacerbated for impoverished survivors in marginalized populations, such as immigrants, residents in remote and rural areas, and sexual and racial/ethnic minorities (see, for instance, O'Neal and Beckman 2017, for an intersectional analysis of the barriers to social services experienced by Latina IPV/A victims). For survivors in rural areas who face geographic isolation and technological deserts, DeKeseredy and colleagues suggest specific recommendations such as transportation subsidies and note the need for broader efforts that include dealing with rural racism and building a more diverse rural economy to expand work opportunities (see DeKeseredy 2015; DeKeseredy and Joseph 2006; DeKeseredy and Schwartz 2009).

Economic dependency on an abuser makes survivors more vulnerable, more likely to stay with or return to their abuser, and less likely to pursue restraining orders (Sanders 2011). Although some research suggests that greater financial autonomy is threatening to abusers and that violence can increase when women work, increase their employability through more education or training, or try to separate their own assets from the abuser's (see Macmillan and Gartner 1999; Moe and Bell 2004), many women I interviewed desired more financial education, more financial independence, and more opportunities to save for goals that would better their lives, such as getting a home of their own, their own transportation, education, or job training. Research findings suggest that asset ownership contributes to enhanced well-being in terms of economic security, household stability, physical health, educational attainment, and civic involvement (Scalon and Page-Adams 2001). Benefits for children are also associated with asset ownership among female-headed households, including their cognitive development, their educational attainment, and parental expectations (Zahn and Sherraden 2001), as is overall financial self-efficacy (Sanders, Weaver, and Schnabel 2007). Yet despite these positive associations with economic, social and psychological benefits, women are less likely than men to own assets (Sanders and Porterfield 2010).

One way to address the economic instability of survivors is to encourage asset-building programs. Initiatives that assist lower-income families in acquiring assets have been around for a couple of decades and strive to encourage savings and retirement plans using Individual Development Accounts (IDAs), which match individual/family contributions to savings accounts by private or government programs, and microenterprise development programs, which match savings to start or support development of a small business (see Sherraden 2001; Sherraden, Sanders, and Sherraden 2004). IPV/A programs that integrate asset-building strategies could provide important ways to combat the devastating consequences of economic abuse and insecurity (Sanders 2011). And indeed community initiatives in this area show positive results (Postmus 2010; Postmus et al. 2013; Sanders and Schnabel 2006). For instance, Sanders and Schnabel (2006) conducted one of the few published reviews of an IDA program designed for IPV/A survivors in St. Louis that coordinated thirteen domestic violence and three homeless service agencies to develop economic services for low-income battered women, including a twelve-hour economic education program and a program that provided matching funds for women's savings. Preliminary reports based on in-depth interviews with thirty early participants in the matched-savings program or the economic education program found that women showed both behavioral changes, such as creating and following a budget, saving consistently, changing their consumer habits, and teaching their own children the importance of saving, and psychological effects, such as increased self-esteem and positive feelings about themselves, pride in setting goals, better focus and motivation to achieve goals, greater self-confidence, future orientation plans, and hope (Sanders 2007, 2010, 2011). These findings suggest that IPV/A survivors' participation in IDA programs could increase their financial stability and in turn increase their safety and future well-being.[3]

Mental Health Services

Far too many of the women related stories about therapists who did not understand the dynamics of IPV/A and saw the couple together without recognizing how the abuser's control manifested in the sessions. Years after the relationship ended, a number of the women—at least a quarter of those I interviewed—craved a group setting where they could receive group counseling or at least talk to other women who had been in similar situations. As time went on, some found it important to grieve the good parts of a bad relationship, a process best understood by other survivors. Others wanted a group to continue to help them recognize their strengths and how far they had come. Longer-term support groups seemed especially welcomed by women who had grown up witnessing their mothers having no power to stop victimization by their fathers. Those who felt that a support group for long-term survivors would be helpful tended to be, not the WIND members, but the women who were not public activists and did not, as a rule, share their personal histories with other people. They wished that crisis hotlines offered an option to be connected with a responder who could just talk and listen to them, instead of being trained to respond mostly to crisis situations with police and shelter information (though of course the women understood the necessity of providing this kind of information). It would be helpful for hotline training to expand to include this option.

Many women benefited from therapy while they were in a shelter or separating from their abuser. Yet after survivors move beyond the immediate crisis and are no longer connected to shelters and victim support services, it can be difficult for them to find a group that is appropriate for long-term survivors, and this is especially a problem for women who cannot afford private therapy. Other models that provide ongoing and long-term support for former addicts (such as Narcotics Anonymous, or Alcoholics Anonymous) or for the grieving (often under the auspices of a church) could be replicated, since activist groups like WIND are not always what survivors seek. Efforts at women's shelters or at other community-based locations to provide low- or no-cost counseling for women who have left IPV/A and moved beyond the immediate crisis should increase. These efforts could support long-term survivors as well as create peer support for women who want to end their relationships but still think living without their abuser is unfathomable. Peer-to-peer "talk" sessions—such as those set up by WIND with residents at local battered women's shelters—can extend some of the peer support and wisdom that activist groups provide their members to women who do not wish to engage in collective activism. They can showcase women's tenacity and fortitude in rebuilding their confidence and inspire victims/survivors still trapped in abusive relationships. As noted earlier, knowing one person who experienced positive growth after ending an abusive relationship can be a catalyst for leaving (Cobb et al. 2006).

Information Technology and Women's Safety

Survivors' economic and psychological well-being depends on their being able to take full advantage of our technological society, whether for job searching or for maintaining connections to workplaces, friends, family, and other resources and sources of support. However, abusers have found ways to weaponize this technology, mostly by using phones, computers, GPS tracking, and social media outlets to stalk, abuse, or harass their exes (for instance, by posting sexualized content online). Eighty-four percent of the IPV/A victims surveyed in an Australian study said that unwanted technology-facilitated contact had an adverse effect on their psychological well-being (Woodlock 2017). While online sites can be helpful and instructive for victims seeking help and connecting with resources, abusers take advantage of easy access to victims despite relationship termination. When survivors have to relocate, close social media accounts, or change phone numbers to avoid contact with their exes, their isolation increases, creating higher levels of psychological distress (Logan and Walker 2009) and depression and suicidal behavior (WHO 2013). Domestic violence organizations have launched campaigns to educate victims of IPV/A about how to block their abuser's attempts to monitor their phone calls, e-mails, and social media and to track their movements. But effective policies and laws must also address this form of coercive control (Woodlock 2017). The communication industry could help respond to the need to protect survivors from technology-facilitated abuse by training workers to recognize such practices and developing safety resources to combat this type of stalking.

Workplaces

Much more is known today about the ramifications of economic abuse and how abusers continue to sabotage survivors' employment after the relationship ends, including violating protection orders. As Dale's story told earlier illustrated, survivors may not be safe at work, even years after the relationship has ended. Many women indicated that their workplaces—though physically located away from their abusers (at least for those able to work outside the home)—were not safe havens. Too many employers know nothing about IPV/A and have taken few or no steps to ensure employees' safety. While several of the women had supervisors or bosses who showed understanding and empathy, most women were terrified to tell their supervisors or coworkers about their abusive exes out of shame and a fear of being fired if there was drama in the workplace. Workplaces should adopt policies that protect workers who are victims of IPV/A and that clearly spell out responses to keep them and coworkers safe in the workplace. Research is available that calculates the costs of IPV/A in the workplace, and various top companies (e.g., Allstate, Liz Claiborne fashions, Verizon, Avon) have made it part of their corporate mission to stop/prevent IPV/A. Helpful guidelines for responding to workplace situations and for following protection orders can be found at www.workplacerespond.org. One suggestion is to make organizational recognition of IPV/A a mandatory part of human resources training (Collins 2011), along the lines of what has been done with the issue of sexual harassment in the workplace (Peled and Krigel 2016).[4]

The Criminal Justice System

Reform efforts are often stymied by the patriarchal nature of the criminal justice system. Though we have some legal remedies to hold offenders accountable, they are often circumvented. Further, what surprised me during this project was that even though funding has been allocated for training justice system personnel about IPV/A, with the aim of transforming victim-blaming and victim-stigmatizing attitudes, so many of the women's stories about their experiences with police and the courts indicated that the actual behavior of system professionals has not caught up with expectations.

Women critiqued the criminal justice system at length. Many had hoped for a more understanding response by law enforcement, but research reveals that police often make their own decisions about what is normative behavior for both victims and offenders and act on the basis of their assumptions (S. Miller 2005; O'Dell 2007; Stalans and Finn 1995), often believing that abused women lack credibility and are somehow to blame for the abuse (DeJong, Burgess-Proctor, and Elis 2008; Goodmark 2008). Some of the women had used force to protect themselves or their children and had been arrested as a result. Meda Chesney-Lind (2006) has described this kind of response as "vengeful equity"—a form of gender-blind treatment by the major institutions of society that fails to see a larger context of inequity (Larance 2007; S. Miller 2005; Osthoff 2002; Pence and Dasgupta 2006). This issue of using gender-neutral proarrest policies must be revisited. Although the criminal justice system's response to treat IPV/A more seriously was lauded initially, given the abysmal record of the legal system in holding batterers accountable and its trivialization of IPV/A cases (Buzawa and Buzawa 2003; Schechter 1982), in the past several decades research has documented that an acontextual response to IPV/A effectively collapses men and women's use of force as one and the same, rather than seeing survivors' motivations of survival and resistance as distinct from preemptive, aggressive, and coercive force (Haviland et al. 2001; Henning and Feder 2004; S. Miller 2005; Rajan and McCloskey 2007). Indeed, as exemplified in the stories of the six women in my study who were arrested or threatened with arrest, survivors' use of force is more likely to occur in response to their abusers' violence or threat of violence and rarely results in the control men have over the women they abuse (see also Larance and Miller 2016). If police followed training to identify the primary aggressor in IPV/A situations, the power asymmetry could be exposed.

Pressure has intensified to urge police and prosecutors to consider context in order to prevent the criminalizing of victimization (see Larance and Miller 2015, 2016; Richie 2000). Primary aggressor training for law enforcement that acknowledges the context and complexity of women's use of force, in addition to a zero-tolerance policy for officer responses that do not address lethality questions, will be most efficacious. Domestic violence specialty courts could also improve equitable treatment, as the Center for Court Innovation (CCI 2013) has advocated.

Although improvements are evident in some jurisdictions, such as intentional coordinated responses involving the courts, justice agencies, and community service providers (Harrell et al. 2009), the system still falls short in its response to IPV/A. For example, in 1999 the National Institute of Justice selected three sites across the nation for Justice Oversight Demonstrations (JODs) where criminal justice agencies formed partnerships with community agencies to develop an effective response to IPV/A that would emphasize the role of the court, and specifically the judge. This response featured *uniform and consistent initial responses to domestic violence offenses*, including proarrest policies, arrest of the primary aggressor, and a coordinated response by law enforcement and victim advocates; *coordinated victim advocacy and services*, including contact by victim advocates as soon as possible after a domestic violence incident, an individualized "safety plan" for the victim, and provision of needed services; and *strong offender accountability and oversight*, including intensive court-based supervision, referral to appropriate batterer intervention programs, and administrative and judicial sanctions and incentives to influence offender behavior. Results, published in 2008, found increased offender accountability for IPV/A (e.g., more probation requirements, increased likelihood of conviction), and victims' greater satisfaction with the police, prosecutor, and courts. Some victims achieved greater understanding of the legal process, and the JODs also increased victim contact with probation agents. These findings suggest continued partnerships between criminal justice agencies and community-based agencies (including nonprofit service providers) can be developed to provide more consistent and uniform responses and to help connect victims to advocates and services more quickly. However, the JODs did not create heightened belief among offenders that IPV would result in negative legal consequences, and victims reported continued barriers to prosecution, including fear of abuser retaliation, as well as scheduling conflicts created by the inflexibility of court appearance dates.

The fear of abuser retaliation at the time of court appearances was a frequently raised concern among the women in my project. Many women pointed out that when they went to court they had to park in the same parking lots, ride the same elevators, and walk through the same door as their exes, a problem faced by most other victims and offenders as well. Courtroom reforms often include separate waiting rooms, but the risks of getting to the waiting room are unaddressed. Some courthouses do arrange to escort high-risk victims to their cars following court appearances, but again, this is not taking into account the entry into court. Further, most courts do not allow cell phones in the courthouse, so this potential safety tool for victims to remain in contact with anyone if they need help is absent as well. Thus there are still many opportunities for courthouse safety reforms.

Civil Courts

The civil court system featured prominently in women's suggestions for overhaul. Women without children, though they were sometimes stalked by their exes, achieved finality with the courts once the relationship ended and any lingering financial or legal issues were resolved. For women with children, however, the process of leaving never really ended. Exes often engaged in "paper abuse," multiplying court actions to harass women and deplete their financial resources. Winnie said that "for the initial six years post-relationship, I did not have a single day without a pending court date." Although Terri had an active Protection from Abuse order (PFA), it expired after a year and "he kept trying to modify the PFA so I kept going back to court, arranging extra child care and taking time off work without pay." Terri's husband continued to drag her into court with frivolous motions: "It is a form of abuse; our file at court, it's as high as my waist. You have to wheel it out on a cart." Weariness over the relentless court procedures was evident in the women's descriptions of feeling beaten down metaphorically by the system after the literal abuse they sustained at the hands of their abusers had ended.

Moreover, courts reinforce the notion that a "real" IPV/A victim is physically abused. Both mediators and judges demand to see evidence and dismiss allegations of abuse without that evidence (E. Rivera, Sullivan, and Zeoli 2012). This introduces a quandary for victims who can document physical abuse but not emotional abuse, even though research has shown that women feel emotional abuse to be more controlling and to have graver, longer-term consequences than physical violence. Many women who experience psychological/emotional abuse and terror from their abusers are unconvincing to the court because their testimonies do not meet arrest or evidentiary standards (see also E. Rivera, Sullivan, and Zeoli 2012).

Negative experiences with the legal system after the relationship add up; deleterious and demeaning interactions between victims/survivors and the courts regarding divorce, custody, and visitation issues can affect women's future willingness to seek help. When the women in Rivera, Sullivan, and Zeoli's (2012, 246) study of women with IPV/A backgrounds seeking a divorce were disbelieved and demeaned in court, they no longer saw the legal system as a viable avenue to pursue to achieve justice or protection for themselves and their children, and "their experiences were so negative they indicated they would not even tell anyone else about the abuse because of the mediators' reaction."

Addressing procedural justice is an important goal if we want to inspire faith in the legal system and encourage victims/survivors to trust judicial and other legal professionals. When victims/survivors feel heard, respected, listened to, and safe, they characterize their experience positively and are more willing to see the court as their ally. This faith in the legitimacy of the system prevails even if the outcome is negative (Tyler 1984, 1988). But when victims/survivors feel they are interrogated or blamed for their victimization, disbelieved or dismissed, this has serious consequences for future help seeking and for belief in the legitimacy of the justice process (S. Herman 2011). In the arena of family court, with custody and visitation decisions at stake, the women I interviewed perceived the justice system as treating them with disrespect and hostility and favoring their abusers. This "second victimization," as described by Rivera, Sullivan, and Zeoli (2012) and Watson and Ancis (2013) and by the women in my study, retraumatizes victims/survivors.

The Family Court Enhancement Project, launched in 2013 as a collaborative effort with the DOJ's Office on Violence against Women, the National Council of Juvenile and Family Court Judges, the National Institute of Justice, and the Battered Women's Justice Project, selected four courts to implement better approaches for keeping IPV/A victims and their children safe throughout and beyond court proceedings. This two-year project captures precisely the custody issues the women voiced time and time again in my interviews, such as the court's failure to identify and understand IPV/A both in court and in third-party assessments; structural and procedural barriers; limited legal and advocacy resources; and the effects of race, class, and gender biases on outcomes.[5]

Success in obtaining a civil protection order is affected by whether a victim/survivor has an attorney. A 2015 study by the Institute for Policy Integrity at the New York University School of Law found that 83 percent of IPV/A victims who had an attorney obtained protection orders, while only 32 percent of those without legal representation did (Rosenberg and Grab 2015). Given how much the women were baffled and frustrated by the court process when they felt they were acting in the best interest of their children, increasing pro bono legal representation for women in civil court would make a difference. At the very least, connecting women with advanced law students or clinics at local law schools could go a long way to balance the scales of justice when offenders with legal representation face victims.

Moreover, the court process for obtaining protection orders often reproduces broader social inequalities. Victims are required to submit a narrative of abuse even when medical and police report documentation is available, and often must frame their narrative without legal assistance. Alesha

Durfee's work shows that orders are usually denied because of "something in the writing," such as insufficient detail or clarity. The assumption is that the narrative requirement is "victim friendly." But it is difficult for victims—who are traumatized, fearful, and sleep-deprived—to testify about their abuse in a public setting in the face of implicit expectations that they should be able to clearly articulate, verbally or in writing, facts about their abuse, and have enough distance from the situation to be able to fully discuss the abuse (Durfee 2015, 472). Durfee (2015) also suggests there is a disconnection between how victims frame their definition of abuse and the goals of the legal system, which can backfire when the court seeks a structure and emphasis that is more formal and legalistic than what victims often provide; this situation is exacerbated for victims lacking legal counsel and tends to result in a lower likelihood of obtaining a protection order. Finally, Durfee (2009) found that gender-based assumptions, such as stereotypical beliefs about what "real" victims were like, biased judges' reading of the narratives. Consequently she recommends that the requirement for narratives of abuse be removed as unnecessarily traumatic and prejudicial to victims and that it be replaced by evidentiary material to support victimization claims as well as checklists to indicate forms of abuse (Durfee 2015, 483–84).

Gun Regulation

The women I interviewed reported that their abusers possessed numerous firearms, even under circumstances where court orders dictated that they were not allowed to do so. Since it has been well established that the presence of firearms in an IPV/A relationship increases the risk of lethal injury or death (J. Campbell et al. 2003; Sorenson and Wiebe 2004), efforts to disarm abusers must be more vigilantly enforced. One court watch project where IPV/A victims sought civil protection orders revealed that when IPV/A victims sought civil protection orders, judges often failed to mention firearm prohibitions (Fleury-Steiner, Miller, and Carcirieri 2017). Given the increase in legal gun ownership reported in 2016 (Jacques 2016), much more needs to be done to ensure victims' safety, despite efforts to increase the scope of background checks and enact new restrictions. Perhaps more judicial monitoring and improvements in court oversight, as well as expanded training for probation officers to better track how guns change hands after protection orders are granted, could assist in this regard and reinforce the laws that are already in place. Zeoli et al.'s (2017) recent study revealed that while twenty-nine states and Washington, D.C., have enacted laws to augment federal law prohibiting abusers under restraining orders from possessing firearms, many laws do not adequately detail to whom firearms must be relinquished, whether the abuser must seek permission to transfer the firearm to a third party, when the dispossession must occur, and who has the authority (law enforcement or courts) to remove the firearm or to order a search and seizure for it. Clearly, these issues must be addressed. In July 2017, Washington became the first state to enact a law requiring victims to be notified when an abuser (either convicted or under an active restraining order) attempts to buy a firearm. This measure not only increases victim safety but also ensures that abusers will be prosecuted (Kahn 2017). Washington's legislation addresses the problem of abusers lying on background checks, a federal offense that is rarely prosecuted, and establishes a grant program to assist authorities in investigations. This is a timely precedent that other states would do well to follow so that abusers' attempts to circumvent court action are no longer tolerated.

PUBLIC AWARENESS CAMPAIGNS

Despite the explosion of material available to the public about IPV/A, many women talked about not having access to resources until a therapist or police officer or university professor provided information. Many of the women did not know about shelters or lived where there were none or considered moving to a shelter too disruptive since they had children in school. Although resources and options have vastly improved in recent years, and the Internet provides quick access to information, there is still a need to provide resource material to people who have limited technological access, live in rural areas, or are terrified to reach out for Internet-based help for fear their abuser can trace their Internet history. Some IPV/A websites include a link to press immediately if someone enters the room who should not see what is onscreen.

Many of the women in my project were younger when their relationships started and lacked public access to resources to learn about healthy and unhealthy relationships. Today, children in school are more technologically savvy and connected to social media, and can easily retrieve information safely on healthy relationships or IPV/A at school or in libraries or community settings. But there is still a need for more public education campaigns to destigmatize victims/survivors and challenge social toleration of abuse.

Many local, state, and national anti-IPV/A campaigns have addressed these issues, and efforts should continue to expand to include the use of social media. Given the safety and vulnerability issues faced by IPV/A victims, innovative strategies that target women-only spaces, such as the posting of resources in bathrooms at gynecological offices, can be especially helpful. A newly enacted 2017 law in Illinois requires hair stylists to receive training in domestic abuse prevention as part of their licensing process because of the close relationships that cosmetologists develop with their clients and the abuse they often see as they style hair or do manicures (Penman 2017).

Religion

Clearly, religious leaders and congregations can play a positive or negative role in situations of IPV/A, and many need more information on the subject. The women's narratives documented how religious institutions that subscribed to traditional gender roles tended to excuse offenders' behavior, offer counseling for the offender or couples counseling, or reinforce the importance of the institution of marriage at the expense of women's safety. This victim blaming often catalyzed women to try to educate their religious community about IPV/A several years after they had ended their abusive relationships. A few women said their ministers or priests had provided understanding and support for them to leave abusive men. Clergy who provide alternative readings of scripture that can support victims/survivors— for example, by challenging the doctrine of wifely submission to husbands or by challenging writings against divorce—can help break the religious coercive control that some abusers employ. Church leaders can also educate and encourage their congregations to offer comfort and practical help to victims/survivors in their midst. The long history of faith communities' commitment to social justice provides the infrastructure to include IPV/A as a community concern. Relatedly, shelters and social service providers may underestimate the importance of the role faith and religion play, particularly for women of color (Fowler and Hill 2004; Gillum, Sullivan, and Bybee 2006; Senter and Caldwell 2002). Women who indicate deeper religiosity tend to stay in their abusive relationships/marriages longer than women with less religiosity, which has implications for intervention as well (Horton, Wilkins, and Wright 1988).

IPV/A AS A PUBLIC HEALTH ISSUE

Although the US surgeon general designated domestic violence as one of the fifteen top public health initiatives as early as 1979, it was not until 1994, when the first Violence against Women Act was passed, that the Centers for Disease Control and Prevention (CDC) and the National Institute of Justice (the research arm of the Department of Justice) collaborated on the National Violence against Women Survey to gather data on the incidence and prevalence of intimate partner violence, sexual violence, and stalking. That same year, the CDC received funds to promote coordinated community responses to prevent IPV/A and to provide rape prevention and education block grants. Many efforts were then made to approach intimate partner abuse as a public health issue as the research findings revealed an epidemic of vast proportions.[6] The CDC strives to combat epidemics with primary, secondary, and tertiary prevention strategies. Primary prevention seeks to prevent injury before it occurs, often by preventing exposure to hazards through legislation, changing behaviors through educating people about healthier habits, and increasing resistance. The stories of the women in this project that highlight their special vulnerability to abuse, especially when they were young and when they came from abusive families, suggest the importance of anti-IPV/A programs beginning in the K-12 years. Children should learn how to engage in safe and respectful relationships, to resolve conflict nonviolently, improve interpersonal communication skills, treat others in nonsexist ways, and develop self-esteem and respect for others. Gender scholar Nan Stein's work is groundbreaking in this regard, as are the CDC-sponsored DELTA (Domestic Violence Prevention Enhancements and Leadership through Alliances) projects.[7] Bruce Taylor et al. (2011) received a federal grant in 2011 to help fifty-five middle schools develop dating violence, sexual violence, and sexual harassment prevention programs to challenge and change violence-supportive attitudes and norms in this age group, with the long-term goal of creating sustainable strategies and programs to address these issues for all youth. Their early findings suggest that school-level interventions reduced dating violence among middle school students by up to 50 percent in thirty public schools in New York City. Given that abuse in adolescent dating relationships is common—the National Survey of Teen Relationships and Intimate Violence found that two-thirds of adolescents experience psychological victimization and one in five experience physical and/or sexual victimization, with perpetration rates for psychological, sexual, and/or physical violence almost as high (B. Taylor and Mumford 2016)—researchers Mumford, Taylor, and Giordano (2017) urge further study on the role of toleration for violence among teen friendship groups and how different norms can be cultivated as a means of prevention.

Many women in my project thought it might be helpful to talk with young people who were just starting to date so they could recognize the warning signs and aspire to have healthy relationships. The women stressed that there must be balance in relationships so that, as Amy said, they would "think about what is the hook that keeps them there. . . . What are you really getting out of it? How can you get it somewhere else since the price tag is too big to stay?"

Katherine also felt the message needed to be proactive when teenagers were just beginning to date, using scare tactics if necessary: "You are going to have to get out of this relationship; you can either do it by choice or someone can carry you out in a body bag." Kristen's cogent suggestion for early education stemmed from her own naïveté: "I wish I had understood power dynamics and finances before I got married, and everyone should know more about the justice system."

To reduce the impact of IPV/A, secondary prevention efforts would detect and treat the injuries, helping survivors return to better health and develop personal strategies to prevent recurrence. Usually we see these efforts emerging during physician exams or screenings (ASPE 2013), and for IPV/A survivors the practice of querying patients about any ongoing issues related to IPV/A can help. Extending the checklist of symptoms or injuries beyond physical ones would better encompass the full range of IPV/A, especially since a number of the women I talked with did not always believe that the emotional abuse "counted" as IPV/A. If patients are not asked the right questions or if medical professionals do not know what to ask or how to follow up—especially if the abuse happened years before—an opportunity is missed to help with long-term resilience. In one research project, outpatient visits by survivors to health care facilities continued for up to sixteen years after abuse (F. Rivera, Anderson, and Fishman 2007); early research on this revealed that fewer than 2 percent of women had been asked about IPV/A by family practice doctors or nurses (Hamberger, Saunders, and Hovey 1992), and only about one-tenth of victims had been identified in emergency settings (Stark, Flitcraft, and Frazier 1979), although these numbers have been improving more recently (Ambuel et al. 2013). Recommendations about screening for IPV/A and providing counseling made by the Institute of Medicine, the US Preventive Services Task Force, and the Department of Health and Human Services have been adopted by the Affordable Care Act.[8] Research on the barriers related to screening and intervention for IPV/A in health care settings reveals that limited training, time constraints, lack of protocols and policies, and differing departmental philosophies of care are often in conflict with screening recommendations, though models for implementing system change and evaluating these efforts are lacking and will take time to develop (Hamberger, Rhodes, and Brown 2015).

Finally, tertiary prevention efforts are needed to help people manage long-term health issues in order to improve quality of life. For IPV/A victims/survivors, this could include grief groups or long-term survivors' groups that encourage emotional support and collective strategies for enhancing well-being—especially given that long-term survivors of IPV/A may not be detected if the abuse effects are not immediately apparent. Again, questions regarding IPV/A should be routinely asked by all physicians, not just gynecologists or primary care physicians or emergency room personnel; a screening survey similar to that of the National Cancer Institute could be extended to IPV/A (Hamberger, Rhodes, and Brown 2015). The use of technology can increase referrals, interventions, medical information exchange, and other tailored health-related services for IPV/A victims/survivors (Hamberger, Rhodes, and Brown 2015).

RESILIENCE AND SOCIAL LOCATION

Although I interviewed a very diverse sample of women, my sample was too small to make it possible for me to draw conclusions about the relationship between resilience and social position (race, class, religion, disability, sexual identity); I have addressed these issues as they manifested in the various themes throughout prior chapters. Despite the small sample size, the analysis sheds light on the multiple and interlocking social locations and oppressions that exacerbate IPV/A. For instance, we know that economic dependence complicates IPV/A and that the lack of financial means continues through the separation process and beyond, especially when women are prevented by their abuser from working or when they must endure protracted custody and visitation court processes. Although even women with more social capital in terms of money or educational attainment could not necessarily escape long-drawn-out legal battles, or paternalism and unjust decisions by police, courts, or service providers, such problems were greatly exacerbated for women of color, lesbians, and women with disabilities, as illustrated in the women's narratives in previous chapters (for example, in chapter 3, when women of color were especially reluctant to bring in police because of fear of the police response and an unwillingness to reveal family dysfunction to their white neighbors). Given important differences in the response of police, courts, and social services to women of different social statuses, even abused women who share other similarities, there is a continued need to provide meaningful sensitivity trainings on this subject to any professionals engaged with abused women. Further explorations with a larger sample of diverse women could offer additional insight about women's intersectional positions and how these affect resilience, growth, and well-being of long-term survivors.

Disability is an important facet of social location with regard to IPV/A. It is well established that IPV/A is associated with psychological and physical health impairment (see Dutton et al. 2006 for a review). For instance, women with a history of IPV/A are three to five times more at risk of depression, suicidal tendencies, and/or PTSD than women with no IPV/A history (Dutton et al. 2006) and a wide range of physical health problems, such as digestive disorders, sleep disorders, heart disease, and migraines, persist long after the abusive relationship ends (Scott-Storey 2011). Additionally, survivors with disabilities are especially vulnerable to psychological, physical, and sexual abuse over their life course compared to their able-bodied counterparts (Shah, Tsitsou, and Woodin 2016) and may be more reluctant to seek help because of fear of not being believed over their able-bodied perpetrator. When children of disabled women are involved, mothers may not seek interventions for fear of being perceived as incompetent caregivers (Priestley 2003). The women with disabilities in this project spoke of how their abusers had often manipulated them by hiding or breaking their assistance tools, such as canes or wheelchairs or eyeglasses and had taunted them with epithets related to their diminished abilities. Some abusers took their wives' disability checks and used them to gamble or buy recreational items. Survivors with disabilities expressed intense guilt about how the abuse affected their children, including, for four of the women, lingering suspicions that their abusers might have caused miscarriages or disabilities in their children, despite these not being confirmed by medical exams. Abusers also often blamed the women for their children's limitations. Though the women fiercely protected them, children with disabilities are also more vulnerable to abuse, and three of the women believed their abusers targeted these children because of their relative weaknesses vis-à-vis the other siblings. Practitioners and criminal justice personnel need additional training to raise their awareness of this population's special risks and to offer a larger repertoire of resources. For instance, the National Center for Victims of Crime offers resource material and webinars geared toward helping service providers better meet the needs of crime victims with disabilities.[9]

FINAL THOUGHTS

What should be clear to other women ending an abusive relationship is that the road ahead will not be easy. Survivors will doubt themselves; though they are relieved to no longer face verbal or physical assaults or threats, they are still fearful of what lies ahead. Yet in light of the women's stories of courage and fortitude and growth, there is cause for optimism: indeed, psychological research on happiness finds that while traumatic events have a negative effect, it is not as great or as long-lasting as one might expect (Gilbert 2005; S. Taylor 1983). A study of survivors in the aftermath of 9/11 (Bonanno, Rennicke, and Dekel 2005) and other studies of survivors of major traumas reveal that most people do well following the events and many believe their lives have been enhanced (Carver 1998; Linley and Joseph 2004; Tedeschi and Calhoun 2004). Though many of these psychological studies revolve around a one-time event, such as a violent crime or a natural disaster, which might be expected to have an impact different from that of abuse, the women I talked to demonstrated steadfast beliefs that the horrific long-term abuse they had endured had mobilized them to find a new direction and that leaving their abuser had given them multiple opportunities to create more fulfilling lives; despite setbacks and discouragements, their exit over time proved to be transformative. The psychologist Norman Rosenthal (2013), who has studied the resilience of Holocaust survivors and apartheid-era South Africans who endured long-term trauma, maintains that adversity can be "a gift" in that dealing with challenges and difficulties can increase people's wisdom and resilience; research on adult survivors of incest finds similar understanding and growth (Himelein and McElrath 1996). This idea of unexpected benefits emerging from adversity resonated with the women too, as evinced by their narratives describing how they had learned something of value from their experiences that helped them interpersonally (with family, friends, employers, coworkers) and that later catalyzed them to help others through collective or individual action. The women's meaning making grew to incorporate the abuse as incidents they did not cause and as experiences that did not define them solely in those terms; regardless of whether the women were public activists or engaged in more private efforts to help others, being a survivor was important, even if not the central theme of their existence. Their journey through the years after leaving abusive relationships exposed structural inequities in familial, religious, economic, and legal institutions that tested their fortitude. But they emerged on the other side of abuse, affected by it but acquiring a deeper understanding of their lives. Vanessa's favorite quote from Khalil Gibran, one that she invoked frequently, also resonates with me: "Out of suffering have emerged the strongest souls; the most massive characters are seared with scars."

Listening to the voices of survivors helps us understand many things: grief and relief are not mutually exclusive; survivors can reassemble a life informed by trauma that is no longer traumatic. They can engage with civic activism or engage in change on a more individual level; these connections are meaningful and reinforce how far they have come. Although the women I interviewed—like all of us—confront challenges and struggles in their lives today, their ability to bounce back from abuse and to thrive underscores their success in nourishing and cultivating hope. Faltering at times did not diminish survivors' determination never to be victims again. Resolute effort to recalibrate their lives and to be free of violence guided their arduous journeys. Some survivors used their unrelenting passion and wisdom to play a public role in challenging IPV/A. Their collective efficacy, captured in the WIND group, demonstrated how they could use their private horrors to assist others in the public arena. Other survivors spoke in a more quiet voice, using their personal efficacy to inspire one victim at a time. But all of the women challenged the systems that rendered them powerless, vowing to never let anyone or anything exert control over them again. They were not always successful, but they persevered, and in the many years following the end of their abusive relationships they learned to take pride in themselves, trust their feelings and other people, reconnect with meaningful people and institutions in their lives, and speak up when necessary.

Even with greater public awareness of IPV/A and the emergence of legal reforms, Rezey (2017), in a study based on data from the National Crime Victimization Survey (a nationally representative sample), concludes that women remain at risk of injury or fatality upon leaving their relationship, with separated women at higher IPV/A risk than nonseparated women. Her findings echo the urgency heard in the women's stories about their thwarted efforts to find help beyond the initial crisis, strengthening the call for social service and legal assistance to extend well beyond the typical time frame.

Our collective expectations to live in a civil and just society mandate greater attention to changing gender and social norms and the unequal distribution of power. The toxicity of the 2016 election season revealed the extent to which our culture still tolerates misogyny, offering the excuse that "boys will be boys" and claiming that women are just too sensitive, with the result that bullies and abusers often enjoy impunity. Measures to prevent and intervene in abusive situations and to sustain women after they leave are vital for addressing IPV/A. Yet, as mentioned in chapter 2, we should be aware that even in nonprofit, pro-women organizations the bureaucratization of funding and leadership can lead to policies that are paternalistic and controlling. Such paternalism shows up as well in civil and criminal court proceedings and among governmental social service providers, reinforcing the women's experience of having been overpowered, controlled, and silenced or belittled by their abuser. Victim-centered policies must not be pushed aside by competing resource and stakeholder demands. We need to be aware of and remain vigilant against alliances that stress control over care and compassion (see Richie 2015). Empowerment for all victims/survivors should guide our efforts on both micro and macro levels.

Though the women in my project were no longer in an abusive relationship, they still confronted common challenges faced by many people in our society: un- or underemployment and economic uncertainty, divorce, struggles with children and other family members, racism, misogyny, homophobia, and so forth. Even during the abusive relationship itself the "expected and ever present" abuse was only one aspect of women's daily challenges of "navigating blended families, trying to get to work on time (if they are fortunate enough to be employed), planning meals on a tight budget, worrying about gas money, scraping funds together for the next birthday party, negotiating caregiving for older family members" (Larance 2012, 209). During the abusive relationship and long after its termination, women succeeded in juggling multiple balls simultaneously, which contributed to their belief that IPV/A was only one part of their life experience and not the core of who they were. Given survivors' ability to tackle different issues on many fronts simultaneously and their tenacity and creativity in doing so, they represent a valuable resource in and of themselves: policy makers should continue to include or invite their voices at municipal, state, and federal levels of legislative bodies and other institutions, including a range of interconnected agencies such as Housing and Urban Development, child protective services, and the Department of Justice.

This book is not the final word on long-term survivorship, but I hope it serves as a framework for developing efficacious policies and listening to women who have experienced and left situations of abuse. They are the true experts on survival strategies, long-term coping, well-being, growth, and resilience, and they inspire others to continue speaking up to inform our understanding and facilitate change.

Notes

1. Though this book focuses on women's relationships and long-term survival strategies given the greater frequency with which women experience IPV/A and their greater likelihood of being seriously injured or killed, men are also victims of relationship violence and abuse (see Houry et al. 2008; H. Straus et al. 2009), including men who are gay, bisexual, or trans (Baker et al. 2013).

2. One of the women in the present study experienced abuse from her female partner. As I noted in a previous work (S. Miller 2005, 25–26), feminist theories of intimate partner violence typically focus on heterosexual couples and exclude lesbians (Renzetti 1999); although some studies indicate that lesbians have similar or higher violence prevalence rates, these studies are often based on small, unrepresentative samples or have not been replicated, so we cannot draw strong conclusions or comparisons to heterosexual women (Balsam, Rothblum, and Beauchaine 2005; Messinger 2011; Renzetti 1992). However, our understanding of same-gender partner violence lags behind that for heterosexual partner violence. Elliott (1996) contends, "The routine and intentional use of intimidation tactics in relationships is not a gender issue but a power one" (quoted in Perilla et al. 2003, 20). Similarly, in their review essay, Baker et al. (2013) argue that gender-based heteronormative assumptions about IPV/A in general may be less helpful in understanding same-sex IPV/A than factors of culture, social structures, social status, and interpersonal dynamics. Still, as "sexism creates an opportunity for heterosexual men to batter women, homophobia creates an opportunity for people in same-gender relationships to batter their partners" (Perilla et al. 2003, 20). Moreover, issues related to self-acknowledgment of being LGBTQ and the related disclosure risks with family, employment, and other social situations make it more difficult for these victims to seek help (S. Miller 2005, 26).

3. I use *agency* here to describe how one is able to exert some choice or power over circumstances, even with constraints. Personal agency is a way to resist or to project one's will over life circumstances (see Showden 2011).

1. FRAMING THE ISSUES

1. Some of these victories include establishing battered women's shelters and shared shelter networks; founding vibrant state coalitions and national networks; creating intervention and treatment programs for men who batter their partners; and passing violence against women legislation that offers greater protection for victims in civil and criminal arenas. In addition, the Centers for Disease Control and Prevention (CDC) funds multiple primary prevention research projects to address the issue of IPV/A in school and community settings.

2. Blankenship (1998, 394–95) uses examples of how the gay community responded to AIDS in the United States by inspiring a social movement, though the black community's response to AIDS was not one of activism. She argues that the difference in mobilization was determined by the structures of power and influence to which these communities had access. People with HIV/AIDS had access to institutions, subcultures, and activist groups important to mounting a public health issue, while the black community's resources included churches, elected officials, and drug treatment advocates, all whom faced practical and ideological struggles in confronting the AIDS crisis.

3. PTSD was measured by the PTSD Checklist Version for Civilians, and resilience was measured by the Connor-Davidson Resilience Scale (2003).

4. This phrase—originally attributed to the philosopher Nietzsche—was popularized in a recent hit song by Kelly Clarkson.

2. SITUATING THE RESEARCH PROJECT

1. For example, I provided the names of some attorneys who might be helpful to women with court issues, and I gathered website information for employment opportunities at my university.

2. WIND's main goals include empowering survivors' voices, being active in promoting change on behalf of survivors, and networking with other survivors. (I do not provide the organization's real name or actual website address because these could reveal geographic information about where some of the women reside.)

3. Despite the debate and movement away from using terms like *domestic violence* and using *IPV/A* instead, here I deliberately use *domestic violence* when talking about this state's coalition and its task forces (like WIND) because that is the language used by most of the state coalitions and the national coalition to define themselves.

4. Other issues include revisions for civil Protection from Abuse (PFA) orders and revisions of the lethality assessment questionnaire. Women offered much personal insight, thinking that there should be more items on the PFA about financial control tactics, cyber/tech stalking, custody issues, and access to guns. They also had language issues about the question "Has violence escalated over the past year," since it suggests that one cannot get a PFA if there has only

been one episode. There was a tremendous wealth of knowledge and experience in the group.

5. VINE was designed in this state for victims and their families to gain access to immediate offender custody status information at every level of the criminal justice system, from probation to long-term incarceration.

6. This realization—after learning about IPV/A during a college class—happened with two other women I interviewed. All three women maintained that they began to believe what they were learning: it was not their fault.

3. "LEAVING THE HORRIBLE FOR THE NOT-SO-HORRIBLE"

1. At the time of the interview Megan was a college graduate, but the family lumped her and her heroin-addicted brother together as losers because she was "the one who ran off and got divorced" and because she had revealed the secret about her abusive marriage, much to her family's dismay.

2. The doctrine of submission is based on a passage in Ephesians 5:21–33 where women are directed to "submit yourselves unto your own husbands, as unto the Lord. For the husband is the head of the wife, even as Christ is the head of the church. . . . Therefore as the church is subject unto Christ, so let the wives be to their own husbands in everything."

3. In particular, the doctrine of submission is often contested, given that there are many possible biblical interpretations (see Bartkowski 1997). It is often used, however, to support husbands' justifications of abuse (see Fortune and Enger 2005).

4. This finding is consistent with other research that found that women who have left violent relationships are profoundly relieved to learn about the abuser's taking responsibility for the violence (see Ulrich 1991; Ferraro and Johnson 1983).

5. Although state laws protecting battered women and housing vary, there are federal law paths available, such as the Violence against Women Act, which specifies that women cannot be denied housing or evicted from their home on the basis of domestic violence, dating violence, sexual assault, or stalking. This law applies only to women and only to those who are living in public or subsidized housing. It also provides these survivors with access to an emergency transfer to another home operated by the same provider if they are in danger. In addition, the Fair Housing Act prohibits discrimination in housing based on gender or other grounds. For example, if an entire household is going to be evicted because of domestic violence against a woman, that eviction can legally be interpreted as discrimination (see "Your Rights as a Tenant," domesticshelters.org, April 8, 2016, https://www.domesticshelters.org/domestic-violence-articles-information/your-rights-as-a-tenant).

4. MEANING MAKING AND POST-TRAUMATIC GROWTH

1. Several women reported that their abuser had engaged in this kind of bargaining, requiring them to perform sexual acts not only in order to protect

their children but also to go to work or to gain some other freedom: for instance, one woman would have to give her abuser a blow job in exchange for being allowed a dinner out with a friend.

2. In the monthly WIND programs, the women's frustration with the continued control the abusers wielded through the children was a common discussion. One woman's daughter committed suicide, leaving behind a young child. The abuser became reinvolved through the courts, asking for custody of the grandchild. Since he had demonstrated no interest in child rearing or custody at the divorce proceeding years earlier, it seemed clear that her ex-husband found a new way to harass his ex-wife, resulting in anxiety, kidnapping fears, and mounting legal bills.

3. Seventy-six percent of their sample were unemployed, 60 percent had achieved higher education (some college or vocational school), and 56 percent were African American. Lim, Valdez, and Lilly (2015, 1082) note that the provision of a monetary reward for participation in the study may have skewed their sample to overrepresent those who were more financially unstable.

4. Gillum, Sullivan, and Bybee's (2006) work is part of a larger longitudinal study in which women had to have experienced some type of IPV/A within the prior four months and had to have at least one minor-age child living with them; the sample included 151 battered women with 45 percent being non-Hispanic white, 38 percent African American, 7 percent Hispanic, 9 percent multiracial, and 1 percent Native American. Though 83 percent of the women at the time of the interview were no longer involved with their abusers, 88 percent had been involved with them when the violence had occurred in the prior four months. The authors found that for women of color greater religious involvement was related to increased social support.

5. Institute for Women's Policy Research, "Politics, Religion and Women's Public Vision," n.d., accessed November 27, 2017, https://iwpr.org/issue /democracy-and-society/civic-political-engagement/politics-religion-womens-public-vision/.

6. The activist history of Quakerism attracted Jayde, who attended "twelve years of Catholic school" decided at age sixteen that "this church sucks with hypocrisy. I remember saying to my father—'There's something wrong with Father X. I think he likes boys a little too much.' My father got mad at me. 'Don't you ever say that about a priest!' . . . Years later, it turns out Father X had been one of the priests that was accused. I found Quakerism through my study of history. I loved that these people helped slaves and were abolitionists. I wanted to join these people."

5. SUPPORT NETWORKS AND STRUCTURAL CHALLENGES

1. This message from a therapist does a disservice to victims of IPV/A but is consistent with that of some pastoral counselors who encourage couples to stick it out, as referenced by several of the women with whom I talked.

2. As I noted previously (S. Miller 2005, 151), Perilla et al. (2002, 21) caution about the risks of using a feminist analysis to explain same-gender IPV/A, maintaining that it can fuel myths such as "(a) gay male violence is logical because men are violent and violence is uncommon in lesbian relationships because women are nonviolent; (b) same-gender partner violence is not as severe as that which men perpetrate against their female partners; (c) as a reflection of heterosexual domestic violence, the perpetrator in homosexual couple must be the 'man' or 'butch' and the victim must be the 'woman' or 'femme.'"

3. This has changed; since 1993, all states no longer have a marital rape exemption, though many states still differentiate marital from nonmarital rape by such policies as shorter penalties, exclusion of nonviolent situations, and shorter reporting periods.

4. This means that the entry appears on her record but the prosecutor decided not to proceed further with the case.

5. In contrast, Joan recounted an instance where the criminal justice system actually reached out to her for input regarding her ex-husband's case. He had applied for a job working in a prison but found out he needed to have his charges pardoned, so he submitted the paperwork to the board of pardons. The board contacted Joan immediately and said that since she was the person who was the victim of his offenses she was invited to "let my voice be heard, the whole nine yards." Joan was able to express her disapproval and even corrected some of his false statements on his job application. He did not ultimately show up at the hearing, so his getting pardoned was moot, but Joan was there and felt validated when asked to participate.

6. Dale frequently phrased it like this because she felt her abuser had killed the person she had been, and she believed that the next time he attempted to kill her he would succeed.

6. PATHS TO SURVIVORSHIP AND SUGGESTIONS FOR POLICY

1. Sandberg (2017) wrote about her struggle to regain her equilibrium after her husband's death and established a nonprofit to assist people in building resilience and finding meaning in the face of adversity (see optionb.org).

2. These included being robbed with a weapon, being physically assaulted by a stranger, witnessing physical assault by a stranger, being physically assaulted by an intimate partner, being threatened with serious physical injury or death, being sexually assaulted, and being stalked (221).

3. Sanders's (2010) evaluation revealed that two-thirds of the 125 women who had IDA accounts met their savings goals and that most received matched funds for housing, education, microenterprise development or retirement withdrawals, though most funds were used to purchase vehicles or make emergency withdrawals to maintain housing or relocate. More research is needed to know how asset building programs affect IPV/A, and efforts also need to address the

expense of operating these kinds of programs (e.g., staffing concerns, finding partners to provide matching funds; see Sanders 2011).

4. The US Department of Justice's Office on Violence against Women funded the Economic Security for Survivors project (2012), which brought together over 1,700 advocates, victim service specialists, and criminal justice professionals with Web-based training and resources to assess their efforts in addressing survivors' economic security. The project also worked with twenty partners across twelve states to educate stakeholders and build partnerships to create more comprehensive coordinated community responses, achieve greater justice through prosecution of economic crimes, and enhance economic advocacy within transitional housing programs (for resources and information, see Institute for Women's Policy Research, "Economic Security for Survivors," n.d., accessed November 20, 2017, https://iwpr.org/issue/special-websites/economic-security-survivors/).

5. US Department of Justice, "Justice Department Selects Four Courts to Identify Promising Practices in Custody and Visitation Decisions in Domestic Violence Cases," press release, November 12, 2013, https://www.justice.gov /opa/pr/justice-department-selects-four-courts-identify-promising-practices-custody-and-visitation.

6. See Centers for Disease Control and Prevention, "Timeline of Violence as a Public Health Problem," last updated March 30, 2015, www.cdc.gov /violenceprevention/overview/timeline.html.

7. See project description at Wellesley Centers for Women, Projects, "Dating Violence Prevention Program for Each Grade in Middle School," directed by Nan Stein and Bruce Taylor, ongoing since 2011, www.wcwonline.org/Active-Projects/a-dating-violence-prevention-program-for-each-grade-in-middle-school.

8. Office on Women's Health, "Health Care Providers and Screening and Counseling for Interpersonal and Domestic Violence," last updated October 15, 2012, https://www.womenshealth.gov/files/documents/fact-sheet-ipv-screening .pdf.

9. See National Center for Victims of Crime, "Responding to Crime Victims with Disabilities: Resource Directory for Service Providers," n.d., https:// victimsofcrime.org/library/resource-directory-victims-with-disabilities/crime-victims-with-disabilities.

References

Abraham, M. 2000. *Speaking the unspeakable: Marital violence among South Asian immigrants in the United States.* New Brunswick, NJ: Rutgers University Press.

Acker, J. 1990. Hierarchies, jobs, bodies: A theory of gendered organizations. *Gender and Society* 4:139–58.

Adams, A. E., M. R. Greeson, A. C. Kennedy, and R. M. Tolman. 2013. The effects of adolescent intimate partner violence on women's educational attainment and earnings. *Journal of Interpersonal Violence* 28 (17): 3283–3300.

Adams, A. E., C. M. Sullivan, D. Bybee, and M. R. Greeson. 2008. Development of the Scale of Economic Abuse. *Violence against Women* 14 (5): 563–88.

Ai, A. L., and C. L. Park. 2005. Possibilities of the positive following violence and trauma: Informing the coming decade of research. *Journal of Interpersonal Violence* 20 (2): 242–50.

Ambuel, B., L. K. Hamberger, C. E. Guse, M. Melzer-Lange, M. B. Phelan, and A. Kistner. 2013. Healthcare can change from within: Sustained improvement in the healthcare response to intimate partner violence. *Journal of Family Violence* 28 (8): 833–47.

American Psychological Association. 1998. *Report of the American Psychological Association Presidential Task Force on Violence and the Family: Issues and dilemmas in family violence.* Washington, DC: American Psychological Association. www.nnflp.org/apa/issue5.html.

———. 2005. Violence and the family: Report of the American Psychological Association—Executive summary. www.nnflp.org/apa/viol&fam.html.

Anderberg, D., and H. Rainer. 2013. Economic abuse: A theory of intrahousehold sabotage. *Journal of Public Economics* 97:282–95.

Andersen, M., and P. H. Collins. 1995. *Race, class, and gender: An anthology.* Belmont, CA: Wadsworth.

Anderson, K. M., L. M. Renner, and F. S. Danis. 2012. Recovery: Resilience and growth in the aftermath of domestic violence. *Violence against Women* 18:1279–99.

214 / *References*

Arizona Coalition against Domestic Violence. 2003. *Battered Mothers' Testimony Project: A human rights approach to child custody and domestic violence.* Phoenix: Arizona Coalition against Domestic Violence. www.thelizlibrary.org /therapeutic-jurisprudence/AZ-Battered-Mothers-Testimony-Project-Report .pdf.

ASPE (Office of the Assistant Secretary for Planning and Evaluation). 2013. Screening for domestic violence in health care settings. Policy Brief, August 1. https://aspe.hhs.gov/report/screening-domestic-violence-health-care-settings.

Baker, N.L., J.D. Buick, S.R. Kim, S. Moniz, and K.L. Nava. 2013. Lessons from examining same-sex intimate partner violence. *Sex Roles* 69 (3–4): 182–92.

Balsam, K.F., E.D. Rothblum, and T.P. Beauchaine. 2005. Victimization over the life span: A comparison of lesbian, gay, bisexual and heterosexual siblings. *Journal of Consulting and Clinical Psychology* 73 (3): 477–87.

Barnett, O.W. 2001. Why battered women do not leave, part 1. *Trauma, Violence, and Abuse* 1 (4): 343–72.

Barrett, B.J., and M. St. Pierre. 2011. Variations in women's help-seeking in response to intimate partner violence: Findings from a Canadian population-based study. *Violence against Women* 17 (1): 47–70.

Bartkowski, J.P. 1997. Debating patriarchy: Discursive disputes over spousal authority among Evangelical family commentators. *Journal for the Scientific Study of Religion* 36:393–410.

Beeble, M.L., D. Bybee, and C.J. Sullivan. 2007. Abusive men's use of children to control their partners and ex-partners. *European Psychologist* 12:54–61.

Beech, N. 2011. Liminality and the practices of identity reconstruction. *Human Relations* 64 (2): 285–302.

Belknap, J. 2015. *The invisible woman: Gender, crime and justice.* Stamford, CT: Cengage.

Belknap, J., H.C. Melton, J.T. Denney, R.E. Fleury-Steiner, and C.M. Sullivan. 2009. The levels and roles of social and institutional support reported by survivors of intimate partner abuse. *Feminist Criminology* 4 (4): 377–402.

Bemiller, M. 2008. When battered mothers lose custody: A qualitative study of abuse at home and in the courts. *Journal of Child Custody* 5:228–55.

Berns, N. 2004. *Framing the victim: Domestic violence, media, and social problems.* New York: Aldine de Gruyter.

Best, J. 1997. Victimization and the victim industry. *Society* 34:9–17.

Black, M.C., K.C. Basile, M.J. Breiding, S.G. Smith, M.L. Walters, M.T. Merrick, and M.R. Stevens. 2011. *National Intimate Partner and Sexual Violence Survey.* Atlanta, GA: Centers for Disease Control and Prevention.

Blankenship, K.M. 1998. A race, class, and gender analysis of thriving. *Journal of Social Issues* 54 (2): 393–404.

Bloom, B., and S. Covington. 2000. Gendered justice: Programming for women in correctional settings. Paper presented at the Annual Meeting of the American Society of Criminology, San Francisco.

Bloom, B., B. Owen, and S. Covington. 2004. Women offenders and the gendered effects of public policy. *Review of the Policy Research* 21:31–48.

Blumer, H. 1969. *Symbolic interaction.* Englewood Cliffs, NJ: Prentice Hall.

Blundo, R. 2002. Mental health: A shift in perspective. In *Resiliency: An integrated approach to practice, policy, and research,* edited by R. R. Greene, 133–52. Washington, DC: NASW Press.

Bonanno, G.A. 2004. Loss, trauma, and human resilience: Have we underestimated the human capacity to thrive after extremely aversive events? *American Psychologist* 59 (1): 20–28.

———. 2005. Resilience in the face of potential trauma. *Current Directions in Psychological Science* 14 (3): 135–38.

Bonanno, G.A., N.P. Field, A. Kovacevic, and S. Kaltman. 2002. Self-enhancement as a buffer against extreme adversity: Civil war in Bosnia and traumatic loss in the United States. *Personality and Social Psychology Bulletin* 28:184–96.

Bonanno, G.A., C. Rennicke, and S. Dekel. 2005. Self-enhancement among high-exposure survivors of the September 11th terrorist attack: Resilience or social maladjustment? *Journal of Personality and Social Psychology* 88:984–98.

Brabeck, K.M., and M.R. Guzman. 2008. Frequency and perceived effectiveness of strategies to survive abuse employed by battered Mexican-origin women. *Violence against Women* 14 (11): 1274–94.

Bradley, R., A.C. Schwartz, and N.J. Kaslow. 2005. Posttraumatic stress disorder symptoms among low-income, African American women with a history of intimate partner violence and suicidal behaviors: Self-esteem, social support, and religious coping. *Journal of Traumatic Stress* 18:685–96.

Brown, L.M., and C. Gilligan. 1992. *Meeting at the crossroads: Women's psychology and girls' development.* Cambridge, MA: Harvard University Press.

Brownridge, D.A., K.L. Chan, D. Hiebert-Murphy, J. Ristock, A. Tiwari, W. Leung, and S.C. Santos. 2008. The elevated risk for non-lethal post-separation violence in Canada: A comparison of separated, divorced, and married women. *Journal of Interpersonal Violence* 23 (1): 117–35.

Brush, L.D. 2011. *Poverty, battered women, and work in U.S. public policy.* New York: Oxford University Press.

Bryan, P.E. 2005. *Constructive divorce.* Washington, DC: American Psychological Association.

Burt, M., and R. Estep. 1981. Who is a victim? Definitional problems in sexual victimization. *Victimology: An International Journal* 6:15–28.

Buzawa, E.S., and C.G. Buzawa. 2003. The scientific evidence is not conclusive: Arrest is no panacea. In *Current controversies on family violence,* edited by R.J. Gelles and D.R. Loseke, 337–56. Newbury Park, CA: Sage Publications.

Cain, M. 1990. Realist philosophy and standpoint epistemologies, or feminist criminology as a successor science. In *Feminist principles in criminology,* edited by L. Gelsthorpe and A. Morris, 124–40. Philadelphia: Open University Press.

Calhoun, L.G., and R.G. Tedeschi, eds. 2006. *Handbook of posttraumatic growth: Research and practice.* Mahwah, NJ: Lawrence Erlbaum.

Campbell, J.C. 2005. Helping women understand their risk in situations of intimate partner violence. *Journal of Interpersonal Violence* 19 (12): 1464–77. doi: 10.1177/0886260504269698.

Campbell, J.C., N. Glass, P.W. Sharps, K. Laughon, and T. Bloom. 2007. Intimate partner homicide: Review and implications of research and policy. *Trauma Violence and Abuse* 8:246. doi: 10.1177/1524838007303505.

Campbell, J.C., D. Webster, J. Koziol-McLain, C. Block, D. Campbell, M.A. Curry, F. Gary, et al. 2003. Risk factors for femicide in abusive relationships: Results from a multisite case control study. *American Journal of Public Health* 93 (7): 1089–97.

Campbell, R., T. Sefl, H.E. Barnes, C.E. Ahrens, S.M. Wasco, and Y. Zaragoza-Diesfeld, Y. 1999. Community services for rape survivors: Enhancing psychological well-being or increasing trauma? *Journal of Consulting and Clinical Psychology* 67 (6): 847–58.

Caputi, J. 1977. The glamour of grammar. *Chrysalis* 4:35–43.

Caputo, R.K. 2005. Religious capital and intergenerational transmission of volunteering as correlates of civic engagement. *Nonprofit and Voluntary Sector Quarterly* 36 (6): 983–1002.

Carlson, B.E. 1984. Children's observations of interparental violence. In *Battered women and their families*, edited by A.R. Roberts, 147–67. New York: Springer.

———. 1991. Outcomes of physical abuse and observation of marital violence among adolescents in placement. *Journal of Interpersonal Violence* 6:526–34.

Carlson, B.E., L.A. McNutt, D.Y. Choi, and I.M. Rose. 2002. Intimate partner abuse and mental health: The role of social support and other protective factors. *Violence against Women* 8:720–45.

Carver, C.S. 1998. Resilience and thriving: Issues, models, and linkages. *Journal of Social Issues* 54:245–66.

Cavendish, J.C. 2000. Church-based community activism: A comparison of black and white Catholic congregants. *Journal for the Scientific Study of Religion* 39:371–84.

CCI (Center for Court Innovation). 2013, Webinar Series: A community's experience addressing the complexity of women's use of force in their intimate heterosexual relationships. September 18. https://courtinnovation.ilinc.com/.

Charles, P., and K.M. Perreira. 2007. Intimate partner violence during pregnancy and 1-year postpartum. *Journal of Family Violence* 22 (7): 609–19.

Chatters, L.M., and R.J. Taylor. 1989. Life problems and coping strategies of older black adults. *Social Work* 34 (4): 313–19.

Chesney-Lind, M. 2002. Criminalizing victimization: The unintended consequences of pro-arrest policies for girls and women. *Criminology and Public Policy* 2 (1): 81–91.

———. 2004. Girls and violence: Is the gender gap closing? VAWnet and National Resource Center on Domestic Violence. August. www.vawnet.org.

———. 2006. Patriarchy, crime and justice: Feminist criminology in an era of backlash. *Feminist Criminology* 1 (1): 6–26.

Chesney-Lind, M., and M. Eliason. 2006. From invisible to incorrigible: The demonization of marginalized women and girls. *Crime, Media and Culture* 2 (1): 29–48.

Chesney-Lind, M., and K. Irwin. 2008. *Beyond bad girls: Gender, violence and hype.* New York: Routledge.

Cobb, A.R., R.G. Tedeschi, L.G. Calhoun, and A. Cann. 2006. Correlates of post-traumatic growth in survivors of intimate partner violence. *Journal of Traumatic Stress* 19:895–903.

Coker, A.L., R. Weston, D.L. Creson, B. Justice, and P. Blakeney. 2005. PTSD symptoms among men and women survivors of intimate partner violence: The role of risk and protective factors. *Violence and Victims* 20:625–43.

Collins, J.C. 2011. Strategy of career interventions for battered women. *Human Resource Development Review* 10 (3): 246–63.

Coser, R. 1959. Some social functions of laughter: A study of humor in a hospital setting. *Human Relations* 12 (2): 171–82.

Crann, S.E., and P.C. Barata. 2016. The experience of resilience for adult female survivors of intimate partner violence: A phenomenological inquiry. *Violence against Women* 22 (7): 853–75.

Crawford, E., H. Liebling-Kalifani, and V. Hill. 2009. Women's understanding of the effects of domestic abuse: The impact of their identity, sense of self and resilience: A grounded theory approach. *Journal of International Women's Studies* 11:63–82.

Creek, S.J., and J.L. Dunn. 2011. Rethinking gender and violence: Agency, heterogeneity, and intersectionality. *Sociology Compass* 5 (5): 311–22.

Crenshaw, K. 1991. Mapping the margins: Intersectionality, identity politics, and violence against women of color. *Stanford Law Review* 43:1251–99.

Crossman, K.A., J.L. Hardesty, and M. Raffaelli. 2016. "He could scare me without laying a hand on me": Mothers' experiences of nonviolent coercive control during marriage and after separation. *Violence against Women* 22 (4): 454–73.

Crowne, S.S., H. Juon, M. Ensminger, L. Burrell, E. McFarlane, and A. Duggan. 2011. Concurrent and long-term impact of intimate partner violence on employment stability. *Journal of Interpersonal Violence* 26 (6): 1282–1304.

Dalton, C., S. Carbon, and N. Olesen 2003. High conflict divorce, violence, and abuse: Implications for custody and visitation decisions. *Juvenile and Family Court Journal* 54 (4): 11–33.

Dasgupta, S.D. 2002. A framework for understanding women's use of nonlethal violence in intimate heterosexual relationships. *Violence against Women* 8:1364–89.

Davidson, J., and M. Chesney-Lind. 2009. Discounting women: Context matters in risk and need assessment. *Critical Criminology* 17 (4): 221–45.

Davis, G. 2011. *Custody evaluators' beliefs about domestic abuse.* Minneapolis, MN: Battered Women's Justice Project.

Davis, M.S., C.S. O'Sullivan, K. Susser, and M.D. Fields. 2011. Custody evaluations when there are allegations of domestic violence. National Criminal Justice Reference Service, Department of Justice. May. www.ncjrs.gov /pdffiles1/nij/grants/2344465.pdf.

Davis, R.E. 2002. "The strongest women": Exploration of the inner resources of abused women. *Qualitative Health Research* 9:1248–63.

Dehan, N., and Z. Lezi. 2009. Spiritual abuse: An additional dimension of abuse experienced by abused Haredi (Ultraorthodox) Jewish wives. *Violence against Women* 15 (11): 1294–1310.

DeJong, C., A. Burgess-Proctor, and L. Elis. 2008. Police officer perceptions of partner violence: An analysis of observational data. *Violence and Victims* 23:683–96.

DeKeseredy, W.S. 2015. New directions in feminist understandings of rural crime. *Journal of Rural Studies* 39:180–89.

DeKeseredy, W.S., and C. Joseph. 2006. Separation/divorce sexual assault in rural Ohio: Preliminary results of an exploratory study. *Violence against Women* 12:301–11.

DeKeseredy, W.S., and M.D. Schwartz. 2009. *Dangerous exits: Escaping abusive relationships in rural America.* New Brunswick, NJ: Rutgers University Press.

Derogatis, L.R. 1994. *Symptom Checklist-90-Revised.* Minneapolis, MN: National Computer Systems, Inc.

Dichter, M.E. 2013. "They arrested me—and I was the victim": Women's experiences with getting arrested in the context of domestic violence. *Women and Criminal Justice* 23:81–98.

Dragiewicz, M. 2011. *Equality with a vengeance.* Boston: Northeastern University Press.

DuBois, B. 1983. Passionate scholarship: Notes on values, knowing, and method in the social sciences. In *Theories for women's studies,* edited by G. Bowers and D.R. Klein, 105–16. London: Routledge and Kegan Paul.

DuBois, D.L., C.A. Bull, M.D. Sherman, and M. Roberts. 1998. Self-esteem and adjustment in early adolescence: A social-contextual perspective. *Journal of Youth and Adolescence* 27:557–83.

Dugard, J. 2011. *A stolen life: A memoir.* New York: Simon and Schuster.

Du Mont, J., T. Forte, M.M. Cohen, I. Hyman, and S. Romans. 2005. Changing help-seeking rates for intimate partner violence in Canada. *Women and Health* 4:1–19.

Dunn, J.L. 2001. Innocence lost: Accomplishing victimization in intimate stalking cases. *Symbolic Interaction* 24:285–313.

———. 2004. The politics of empathy: Social movements and victim repertoires. *Sociological Focus* 37:235–50.

———. 2005. "Victims" and "survivors": Emerging vocabularies of motives for "battered women who stay." *Sociological Inquiry* 75:1–30.

———. 2008. Accounting for victimization: Social constructionist perspectives. *Sociology Compass* 2 (5): 1601–20.

Durfee, A. 2009. Victim narratives, legal representation, and domestic violence civil protection orders. *Feminist Criminology* 4:7–31.

———. 2015. "Usually it's something in the writing": Reconsidering the narrative requirement for protection order petitions. *University of Miami Race and Social Justice Law Review* 5:469.

Dutton, M.A., and R. Greene. 2010. Resilience and crime victimization. *Journal of Traumatic Stress* 23 (2): 215–22.

Edelson, J. L. 1999. The overlap between child maltreatment and woman battering. *Violence against Women* 5:134–54.

Eisen, S. A., K. H. Griffith, H. Xian, J. F. Scherrer, I. D. Fischer, and S. Chantarujikapong. 2014. Lifetime and 12-month prevalence of psychiatric disorders in 8,169 male Vietnam War era veterans. *Military Medicine* 169:896–902.

Eisenstein, J., and H. Jacob. 1977. *Felony justice: An organizational analysis of criminal courts.* Boston: Little, Brown.

Eisikovits, Z., E. Buchbinder, and M. Mor. 1998. "What it was won't be anymore": Reaching the turning point in coping with intimate violence. *Affilia* 13 (4): 411–34.

Ellison, C. G., and R. J. Taylor. 1996. Turning to prayer: Social and situational antecedents of religious coping among African Americans. *Review of Religious Research* 38 (2): 111–31.

Faver, C. A. 2004. Relational spirituality and social caregiving. *Social Work* 49 (2): 241–49.

Feiring, C., L. Taska, and K. Chen. 2002. Trying to understand why horrible things happen: Attribution, shame, and symptom development following sexual abuse. *Child Maltreatment* 7:25–39. doi:10.1177./1077559502007001003.

Ferraro, K. L., and J. M. Johnson. 1983. How women experience battering: The process of victimization. *Social Problems* 80:325–37.

Fiol, C. M. 2002. Capitalizing on paradox: The role of language in transforming organizational identities. *Organization Science* 13 (6): 653–66.

Flasch, P., C. E. Murray, and A. Crowe. 2017. Overcoming abuse: A phenomenological investigation of the journey to recovery from past intimate partner violence. *Journal of Interpersonal Violence* 32 (22): 3373–3401.

Flavin, J. 2001. Feminism for the mainstream criminologist: An invitation. *Journal of Criminal Justice* 27:271–85.

Fleury, R. E., C. M. Sullivan, and D. I. Bybee. 2000. When ending the relationship doesn't end the violence: Women's experiences of violence by former partners. *Violence against Women* 6:1363–83. doi: 10.1177/1077801002218369s.

Fleury-Steiner, R. E., B. D. Fleury-Steiner, and S. L. Miller. 2011. More than a piece of paper? Protection orders as a resource for battered women. *Sociology Compass* 5 (7): 512–24.

Fleury-Steiner, R. E., S. L. Miller, and A. Carcirieri. 2017. Calling the shots: How family courts address the firearms ban in protection orders. *Violence against Women* 23 (9): 1140–51.

Florian, V., M. Mikulincer, and O. Taubman. 1995. Does hardiness contribute to mental health during a stressful real-life situation: The roles of appraisal and coping. *Journal of Personality and Social Psychology* 68:687–95.

Fontana, A. and J. H. Frey. 1994. Interviewing: The art of science. In *The Handbook of Qualitative Research,* edited by N. Denzin and Y. Lincoln, 361–76. Thousand Oaks, CA: Sage Publications.

Fowler, D. N. and H. M. Hill. 2004. Social support and spirituality as culturally relevant factors in coping among African American women survivors of partner abuse. *Violence against Women* 10 (11): 1267–82.

Frattaroli, J. 2006. Experimental disclosure and its moderators: A meta-analysis. *Psychological Bulletin* 132 (6): 823–65.

Fortune, M. M., and C. G. Enger. 2005. *Violence against women and the role of religion.* Harrisburg, PA: National Online Research Center on Violence against Women.

Gavey, N. 1999. "I wasn't raped, but . . .": Revisiting definitional problems in sexual victimization. In *New versions of victims: Feminists struggle with the concept,* edited by S. Lamb, 57–81. New York: NYU Press.

Gay, L. R., and P. Airasian. 2003. *Educational research: Competencies for analysis and applications.* Upper Saddle River, NJ: Merrill Prentice Hall.

Gelsthorpe, L. 1990. Feminist methodologies in criminology. In *Feminist perspectives in criminology,* edited by L. Gelsthorpe and A. Morris, 89–106. Philadelphia: Open University Press.

Giesbrecht, N., and I. Sevcik. 2000. The process of recovery and rebuilding among abused women in the conservative Evangelical subculture. *Journal of Family Violence* 15:229–48.

Gilbert, D. 2005. *Stumbling on happiness.* New York: Random House.

Gilfus, M. E. 1999. The price of the ticket: A survivor-centered appraisal of trauma theory. *Violence against Women* 5:1238–57.

Gillum, T., C. Sullivan, and D. Bybee. 2006. The importance of spirituality in the lives of domestic violence survivors. *Violence against Women* 12 (3): 240–50.

Gilson, S. F., E. DePoy, and E. P. Cramer. 2001. Linking the assessment of self-reported functional capacity with abuse experiences of women with disabilities. *Violence against Women* 7 (4): 418–31.

Goffman, E. 1963. *Stigma: Notes on the management of a spoiled identity.* Englewood Cliffs, NJ: Prentice Hall.

———. 1974. *Frame analysis.* New York: Harper and Row.

Gondolf, E. W., and E. R. Fisher. 1988. *Battered women as survivors: An alternative to treating learned helplessness.* Lexington, MA: Lexington Books.

Goodman, L. A., M. A. Dutton, K. Weinfurt, and S. Cook. 2003. The Intimate Partner Violence Strategies Index: Development and application. *Violence and Victims* 9:163–86.

Goodman, L. A., and D. Epstein. 2008. *Listening to battered women: A survivor-centered approach to advocacy, mental health, and justice.* Washington, DC: American Psychological Association.

———. 2011. The justice system response to domestic violence. In *Violence against women and children: Navigating solutions,* edited by M. P. Koss, J. W. White, and A. E. Kazdin, 2:215–36. Washington, DC: American Psychological Association.

Goodmark, L. 2008. When is a battered woman not a battered woman? When she fights back. *Yale Journal of Law and Feminism* 20 (75): 75–129.

———. 2012. *A troubled marriage: Domestic violence and the legal system.* New York: NYU Press.

———. 2013. Transgender people, intimate partner abuse, and the legal system. *Harvard Civil Rights–Civil Liberties Law Review* 48:51–104.

Gover, A.G., E.A. Tomsich, and T.N. Richards. 2015. Victimization and help-seeking among survivors of intimate partner violence. *Oxford Handbooks Online.* doi: 10.1093/oxfordhb/9780199935383.013.58.

Graetz, N. 1998. *Silence is deadly: Judaism confronts wifebeating.* Northvale, NJ: Jason Aronson.

Graham-Bermann, S.A., and J. Seng. 2005. Violence exposure and traumatic stress symptoms as additional predictors of health problems in high-risk children. *Journal of Pediatrics* 146 (3): 309–10.

Gregory, K., N. Nnawulezi, and C.M. Sullivan. 2017. Understanding how domestic violence shelter rules may influence survivor empowerment. *Journal of Interpersonal Violence.* Prepublished October 3. doi: 10.1177/0886260517730561.

Grimké, A.E. [1836] 2016. *Appeal to the Christian women of the South.* New York: Firework Press.

Gutiérrez, G. [1973] 1988. *A theology of liberation: History, politics, and salvation.* Edited and translated by Sister Caridad Inda and John Eagleson. 15th anniversary ed. Maryknoll, NY: Orbis Books.

Gwinn, C. 2006. Domestic violence and firearms. *Evaluation Review* 30 (3): 237–44. doi: 10.1177/0193841X06287818.

Hahn, J.W., M.C. McCormick, J.G. Silverman, E.B. Robinson, and K.C. Koenen. 2014. Examining the impact of disability status on intimate partner violence victimization in a population sample. *Journal of Interpersonal Violence* 29:3063–85.

Hamberger, L.K., K. Rhodes, and J. Brown. 2015. Screening and intervention for intimate partner violence in healthcare systems: Creating sustainable system-level programs. *Journal of Women's Health* 24 (1): 86–91. doi: 10.1089/jwh.2014.4861.

Hamberger, L.K., D.G. Saunders, and M. Hovey. 1992. Prevalence of domestic violence in community practice and rate of physician inquiry. *Family Medicine* 24:83–87.

Hamby, S. 2014. *Battered women's protective strategies: Stronger than you know.* New York: Oxford University Press.

Haney, L. 1996. Homeboys, babies, men in suits: The state and the reproduction of male dominance. *American Sociological Review* 61 (5): 759–78.

Hannah, M.T., and B. Goldstein. 2010. *Domestic violence, abuse, and child custody: Legal strategies and policy issues.* Kingston, NJ: Civic Research Institute.

Hardesty, J.L. 2002. Separation assault in the context of postdivorce parenting: An integrative review of the literature. *Violence against Women* 8 (5): 597–625. doi: 10.1177/10778012200800505.

Hardesty, J.L., and L.H. Ganong. 2006. How women make custody decisions and manage co-parenting with abusive former husbands. *Journal of Social and Personal Relationships* 23:543–63. doi: 10.1177/0265407506065983.

Hardesty, J.L., L. Khaw, M.D. Ridgway, C.L. Weber, and T. Miles. 2013. Coercive control and abused women's decisions about their pets when seeking shelter. *Journal of Interpersonal Violence* 28 (13): 2617–39.

Harrell, A., C. Visher, L. Newmark, and Y. Yahner. 2009. *The Judicial Oversight Demonstration: Culminating report on the evaluation.* Washington, DC: National Institute of Justice.

Harris, F.C. 1994. Something within: Religion as a mobilizer of African-American political activism. *Journal of Politics* 56 (1): 42–68.

Harrison, C. 2008. Implacably hostile or appropriately protective: Women managing child contact in the context of domestic violence. *Violence against Women* 14:381–405.

Hart, B. 1990. Gentle jeopardy: The further endangerment of battered women and children in custody mediation. *Mediation Quarterly* 7:326–27.

Harvey, J., K. Orbuch, D. Chwalisz, and G. Garwood. 1991. Coping with sexual assault: The roles of account-making and confiding. *Journal of Traumatic Stress* 4 (4): 515–31.

Haselschwerdt, M.L., J.L. Hardesty, and J.D. Hans. 2011. Custody evaluators' beliefs about domestic violence allegations during divorce: Feminist and family violence perspectives. *Journal of Interpersonal Violence* 26:1694–1719.

Hassouneh-Phillips, D.S. 2001. "Marriage is half of faith and the rest is fear Allah": Marriage and spousal abuse among American Muslims. *Violence against Women* 7:927–47.

Haviland, M., V. Frye, V. Rajah, J. Thukral, and M. Trinity. 2001. *The Family Protection and Domestic Violence Intervention Act of 1995: Examining the effects of mandatory arrest in New York City.* New York: Urban Justice Center.

Hayes, B.E. 2012. Abusive men's indirect control of their partner during the process of separation. *Journal of Family Violence* 27 (4): 333–44.

Heim, S., H. Grieco, S. DiPaola, and R. Allen. 2002. *California National Organization for Women: Family court report.* June 26. Revised September 26. Sacramento: California NOW. www.centerforjudicialexcellence.org/wp-content/uploads/2013/12/California-NOW-Family-Court-Report-2002-2.pdf.

Hellmuth, J.C., K.C. Gordon, G.L. Stuart, and T.M. Moore. 2013. Risk factors for intimate partner violence during pregnancy and postpartum. *Archives of Women's Mental Health* 16 (1): 19–27. doi:10.1007/s00737–012–0309–8.

Henning, K., and L. Feder. 2004. A comparison of men and women arrested for domestic violence: Who presents the greater threat? *Journal of Family Violence* 19:69–80.

Herman, J.L. 1992. *Trauma and recovery.* New York: Basic Books.

Herman, S. 2011. *Parallel justice for victims of crime.* Washington, DC: National Center for Victims of Crime.

Himelein, M.J., and J.A. McElrath. 1996. Resilient child sexual abuse survivors: Cognitive coping and illusion. *Child Abuse and Neglect* 20:747–58.

Holdaway, S. 1984. *Inside the British police.* Oxford: Basil Blackwell.

Holstein, J.A., and G. Miller. 1997. Rethinking victimization: An interactional approach to victimology. In *Social problems in everyday life,* edited by G. Miller and J.A. Holstein, 25–47. Greenwich, CT: JAI.

hooks, bell. 2000. *Feminist theory: From margin to center.* London: Pluto Press.

Horton, A.L., M.M. Wilkins, and W. Wright. 1988. Women who ended abuse: What religious leaders and religion did for these victims. In *Abuse and religion: When praying isn't enough*, edited by A. Horton and J. Williamson, 235–46. New York: Heath.

Hotaling, G.T., and D.B. Sugarman. 1986. An analysis of risk markers in husband to wife violence: The current state of knowledge. *Violence and Victims* 1 (2): 101–24.

Houry, Y., K.V. Rhodes, R.S. Kemball, L. Click, C. Cerulli, L.A. McNutt, et al. 2008. Differences in female and male victims and perpetrators of partner violence with respect to WEB scores. *Journal of Interpersonal Violence* 23 (8): 1041–55.

Huemann, M. 1977. *Plea bargaining: The experiences of prosecutors, judges, and defense attorneys*. Chicago: University of Chicago Press.

Humphreys, J. 2003. Resilience in sheltered battered women. *Issues in Mental Health Nursing* 24:137–52.

Irwin, K., and M. Chesney-Lind. 2008. Girls' violence: Beyond dangerous masculinity. *Sociology Compass* 2 (3): 837–55.

Jacques, J. 2016. Pew research poll shows sharp increase in gun ownership. August 29. Bearing Arms, news, August 29. https://bearingarms.com/jenn-j/2016/08/29/pew-pew-research-poll-shows-sharp-increase-gun-ownership/.

Jaffe, P.G., N.K. Lemon, and S.E. Poisson. 2003. *Child custody and domestic violence: A call for safety and accountability*. Thousand Oaks, CA: Sage Publications.

Janoff-Bulman, R. 1992. *Shattered assumptions: Towards a new psychology of trauma*. New York: Free Press.

———. 2006. Schema-change perspectives on posttraumatic growth. In *Handbook of posttraumatic growth: Research and practice*, edited by L.G. Calhoun and R.G. Tedeschi, 81–99. Mahwah, NJ: Lawrence Erlbaum.

Jasinski, J.L. 2004. Pregnancy and domestic violence: A review of the literature. *Trauma, Violence, and Abuse* 5:47–64.

Johnson, M.P., J.M. Leone, and Y. Xu. 2014. Intimate terrorism and situational couple violence in general surveys: Ex-spouses required. *Violence against Women* 20:186–207.

Johnson, S. 1989. *Wildfire: Igniting the she/volution*. Albuquerque, NM: Wildfire Books.

Kahn, M. 2017. Washington will be the first state to alert victims when a domestic abuser tries to buy a gun. *Trace*, July 15. https://www.thetrace.org/2017/07/washington-domestic-violence-laws-alert-abusers-guns/.

Kangagaratnam, P., R. Mason, I. Hyman, L. Manuel, H. Berman, and B. Toner. 2012. Burden of womanhood: Tamil women's perceptions of coping with intimate partner violence. *Journal of Family Violence* 27:647–58.

Karmen, A. 2013. *Crime victims: An introduction to victimology*. 8th ed. Belmont, CA: Wadsworth.

Kaufman, C.G. 2003. *Sins of omission: The Jewish community's reaction to domestic violence*. Boulder, CO: Westview.

Kelly, L., N. Sharp, and R. Klein. 2014. *Finding the costs of freedom: How women and children rebuilt their lives after domestic violence*. London: Child and Woman Abuse Studies Unit.

Kernic, M.A., D.J. Monary-Ernsdorff, J.K. Koepsell, and V.L. Holt. 2005. Children in the crossfire: Child custody determinations among couples with a history of intimate partner violence. *Violence against Women* 11:991–1021.

Knickmeyer, N., H.M. Levitt, S.G. Horne, and G. Bayer. 2003. Responding to mixed messages and double binds: Religious oriented coping strategies of Christian battered women. *Religion and Abuse* 5:29–54.

Kobasa, S.C., S.R. Maddi, and S. Kahn. 1982. Hardiness and health: A prospective study. *Journal of Personality and Social Psychology* 108:168–77.

Koss, M.P. 2014. The RESTORE program of restorative justice for sex crimes: Vision, process, and outcomes. *Journal of Interpersonal Violence* 29 (9): 1623–60.

Krueger, R. 1994. *Focus groups: A practical guide for applied research*. 2nd ed. Newbury Park, CA: Sage Publications.

Lamb, S. 1999a. Constructing the victim: Popular images and lasting labels. In *New versions of victims: Feminists struggle with the concept*, edited by S. Lamb, 108–38. New York: NYU Press.

———. 1999b. *The trouble with blame: Victims, perpetrators, and responsibility*. Cambridge, MA: Harvard University Press.

Larance, L.Y. 2007. When she hits him: Why the institutional response deserves reconsideration. *Violence against Women Newsletter: Prosecuting Attorney's Association of Michigan* 5 (4): 11–19.

———. 2012. Commentary on Wilson, Woods, Emerson, and Donenberg: The necessity for practitioner vigilance in assessing the full-context of an individual's life experiences. *Psychology of Violence* 2 (2): 208–10.

Larance, L.Y., and S.L. Miller. 2015. Finding the middle ground: Re-imagining responses to women's use of force. *University of Miami Race and Social Justice Law Review* 5:437–43.

———. 2016. In her own words: Women describe their use of force resulting in court-ordered intervention. *Violence against Women*. doi: 10.1177 /1077801216662340.

Lee, E. 2004. The way of being a social worker: Implications for Confucianism to social work, education and clinical practice. *Smith College Studies in Social Work* 74 (2): 393–408.

Lee, E.K.O., and C. Barrett. 2007. Integrating spirituality, faith, and social justice in social work practice and education: A pilot study. *Journal of Religion and Spirituality in Social Work: Social Thought* 26 (2): 1–21.

Leisenring, A. 2006. Confronting "victim" discourses: The identity work of battered women. *Symbolic Interaction* 29 (3): 307–30.

Lerner, M.J. 1980. The belief in a just world. In *The belief in a just world: A fundamental delusion*, chap. 1. New York: Springer.

Lesser, B. 1990. Attachment and situational factors influencing battered women's return to their mates following a shelter program. In *Research explorations in adult attachment,* edited by K. Pottharst, 81–128. New York: Peter Lang.

Levy, B., ed. 1991. *Dating violence: Young women in danger.* Seattle, WA: Seal Press.

Lewin, T. 1992. Feminists wonder if it was progress to become "victims." *New York Times,* May 10.

Lichter, E.L., and L.A. McCloskey. 2004. The effects of childhood exposure to marital violence on adolescent gender-role beliefs and dating violence. *Psychology of Women Quarterly* 28 (4): 344–57.

Lilly, M.M., C.E. Valdez, and S.A. Graham-Bermann. 2011. The mediating effect of world assumptions on the relationship between trauma exposure and depression. *Journal of Interpersonal Violence* 26:2499–2516.

Lim, B.II., C.E. Valdez, and M.M. Lilly. 2015. Making meaning out of interpersonal victimization: The narratives of IPV survivors. *Violence against Women* 21 (9): 1065–86.

Linley, P.A., and S. Joseph. 2004. Positive change following trauma and adversity: A review. *Journal of Traumatic Stress* 17:11–21.

Lofland, J., and L.J. Lofland. 1995. *Analyzing social settings: A guide to qualitative observation and analysis.* 3rd ed. Belmont, CA: Wadsworth.

Logan T.K., L. Shannon, J. Cole, and R. Walker. 2006. The impact of differential patterns of physical violence and stalking on mental health and help-seeking among women with protective orders. *Violence against Women* 12 (9): 866–86.

Logan, T., and R. Walker. 2009. Partner stalking: Psychological dominance or business as usual? *Trauma, Violence, and Abuse* 10 (3): 247–70.

Loseke, D.R. 1992. *The battered woman and shelters: The social construction of wife abuse.* Albany: State University of New York Press.

———. 2003. *Thinking about social problems: An introduction to constructionist perspectives.* New York: Aldine de Gruyter.

Lund, E.M. 2011. Community-based services and interventions for adults with disabilities who have experienced interpersonal violence: A review of the literature. *Trauma, Violence, and Abuse* 12:171–82.

Lutgen-Sandvik, P. 2008. Intensive remedial identity work. *Organization* 15 (1): 97–120.

Luthar, S.S., D. Cicchetti, and B. Becker. 2000. The construct of resilience: A critical evaluation and guidelines for future work. *Child Development* 71:543–62.

Macini, A.D., and G.A. Bonanno. 2006. Resilience to potential trauma: Toward a lifespan approach. In *Handbook of adult resilience,* edited by J.W. Reich, A.J. Zautra, and J.S. Hall, 258–80. New York: Guilford Press.

Macmillan, R., and R. Gartner. 1999. When she brings home the bacon: Labor-force participation and the risk of spousal violence against women. *Journal of Marriage and Family* 61 (4): 947–58.

Macy, R., M. Giattina, S. Parish, and C. Crosby. 2010. Domestic violence and sexual assault services: Historical concerns and contemporary challenges. *Journal of Interpersonal Violence* 25:3–32.

Markowitz, F. E. 2001. Attitudes and family violence: Linking intergenerational and cultural theories. *Journal of Family Violence* 16 (2): 205–18.

Martin, P. Y. 2005. *Rape work: Victims, gender, and emotions in organization and community context.* New York: Routledge.

Massey, S., A. Cameron, S. Ouellette, and M. Fine. 1998. Qualitative approaches to the study of thriving: What can be learned? *Journal of Social Issues* 54:337–55.

Masten, Ann S. 1994. Resilience in individual development: Successful adaptation despite risk and adversity. In *Educational resilience in inner-city America: Challenges and prospects,* edited by M. C. Wang and E. W. Gordon, 3–25. Hillsdale, NJ: Lawrence Erlbaum.

———. 2007. Resilience in developing systems: Progress and promise as the fourth wave rises. *Developmental Psychopathology* 19:921–30.

Mattis, J. S. 2000. African American women's definitions of spirituality and religiosity. *Journal of Black Psychology* 26 (1): 101–22.

Mattis, J. S., R. J. Taylor, and L. M. Chatters. 2001. Are they truly not religious? A multi-method analysis of the attitudes of religiously noninvolved African American women. *African American Research Perspectives* 7 (1): 90–103.

Max, W., D. P. Rice, E. Finkelstein, R. A. Bardwell, and S. Leadbetter. 2004. The economic toll of intimate partner violence against women in the United States. *Violence and Victims* 19 (3): 259–72.

McDermott, M. J., and J. Garofalo. 2004. When advocacy for domestic violence victims backfires: Types and sources of victim disempowerment. *Violence against Women* 10 (11): 1245–66.

McLeer, A. 1998. Saving the victims: Recuperating the language of the victim and reassessing global feminism. *Hypatia* 13:41–55.

McMillen, J. C., S. Zuravin, and G. Rideout. 1995. Perceived benefit from child abuse. *Journal of Consulting and Clinical Psychology* 63:1037–43. doi: 10.1037/0022–006X.63.6.1037.

Meadows, L. A., N. J. Kaslow, M. P. Thompson, and G. J. Jurkovic. 2005. Protective factors against suicide attempt risk among African American women experiencing intimate partner violence. *American Journal of Community Psychology* 36:109–21.

Mechanic, M., T. Weaver, and P. Resick. 2008. Mental health consequences of intimate partner abuse: A multidimensional assessment of four different forms of abuse. *Violence against Women* 14:634–54.

Melbin, A., C. M. Sullivan, and D. Cain. 2003. Transitional supportive housing programs: Battered women's perspectives and recommendations. *Affilia* 8 (4):445–60.

Meloy, M. L., and S. L. Miller. 2011. *The victimization of women: Law, policies, and politics.* New York: Oxford University Press.

Melton, H. C. 2004. Stalking in the context of domestic violence: Findings on the criminal justice system. *Women and Criminal Justice* 15 (3–4): 33–58.

———. 2007. Stalking in the context of intimate partner abuse: In the victims' words. *Feminist Criminology* 2 (4): 347–63.

Messinger, A.M. 2011. Invisible victims: Same sex IPV in the National Violence against Women Survey. *Journal of Interpersonal Violence* 26 (11): 2228–43.

Miller, E., M.R. Decker, H.L. McCauley, D.J. Tancredi, R.R. Levenson, J. Waldman, P. Schoenwald, and J.G. Silverman. 2010. Pregnancy coercion, intimate partner violence and unintended pregnancy. *Contraception* 81 (4): 316–22.

Miller, E., B. Jordan, R. Levenson, and J.G. Silverman. 2010. Reproductive coercion: Connecting the dots between partner violence and unintended pregnancy. *Contraception* 81 (6): 457–59. www.arhp.org/publications-and-resources/contraception.journal/june-2010.

Miller, S.L. 2001. The paradox of women arrested for domestic violence: Criminal justice professionals and service providers respond. *Violence against Women* 7 (12): 1339–76.

———. 2005. *Victims as offenders: The paradox of women's violence in relationships.* New Brunswick, NJ: Rutgers University Press.

Miller, S.L., and N.L. Smolter. 2011. "Paper abuse": When all else fails, batterers use procedural stalking. *Violence against Women* 17 (5): 637–50.

Minow, M. 1993. Surviving victim talk. *UCLA Law Review* 40:1411–45.

Moe, A.M. 2009. Battered women, children, and the end of abusive relationships. *Affilia* 24 (3): 244–56.

Moe, A.M., and P.P. Bell. 2004. Abject economics: The effects of battering and violence on women's work and employability. *Violence against Women* 10:29–55.

Molina, Y., J.C. Yi, J. Martinez-Gutierrez, K.W. Reding, J.P. Yi-Frazier, and A.R. Rosenberg. 2014. Resilience among patients across the cancer continuum: Diverse perspectives. *Clinical Journal of Oncology Nursing* 18 (1): 93–101. doi: 10.1188/14.CJON.93–101.

Morgan, J.K., and S.L. Desmaris. 2017. Associations between time since event and posttraumatic growth among military veterans. *Military Psychology,* prepublished March 2017. doi: 10.1037/mil0000170.

Morrill, A.C., J. Dai, S. Dunn, I. Sung, and K. Smith. 2005. Child custody and visitation decisions when the father has perpetrated violence against the mother. *Violence against Women* 11:1076–1107. doi: 10.1177/1077801205278046.

Moylan, C.A., T.I. Herrenkohl, C. Sousa, E.A. Tajima, R.C. Herrenkohl, and M.J. Russo. 2010. The effects of child abuse and exposure to domestic violence on adolescent internalizing and externalizing behavior problems. *Journal of Family Violence* 25 (1): 53–63.

Mumford, E.A., B.G. Taylor, and P.C. Giordano. 2017. Perpetration of adolescent dating relationship abuse: The role of conditional tolerance for violence and friendship factors. *Journal of Interpersonal Violence,* prepublished February 1. http://journals.sagepub.com/doi/abs/10.1177/0886260517693002.

Murray, S.B. 1988. The unhappy marriage of theory and practice: An analysis of a battered women's shelter. *National Women's Studies Association Journal* 1 (1): 75–92.

Naples, N. 2003. *Feminism and method: Ethnography, discourse analysis and activist research*. New York: Routledge.

Nash, S.T. 2006. The changing of the gods: Abused Christian wives and their hermeneutic revision of gender, power, and spousal conflict. *Qualitative Sociology* 29:195–209.

Nason-Clark, N. 1997. *The battered wife: How Christians confront family violence*. Louisville, KY: Westminster John Knox Press.

National Center for Injury Prevention and Control. 2003. *Costs of intimate partner violence against women in the United States*. Atlanta, GA: Centers for Disease Control and Prevention. www.cdc.gov/violenceprevention/pdf /IPVBook-a.pdf.

National Domestic Violence Hotline. 2013. 50 obstacles to leaving: 1–10. June 13. www.thehotline.org/2013/06/10/50-obstacles-to-leaving-1–10/.

Neilson, L.C. 2004. Assessing mutual partner-abuse claims in child custody and access claims. *Family Court Review* 42:411–38.

Newman, M.G., and A.A. Stone. 1996. Does humor moderate the effects of experimentally-induced stress? *Annals of Behavioral Medicine* 18 (2): 101–9.

Nichols, A. 2011. Gendered organizations: Challenges for domestic violence victim advocates and feminist advocacy. *Feminist Criminology* 6 (2): 111–31.

O'Dell, A. 2007. Why do police arrest victims of domestic violence: The need for comprehensive training and investigative protocols. *Journal of Aggression, Maltreatment and Trauma* 15:53–73.

O'Leary, V.E. 1998. Strength in the face of adversity: Individual and social thriving. *Journal of Social Issues* 54 (2): 425–46.

O'Leary, V.E., and J.R. Ickovics. 1995. Resilience and thriving in response to challenge: An opportunity for a paradigm shift in women's health. *Women's Health: Research on Gender, Behavior and Policy* 1:121–42.

O'Neal, E.N., and L.O. Beckman. 2017. Intersections of race, ethnicity, and gender: Reframing knowledge surrounding barriers to social services among Latina intimate partner violence victims. *Violence against Women* 23 (5): 643–65.

Orbdlik, A.J. 1942. Gallows humor: A sociological phenomenon. *American Journal of Sociology* 47:709–16.

Orenstein, P. 1994. *Schoolgirls: Young women, self-esteem, and the confidence gap*. New York: Random House.

Orth, U. 2002. Secondary victimization of crime victims by criminal proceedings. *Social Justice Research* 15 (4): 313–25.

Osthoff, S. 2002. But, Gertrude, I beg to differ, a hit is not a hit is not a hit. *Violence against Women* 8:1521–44.

Ovrelid, B. 2008. The cultivation of moral character: A Buddhist challenge to social workers. *Ethics and Social Welfare* 2 (3): 243–61.

Pagelow, M.D. 1993. Justice for victims of spouse abuse in divorce and child custody cases. *Violence and Victims* 8 (1): 69–83.

Park, C.L., and C.J. Blumberg. 2002. Disclosing trauma through writing: Testing the meaning-making hypothesis. *Cognitive Therapy and Research* 26 (5): 597–616.

Park, J.Z., and C. Smith. 2000. "To whom much has been given . . .": Religious capital and community voluntarism among churchgoing Protestants. *Journal for the Scientific Study of Religion* 39 (3): 272–86.

Parker-Pope, T. 2015. Writing your way to happiness. *New York Times,* January 20, D6.

Patton, M.Q. 1990. *Qualitative evaluation and research methods.* 2nd ed. Newbury Park, CA: Sage Publications.

Pearl, R. 2013. Domestic violence: The secret killer that costs $8.3 billion annually. *Forbes,* December 5. https://www.forbes.com/sites/robertpearl/2013 /12/05/domestic-violence-the-secret-killer-that-costs-8–3-billion-annually /#9fcffff4681f.

Peled, E., and K. Krigel. 2016. The path to economic independence among survivors of intimate partner violence: A critical review of the literature and courses for action. *Aggression and Violent Behavior* 31:127–35.

Pence, E., and S.D. Dasgupta. 2006. *Re-examining "battering": Are all acts of violence against intimate partners the same?* Duluth, MN: Praxis International.

Penelope, J. 1990. *Speaking freely: Unlearning the lies of the fathers' tongues.* New York: Teachers College Press.

Penman, M. 2017. With new law, Illinois stylists join the fight against domestic violence. Morning Edition, January 1, NPR. https://www.npr.org/sections /thetwo-way/2017/01/01/507770649/with-new-law-illinois-stylists-join-the-fight-against-domestic-violence.

Pennebaker, J.W., and J.M. Smyth. 2016. *Opening up by writing it down: How expressive writing improves health and eases emotional pain.* New York: Guilford Press.

Perilla, J., K. Frndak, D. Lillard, and C. East. 2003. A working analyses of women's use of violence in the context of learning, opportunity, and choice. *Violence against Women* 9 (1): 10–46.

Pleck, E. 1987. *Domestic tyranny: The making of social policy against family violence from colonial times to the present.* New York: Oxford University Press.

Pogrebin, M.R., and E.D. Poole. 1988. Humor in the briefing room: A study of the strategic uses of humor among police. *Journal of Contemporary Ethnography* 17 (2): 183–210.

Postmus, J.L. 2010. Economic empowerment of domestic violence survivors. VAWnet. National Resource Center on Domestic Violence and Pennsylvania Coalition against Domestic Violence, Harrisburg, PA. October. www.ncdsv .org/images/VAWnet_EcoEmpowermentDVSurvivors_10–2010.pdf.

Postmus, J.L., S.B. Plummer, S. McMahon, and K.A. Kurlo. 2013. Financial literacy: Building economic empowerment with survivors of violence. *Journal of Family and Economic Issues* 34 (3): 275–84.

Postmus, J.L., S.B. Plummer, S. McMahon, N.S. Murshid, and M.S. Kim. 2012. Understanding economic abuse in the lives of survivors. *Journal of Interpersonal Violence* 27 (3): 411–30.

Potter, H. 2007. Battered black women's use of religious services and spirituality for assistance in leaving abusive relationships. *Violence against Women* 13 (3): 262–84.

Priestley, M. 2003. *Disability: A life course approach.* Cambridge: Polity Press.

Profit, N.J. 1996. "Battered women" as "victims" and "survivors." *Canadian Social Work Review* 13:23–38.

Rajan, M., and K.A. McCloskey. 2007. Victims of intimate partner violence: Arrest rates across recent studies. *Journal of Aggression, Maltreatment and Trauma* 15 (3–4): 27–52.

Randall, M. 2004. Domestic violence and the construction of "ideal victims": Assaulted women's "image problems" in law. *Saint Louis University Public Law Review* 23 (1): 107–54.

Raphael, J. 2000. *Saving Bernice: Battered women, welfare, and poverty.* Boston: Northeastern University Press.

Renner, L.M. 2009. Intimate partner violence victimization and parenting stress: Assessing the mediating role of depressive symptoms. *Violence against Women* 15 (11): 1380–1401.

Renzetti, C.M. 1992. *Violent betrayal: Partner abuse in lesbian relationships.* Newbury Park, CA: Sage Publications.

———. 1999. The challenges to feminism posed by women's use of violence in intimate relationships. In *New versions of victims: Feminists struggle with the concept,* ed. S. Lamb, 42–56. New York: New York University Press.

Rezey, M.L. 2017. Separated women's risk for intimate partner violence: A multiyear analysis using the National Crime Victimization Survey. *Journal of Interpersonal Violence,* prepublished February 21. doi: 10.1177/0886260517692334.

Richie, B.E. 1996. *Compelled to crime: The gender entrapment of battered black women.* New York: Routledge.

———. 2000. A black feminist reflection on the antiviolence movement. *Signs* 25:1133–37.

———. 2015. Reimagining the movement to end gender violence: Anti-racism, prison abolition, women of color feminisms, and other radical visions of justice (transcript). *University of Miami Race and Social Justice Law Review* 5:257–73.

Rivera, E.A., C.M. Sullivan, and A.M. Zeoli. 2012. Secondary victimization of abused mothers by family court mediators. *Feminist Criminology* 7 (3): 234–52.

Rivera, F.P., M.L. Anderson, P. Fishman, A.E. Bonomi, R.J. Reid, D. Carrell, and R.S. Thompson. 2007. Healthcare utilization and costs for women with a history of intimate partner violence. *American Journal of Preventive Medicine* 32 (2): 89–96.

Roisman, G.I. 2005. Conceptual clarifications in the study of resilience. *American Psychologist* 60:264–65.

Rose, L. E., and J. Campbell. 2000. The role of social support and family relationships in women's responses to battering. *Health Care for Women International* 2 (1): 27–39.

Rosenberg, J. S., and D. A. Grab. 2015. *Supporting survivors: The economic benefits of providing civil legal assistance to survivors of domestic violence.* New York: Institute for Policy Integrity. http://policyintegrity.org /files/publications/SupportingSurvivors.pdf.

Rosenthal, N. E. 2013. *The gift of adversity: The unexpected benefits of life's difficulties, setbacks, and imperfections.* New York: Penguin.

Rotton, J., and M. Shats. 1996. Effects of state humor, expectancies, and choice on postsurgical mood and self-medication: A field experiment. *Journal of Applied Social Psychology* 26 (20): 1775–94.

Saakvitne, K. W., H. Tennen, and G. Affleck. 1998. Exploring thriving in the context of clinical trauma theory: Constructivist self-development theory. *Journal of Social Issues* 54:279–99.

Sabina, C., C. A. Cuevas, and J. L. Schally. 2012. Help-seeking in a national sample of victimized Latino women: The influence of victimization types. *Journal of Interpersonal Violence* 27 (1): 40–61.

Saltzman, L. E., C. H. Johnson, B. C. Gilbert, and M. M. Goodwin. 2003. Physical abuse around the time of pregnancy: An examination of prevalence and risk factors in 16 states. *Maternal and Child Health Journal* 7 (1): 31–43.

Sandberg, S., and A. Grant. 2017. *Option B: Facing adversity, building resilience, and finding joy.* New York: Random House.

Sanders, C. K. 2007. *Domestic violence, economic abuse and implications of a program for building economic resources for low-income women: Findings from interviews with participants in a women's economic action program.* CSD Research Report 07–12. St. Louis, MO: Washington University in St. Louis, Center for Social Development. http://csd.wustl.edu/Publications /Documents/RP07–12.pdf.

———. 2010. *Savings outcomes of an IDA program for survivors of domestic violence.* Research report. St. Louis, MO: Washington University, Center for Social Development. http://csd.wustl.edu/Publications/Documents /RP10–42.pdf.

———. 2011. *Asset building programs for domestic violence survivors.* Harrisburg, PA: VAWnet, National Resource Center on Domestic Violence. www.vawnet.org.

———. 2015. Economic abuse in the lives of women abused by an intimate partner: A qualitative study. *Violence against Women* 1 (21): 3–29.

Sanders, C. K., and S. Porterfield. 2010. The "ownership society" and women: Exploring female householders' ability to accumulate assets. *Journal of Family and Economic Issues,* 31 (1): 90–106.

Sanders, C. K., and M. Schnabel. 2006. Organizing for economic empowerment of battered women: Women's Savings Accounts. *Journal of Community Practice* 14 (3): 47–68.

Sanders, C.K., T.L. Weaver, and M. Schnabel. 2007. Economic education for battered women: An evaluation of outcomes. *Affilia* 22 (3): 240–54.

Sauber, E.W., and K.M. O'Brien. 2017. Multiple losses: The psychological and economic well-being of survivors of intimate partner violence. *Journal of Interpersonal Violence*, prepublished May 3. doi: 10.1177/0886260517706760.

Saunders, D.G., K.C. Faller, and R.M. Tolman. 2011. *Custody evaluators' beliefs about domestic abuse in relation to custody outcomes.* Washington, DC: National Institute of Justice.

Scalon, E., and D. Page-Adams. 2001. Effects of asset holdings on neighborhoods, families, and children: A review of research. In *Building assets: A report on the asset-development and IDA field,* edited by R. Boshara, 35–50. . Washington, DC: Corporation of Enterprise Development.

Schechter, S. 1982. *Women and male violence: The visions and struggles of the battered women's movement.* Boston: South End.

Schneider, E. 1993. Feminism and the false dichotomy of victimization and agency. *New York Law School Review* 38:387–99.

Schrag, E. 2015. Economic abuse and later material hardship: Is depression a mediator? *Affilia* 30 (3): 341–51.

Scott-Storey, K. 2011. Cumulative abuse: Do things add up? An evaluation of the conceptualization, operationalization, and methodological approaches in the study of the phenomenon of cumulative abuse. *Trauma, Violence, and Abuse* 12 (3): 135–50.

Senter, K.E., and K. Caldwell. 2002. Spirituality and the maintenance of change: A phenomenological study of women who leave abusive relationships. *Contemporary Family Therapy* 24 (4): 543–64.

Sev'er, A. 1997. Recent or imminent separation and violence against women: A conceptual overview and some Canadian examples. *Violence against Women* 3 (6): 566–89.

Shah, S., L. Tsitsou, and S. Woodin. 2016. Hidden voices: Disabled women's experiences of violence and support over the life course. *Violence against Women* 22 (10): 1189–210.

Sharp, S. 2009. Escaping symbolic entrapment, maintaining social identities. *Social Problems* 56:267–84.

———. 2014. Resisting religious coercive control. *Violence against Women* 20 (12): 1407–27.

Sharp-Jeffs, N., L. Kelly, and R. Klein. 2017. Long journeys toward freedom: The relationship between coercive control and space for action. Measurement and emerging evidence. *Violence against Women*, prepublished February 2. doi: 10.1177/1077801216686199.

Shaw, S., L. Tsitsou, and S. Woodin. 2016. Hidden voices: Disabled women's experiences of violence and support over the life course. *Violence against Women* 22 (10): 1189–1210.

Sherraden, M.S. 2001. *Assets and the poor: A new American welfare policy.* Armonk, NY: M.E. Sharpe.

Sherraden, M.S., C.K. Sanders, and M. Sherraden. 2004. *Kitchen capitalism: Microenterprise in poor households*. Albany: State University of New York Press.

Short, L.M., P.M. McMahon, D.D. Chervin, G.A. Shelley, N. Lezin, and K.S. Sloop. 2000. Survivors' identification of protective factors and early warning signs for intimate partner violence. *Violence against Women* 6:272–85.

Shotter, J. 2008. Dialogism and polyphony in organizing theorizing in organization studies. *Organization Studies* 29 (4): 501–24.

Showden, C.A. 2011. *Choices women make: Agency in domestic violence, assisted reproduction, and sex work*. Minneapolis: University of Minnesota Press.

Silver, R.L., C. Boon, and M.H. Stones. 1983. Searching for meaning in misfortune: Making sense of incest. *Journal of Social Issues* 39 (2): 81–101.

Singletary, J.E. 2005. The praxis of social work: A model of how faith informs practice informs faith. *Social Work and Christianity* 32 (1): 56–72.

Sleeper, J. 2007. A civic decline, but from what? America's exceptional understandings of civil society. *International Journal of Public Administration* 30:671–82.

Slote, K.Y., C. Cuthbert, C.J. Mesh, M.G. Driggers, L. Bancroft, and J.G. Silverman. 2005. Battered mothers speak out: Participatory human rights documentation as a model for research and activism in the United States. *Violence against Women* 11:1267–1395.

Smart, E. 2013. *My story*. New York: St. Martin's Press.

Smith, D.E. 1989. *The everyday world as problematic: A feminist sociology*. Dartmouth, MA: Northeastern University Press.

Smith, J.A. 1995. Semi-structured interviewing and qualitative analysis. In *Rethinking methods in psychology*, edited by J.A. Smith, R. Harre, and L.V. Langenhorne, 9–26. London: Sage Publications.

Smith, T.W., and J. Son. 2015. *General Social Survey Final Report: Trends in gun ownership in the United States, 1972–2014*. March. Chicago: NORC.

Smith-Marek, E.N., B. Cafferky, P. Dharnidharka, A.B. Mallory, M. Dominguez, J. High, S.M. Stith, and M. Mendez. 2015. Effects of childhood experiences of family violence on adult partner violence: A meta-analytic review. *Journal of Family Theory Review* 7:498–519. doi: 10.1111/jftr.12113.

Snodgrass, S. 1998. A personal account. *Journal of Social Issues* 54 (2): 373–80.

Sorenson, S.B., and D.J. Wiebe. 2004. Weapons in the lives of battered women. *American Journal of Public Health* 92 (8): 1412–17.

Southworth, C., J. Finn, S. Dawson, C. Fraser, and S. Tucker. 2007. Intimate partner violence, technology, and stalking. *Violence against Women* 25 (7): 842–56.

Spender, D. 1980. *Man-made language*. London: Routledge and Kegan Paul.

Stalans, L.J., and M.A. Finn. 1995. How novice and experienced officers interpret wife assaults: Normative and efficiency frames. *Law and Society Review* 29:287–321.

Stark, E. 2007. *Coercive control: How men entrap women in personal life.* New York: Oxford University Press.

Stark, E., A. Flitcraft, and W. Frazier. 1979. Medicine and patriarchal violence: The social construction of a "private" event. *International Journal of Health Service* 9:461–93.

Straus, H., C. Cerulli, L.A. McNutt, K.V. Rhodes, K.R. Conner, R.S. Kemball, N.J. Kaslow, and D. Houry. 2009. Intimate partner violence and functional health status: Associations with severity, danger, and self-advocacy behaviors. *Journal of Women's Health* 18 (5): 625–31.

Straus, M.A. 1992. *Children as witnesses to marital violence: A risk factor for lifelong problems among a nationally representative sample of American men and women.* Columbus, OH: Ross Laboratories.

Strauss, A.L. 1987. *Qualitative analysis for social scientists.* New York: Cambridge University Press.

Strauss, A.L., and J. Corbin. 1990. *Basics of qualitative research: Grounded theory procedures and techniques.* Thousand Oaks, CA: Sage Publications.

Stroebe, M.S., and W. Stroebe. 1983. "Who suffers more?" Sex differences in health risks of the widowed. *Psychological Bulletin,* 93:279–301.

Stroebe, W., and M.S. Stroebe. 1993. Determinants in adjustment to bereavement in younger widows and widowers. In *Handbook of bereavement,* edited by M.S. Stroebe, W. Stroebe, and R.O. Hansson, 208–66. New York: Cambridge University Press.

Swan, S.C., and D.L. Snow. 2002. A typology of women's use of violence in intimate relationships. *Violence against Women* 8 (3): 286–319.

Sylaska, K.M., and K.M. Edwards. 2014. Disclosure of intimate partner violence to informal social support network members: A review of the literature. *Trauma, Violence, and Abuse* 5 (1): 3–21.

Taillieu, T.A., and D.A. Brownridge. 2014. Review: Intimate partner violence is associated with termination of pregnancy. *Evidence Based Nursing* 18 (1). doi: 10.1136/eb-2014–101779.

Taylor, B.G., and E.A. Mumford. 2016. A national descriptive portrait of adolescent relationship abuse: Results from the National Survey on Teen Relationships and Intimate Violence. *Journal of Interpersonal Violence* 31 (6): 963–88.

Taylor, B.G., N.D. Stein, D. Woods, and E. Mumford. 2011. *Shifting boundaries: Final report on an experimental evaluation of a youth dating violence prevention program in New York City middle schools.* Washington, DC: Police Executive Research Forum, US Department of Justice.

Taylor, D.H., M.V. Stoilkov, and D.J. Greco. 2008. Ex parte domestic violence orders of protection: How easing access to judicial process has eased the possibility for abuse of the process. *Kansas Journal of Law and Public Policy* 18 (1): 83–133.

Taylor, S.E. 1983. Adjustment to threatening events: A theory of cognitive adaptation. *American Psychologist* 38:1161–73.

Tedeschi, R.G., and L.G. Calhoun. 1996. The Posttraumatic Growth Inventory: Measuring the positive legacy of trauma. *Journal of Traumatic Stress* 9 (3): 455–71.

———. 2003. Routes to posttraumatic growth through cognitive processing. In *Promoting capabilities to manage post-traumatic stress: Perspectives on resilience,* edited by D. Paton, J.M. Violanti, and L.M. Smith, 12–26. Springfield, IL: Charles C. Thomas.

———. 2004. Posttraumatic growth: Conceptual foundations and empirical evidence. *Psychological Inquiry* 15:1–18.

Tjaden, P., and N. Thoennes. 2000. *Extent, nature, and consequences of intimate partner violence: Findings from the National Violence against Women Survey.* Washington, DC: US Department of Justice, Office of Justice Programs.

Tobolowsky, P.M., D.E. Beloof, M.T. Gaboury, A.L. Jackson, and A.G. Blackburn. 2016. *Crime victim rights and remedies.* Durham, NC: Carolina Academic Press.

Toews, M.L., and A.M. Bermea. 2017. I was naïve in thinking, "I divorced this man, he is out of my life": A qualitative exploration of post-separation power and control tactics experienced by women. *Journal of Interpersonal Violence* 32 (14): 2166–89.

Turner, B. 1967. *The forest of symbols: Aspects of Ndembu ritual.* Ithaca, NY: Cornell University Press.

Tyler, T.R. 1984. The role of perceived injustice in defendants' evaluations of their courtroom experience. *Law and Society Review* 18 (1): 51–74.

———. 1988. What is procedural justice? Criteria used by citizens to assess the fairness of legal procedures. *Law and Society Review* 22 (1): 103–35.

Ullman, S.E. 2005. Interviewing clinicians and advocates who work with sexual assault survivors: A personal perspective on moving from quantitative to qualitative research methods. *Violence against Women* 11 (9): 1113–39.

Ulrich, Y.C. 1991. Women's reasons for leaving abusive spouses. *Health Care for Women International* 12:465–73.

Ungar, M. 2004. A constructionist discourse on resilience: Multiple contexts, multiple realities among at-risk children and youth. *Youth and Society* 35:341–65.

Valdez, C.E., and M.M. Lilly. 2015. Posttraumatic growth in survivors of intimate partner violence: An assumptive world process. *Journal of Interpersonal Violence* 30 (2): 215–31.

Valli, R. 2007. Resistance as edgework in violent intimate relationships of drug-involved women. *British Journal of Criminology* 47:196–213.

Van der Kolk, B.A. 2015. *The body keeps the score: Brain, mind, and body in the healing of trauma.* New York: Penguin Books.

Varcoe, C., and L.G. Irwin. 2004. "If I killed you, I'd get the kids": Women's survival and protection work with child custody and access in the context of woman abuse. *Qualitative Sociology* 227 (1): 77–99.

Verba, S., K. L. Schlozman, and H. Brady. 1995. *Voice and equality: Civic voluntarism in American politics*. Cambridge, MA: Harvard University Press.

Verba, S., K. L. Schlozman, H. Brady, and N. H. Nie. 1993. Race, ethnicity and political resources: Participation in the United States. *British Journal of Political Science* 23 (4): 453–97.

Velonis, A. J. 2016. "He never did anything you typically think of as abuse": Experiences with violence in controlling and non-controlling relationships in a non-agency sample of women. *Violence against Women* 22 (9): 1031–54.

Vidgor, E. R., and J. Mercy. 2006. Do laws restricting access to firearms by domestic violence offenders prevent intimate partner homicide? *Evaluation Review* 30 (3): 313–46. doi: 0.1177/0193841x06287307.

Wagnild, G., and H. M. Young. 1993. Development and psychometric evaluation of the Resilience Scale. *Journal of Nursing Measurement* 1:165–78.

Waldrop, A. E., and P. A. Resick. 2004. Coping among adult female victims of domestic violence. *Journal of Family Violence* 19 (5): 291–302.

Walker, L. E. 1979. *The battered woman*. New York: Harper Perennial.

———. 1984. *The battered woman syndrome*. New York: Springer.

Walker, L. E., and A. Browne. 1985. Gender and victimization by intimates. *Journal of Personality* 53 (2): 179–95.

Watson, L. B., and J. R. Ancis. 2013. Power and control in the legal system: From marriage/relationship to divorce and custody. *Violence against Women* 19 (2): 166–86.

Webster, D. W., S. Frattaroli, J. S. Vernick, C. O'Sullivan, J. Roehl, and J. C. Campbell. 2010. Women with protective orders report failure to remove firearms from their abusive partners: Results from an exploratory study. *Journal of Women's Health* 19 (1): 93–98. doi: 10.1089/jwh.2007.0530.

Weiss, G. 2008. An interview with Professor Gail Weiss. *International Postgraduate Journal of Philosophy* 1:3–8.

Weisz, A. N. 1999. Legal advocacy for domestic violence survivors: The power of an informative relationship. *Families in Society* 80:138–47.

West, C., and S. Fenstermaker. 1995. Doing difference. *Gender and Society* 9:8–37.

West, T. C. 1999. *Wounds of the spirit: Black women, violence, and resistance ethics*. New York: New York University Press.

Whittle, A., F. Mueller, and A. Mangan. 2009. Storytelling and character: Victims, villains and heroes in a case of technological change. *Organization* 16 (3): 425–42.

WHO (World Health Organization). 2013. *Responding to intimate partner violence and sexual violence against women: WHO clinical and policy guidelines*. Geneva: WHO Press.

Williams, N. R. (2002). Surviving violence: Resilience in action at the micro level. In *Resiliency: An integrated approach to practice, policy and research*, edited by R. R. Greene, 195–215. Washington: NASW Press.

Wilson, T.D. 2015. *Redirect: Changing the stories we live by.* New York: Little, Brown.

Wood, L. 2017. "I look across from me and I see me": Survivors as advocates in intimate partner violence agencies. *Violence against Women* 23 (3): 309–29.

Woodlock, D. 2017. The abuse of technology in domestic violence and stalking. *Violence against Women* 23 (5): 584–602.

Wright, C.V., S. Perez, and D. Johnson. 2010. The mediating role of empowerment for African American women experiencing intimate partner violence. *Psychological Trauma: Theory, Research, Practice, and Policy* 2:266–72.

Wuest, J., and M. Merrit-Gray. 2011. Beyond survival: Reclaiming self after leaving an abusive male partner. *Canadian Journal of Nursing Research* 32:79–94.

Ybema, S., T. Keenoy, C. Oswick, A. Beverungen, N. Ellis, and I. Sabelis. 2009. Articulating identities. *Human Relations* 63 (3): 299–322.

Young, M.D. 2007. Finding meaning in the aftermath of trauma: Resilience and posttraumatic growth in female survivors of intimate partner violence. PhD diss., University of Montana. http://scholarworks.umt.edu/cgi/viewcontent.cgi?article=1468&context=etd.

Yount, K.M., and L. Li. 2009. Women's "justification" of domestic violence in Egypt. *Journal of Marriage and Family* 71 (5): 1125–40.

Zahn, M., and M. Sherraden. 2001. Assets, expectations, and children's educational achievement in female-headed households. *Social Service Review* 77 (2): 191–112.

Zeoli, A.M., S. Frattaroli, K. Roskam, and A.K. Herrera. 2017. Removing firearms from those prohibited from possession by domestic violence restraining orders: A survey and analysis of state laws. *Trauma, Violence, and Abuse*, prepublished February 22. doi: 10.1177/1524838017692384.

Zeoli, A.M., E.A. Rivera, C.M. Sullivan, and S. Kubiak. 2013. Post-separation abuse of women and their children: Boundary-setting and family court utilization among victimized mothers. *Journal of Family Violence* 28 (6): 547–60.

Zijderveld, A.C. 1968. Jokes and their relation to social reality. *Social Research* 35:268–311.

Zorza, J. 2007. The "friendly parent" concept: Another gender biased legacy from Richard Gardner. *Domestic Violence Report* 12 (5): 65–78.

Zweig, J., and M. Burt. 2007. Predicting women's perceptions of domestic violence and sexual assault agency helpfulness: What matters to program clients? *Violence against Women* 13:1149–78.

Index

abduction, 88, 97, 166, 174, 210n2

Abigayle: activism and, 125; arrests and, 77, 88, 154, 157; children and, 63; courts and, 157; demographics and, 34*table*; empowerment and, 125; faith and, 120; finances and, 125; guns and, 68; police and, 154; self-defense and, 157; siblings and, 134; on survivorship, 181

abolitionists, 123, 210n6

abortion, 60, 63, 98

abuse: abusers/ex-partners and, 49, 94–95; activism and, 36; adolescents and, 200; African Americans and, 59, 114; breakups and, 165; Celeste and, 44, 134; children and, 88–89, 92, 97, 102–5; Christianity and, 65–66; churches/religious communities and, 119, 138–40, 142, 171; class and, 59; courts and, 195; the criminal/(in)justice/legal system and, 106–7, 147, 166, 171; custody and, xx; Dale and, 159; disabilities and, 65, 98, 203; divorces and, 169–70; documentation and, 195; Elizabeth and, 98, 148–50; epiphanies and, 51; faith and, 119; families of origin and, 53, 62, 122, 179, 200; feminine norms/socialization and, 53; health care and, 187; information technologies and, 191; Jazzy on, 62; Jenny and, 48, 125; judges and, 106–

7, 195; leaving and, xvii, xx; management of, 87; meaning making and, 180, 204; mediators and, 195; miscarriages and, 60, 65, 98; Naomi and, 64, 122; narratives and, 37–38; obstacles and, 131; parents and, 58–59; participants/samples and, 32, 36; Pepper and, 61; pregnancies and, 65; self-blame and, 178; self-efficacy and, 64; social media and, 128; social services and, 171; social structures and, 9; stereotypes and, 59; stigmas and, 9; *A Stolen Life* (Dugard) and, 37; Tina and, 47, 155–56; victim narratives (protection orders) and, 196–97; victims and, 196–97; vulnerabilities and, 200; weapons and, 92; wifely submission doctrine and, 209n3; Winnie and, 136–37; women and, 12–13, 25, 206. *See also* post-abuse; Protection from Abuse (PFA); restraining orders

abusers: abduction and, 88, 97, 166, 174, 210n2; abuse and, 49; accountability and, 91–92, 209n4; affairs and, 58, 75, 80; anger and, 56; arrests and, 82–83, 150, 164; battered women and, 3, 4, 16; breakups and, 165; child abuse and, 100–105; children and, 47–48, 75, 76, 77, 88–89, 97–109, 165, 168–69,

239

children *(continued)*
  Florence and, 100–101, 102; guns and, 67; hopes and, 182; humor and, 79; information technologies and, 198; IPV/A and, xvii, 102, 167–68; Jazzy and, 102–3; Joan and, 54, 100; Julia and, 104, 105–6; just world hypothesis and, 175; Katherine and, 46, 98, 103, 105; leaving and, 51, 63, 88, 93, 97, 105–6; meaning making and, 176; Megan and, 54, 88, 97, 101, 155, 169; neglect and, 102; participants and, 32–33, 34–35*table*; physical violence and, 100; post-traumatic growth and, xv–xvi, 97–109; pregnancies and, 57; protections and, 86, 101, 104, 129, 209n1; Reeva and, 65, 74, 87, 98, 168; religion and, 141; resilience and, xviii, 15; Robyn and, 99–100, 104; Rosa and, 107; sabotage and, 107; safety and, xvi, 7, 14, 97, 161, 164, 166–67; Sara and, 87, 104; separations and, 97, 107; shelters and, 9, 145, 198; suicides and, 163–64, 210n2; survivors and, 109; Terri and, 109; Tina and, 101, 168; trauma and, 7, 103–4; (un)healthy relationships and, 200; use of force and, 4; Vanessa and, 101, 111, 168–69; victim identities and, 42; victims/survivors and, 102; violence and, 86, 88, 94, 103–4, 184; violence normalcy and, 60–62; vulnerabilities and, 51, 63; well-being and, 102; WIND and, 27; Winnie and, 44, 56, 88, 103–4, 105, 163–64. *See also* child abuse; custody; visitations; women and children
child sexual abuse, 7, 99–101, 109–11, 117, 179, 187. *See also* molestation
child support: abusers and, 47–48, 74–75, 77, 106, 129, 166; control and, 106; courts and, 166, 170, 171, 182; Danielle and, 187; economic abuse and, 71, 74–75; Joan and, 75, 87; participants and, 32; power and, 106; Tina and, 77–78; Winnie and, 140; women and, 170

Christianity, xv, 65–66, 74, 139–40. *See also* wifely submission doctrine
churches, 138–44; abuse and, 142; activism and, 123–24, 127; African Americans and, 113–14, 122–24, 208n2; Amy and, 140–41; Anita and, 123, 128, 144; coping and, 116; Danielle and, 123, 142–43; divorces and, 139, 142; domestic violence and, 123, 128, 141, 144; Elizabeth and, 128; Florence and, 119, 143; help-seeking and, 143; IPV/A and, 123, 128, 140; Joan and, 54, 65, 141–42; Julia and, 139–40; long-term survivorship and, 131; meaning making and, 109; Naomi and, 144; post-abuse and, 180; Reeva and, 143; resilience and, 113, 131; Robyn and, 143; self-blame and, 179; social justice and, 124; as supports/networks, 114, 123, 138–44; survivors and, 185–86; Tina and, 140; Tyler Clementi Foundation and, 1; Winnie and, 140; women and, 139. *See also* clergy; faith; religion; religious communities
Chwalisz, D., 178
Cichetti, D., 176
civil courts. *See* courts; family courts
civil justice systems. *See* attorneys; courts; (in)justice system, the; judges; legal representation; legal system, the
civil protection orders. *See* Protection from Abuse (PFA); protection orders; restraining orders
civil rights movement, 123
class: abuse and, 59; African Americans and, 59; courts and, 196; the criminal justice system and, xxi; feminism and, 19, 40; gender and, 6; participants and, 33; police and, 154; policies and, 186–87; post-traumatic growth and, 112; resilience and, 202; thriving and, 19; WIND and, 20, 128
Clementi, Tyler, 1

victims/survivors: abusers and, 165; abusive relationships and, 25; agency and, xv; arrests and, 154–55; children and, 102; clergy and, 199; courts and, 159, 161–62, 195–96; the criminal justice/(in)justice/legal system and, 147–48, 171, 195–96; data collection and, 25; economic abuse and, 70; empowerment and, 11, 206; epiphanies and, 86; faith and, 129; fears and, 66; feminist research design and, 40; identities and, 13, 174; meaning making and, 22–23, 129; narratives and, 38; paper abuse and, 165; peer support and, xiv, 191; public awareness and, 28, 198; recommendations and, xxi; religion/religious communities and, 66, 171; resilience and, 19; samples and, 36–37; self-defense and, 158; self-identities and, 41–50; semantics and, xvii, 14; social services and, 171; stigmas and, 13, 198; support groups and, 201–2; supports and, 173, 179; trauma and, 196; victimology and, 12; women and, 14
VINE (Victim Information and Notification Everyday), 29, 209n5
violence: abusers and, 59–60; adolescents and, 200; African Americans and, 113–14; alcohol and, 98; battered women's movements and, 8; breakups and, 165; Celeste and, 44; challenges and, 20; children and, 86, 88, 94, 103–4, 184; Ellen and, 53; emotional abuse and, 42; employment and, 189; euphemisms, 11; families and, 51; families of origin and, 51, 59–62; gender and, 211n2; homosexuality and, 207n2, 211n2; IPV/A and, 51; Joan and, 87; leaving and, xvii, 12, 51; legislation and, 208n1; males and, 11; meaning making and, 111–12; Megan and, 61; National Violence Against Women survey, 199–200; obstacles and, 131; Office on Violence against Women, 196; participants and, 32–33; Pepper and, 45, 61; Protection from Abuse (PFA) and, 208n4; research and, 39; self-defense and, 157; social structures and, 9, 184; survivors and, 13, 14; use of force and, 193; WIND and, 124; Winnie and, 43–44, 56; women and, 27, 184; workplace violence, 46–47. *See also* separation violence; urban violence
Violence against Women Act (1994), 66, 199–200, 209n5
violence normalcy, 5, 60–62, 111–12, 175, 185
visitations: abusers and, 51, 106–7, 129, 166–67; Celeste and, 166; children and, 166–67; control and, 106; courts and, 51, 108, 163, 166–67, 167–68, 170, 182, 195; Danielle and, 166–67; family courts and, 196; fears and, 94, 95; harassment and, 165; Naomi and, 109; participants and, 32; power and, 106; survivors and, 185; women and, 170, 186, 202
volunteers. *See* activism
vulnerabilities, 52–64; abuse and, 200; abusers and, 51; age and, 52–54, 58; children and, 51, 63; dating experience and, 51, 52, 53, 56–57; disabilities and, 51, 63–64; education and, 52, 91; epiphanies and, 91; families and, 53, 56, 59; families of origin and, 51, 59–62; good fronts and, 55–56; Haley and, 54; IPV/A and, 52; isolation and, 53, 55, 57, 58, 91; Jayde and, 54–55; Jenny and, 57; Katherine and, 63; marriages and, 55–56, 57; neglect and, 60, 62; parents and, 58–59; pregnancies and, 56, 57, 60, 62, 63; race and, 52; Reeva and, 54; resources and, 62, 91; romance and, xx, 54, 56; Sara and, 57–58; self-esteem and, 59; shame and, 58; single mothers and, 63; Terri and, 53; violence normalcy and, 60–62; WIND and, 52; Winnie and, 55–56. *See also* warning signs
vulnerability/deficit models, 15